CLEAN HOME, GREEN HOME

KNACK®

CLEAN HOME, GREEN HOME

The complete illustrated guide to an eco-friendly home

KIMBERLY DELANEY

KNACK®
MAKE IT EASY

Guilford, Connecticut
An imprint of The Globe Pequot Press

Cover photos by (from left to right) GoodMood Photo/shutterstock, Liv friis-larsen/shutterstock, Barbro Wickström/shutterstock, photos.com
Back cover photos by (from left to right) Svetlana Larina/shutterstock, Domenico Gelermo/shutterstock, Ints Vikmanis|Dreamstime.com, Carole Drong
Photo research by Anna Adesanya
Additional photo research by Mary Rischer
Text design by Paul Beatrice
Special Photography by Carole Drong

CIP DATA: A catalogue record for this book is available from the British Library

Delaney, Kimberly.
  Knack clean home, green home : the complete illustrated guide to eco-friendly homekeeping / Kimberly Delaney.
    p. cm.
  ISBN 978-0-7627-5694-0
1. House cleaning. 2. Green products. I. Title.
TX324.D443 2009
648'.5--dc22

Globe Pequot Press International
Footprint Handbooks
6 Riverside Court
Lower Bristol Road
Bath
BA2 3DZ
UK
T+44(0)1225 469141
F+44(0)1225 469461

The following manufacturers/names appearing in *Knack Clean Home, Green Home* are trademarks:
Can-O-Worms, Forest Stewardship Council©, Formica®, Leaping Bunny™, Printed with Soy Ink™, Pyrex®, Tetra Pak™

Printed in India by Replika Press Pvt Ltd

About the author

Kimberley Delaney is a freelance writer for numerous magazines. She also co-authors and edits books and maintains a blog, 'A Greener Shade of Clean' on Lime.com. She lives in Santa Cruz, California, USA, with her husband and daughter.

CONTENTS

INTRODUCTION
The Green-Cleaning Mindset

INTRODUCTION

With ever more news coming out about dangerous toxins in common household products, it's easy to feel either a little overwhelmed or a little over it. After all, if some of the most common and best-selling household products have hazardous chemicals in them, what can we do about it? Luckily, one of the simplest ways to have a big impact on the health of your family and the environment is to 'green' your cleaning. Contrary to what many people assume about green cleaning, it actually doesn't have to cost any more, take more time, or mean you have to compromise on what you think of as clean. But green cleaning does require a shift in how we define 'clean'.

'Clean' in the conventional sense means free of dirt and germs. It's about how the surfaces and objects in your home look. Are the appliances shiny? The cupboards free of fingerprints? The windows clean and clear? When you go green, the definition of clean expands, and, by this new definition, many chemical-laden products might not be considered cleaners at all. A clean green home is still one that is free of dirt and germs, but also one that is free of toxic pollution.

1. Green cleaning is about air quality

The difference between green cleaning and just cleaning can be boiled down to the simple rule that when

What Is a Toxin?

What is a toxin? A chemical that irritates your skin, burns your eyes or causes human illness or injury when inhaled, swallowed or absorbed through the skin. While any chemical can be toxic if you drink the whole bottle, the toxins we refer to in this book are those that have been shown to have or are strongly suspected of having health or environmental consequences even when used according to the directions on the pack.

you finish green cleaning a room, the air should be as clean or cleaner than when you started. That means no more toxic chemicals to shine surfaces or remove dirt or grease. Using products that pollute the air is not cleaning. It's polluting.

In the green-cleaning mindset, sleeping in a clean bedroom means the shelves and furniture are well dusted, the mirror and windows are streak-free, the blinds and curtains are clean, as are the floor and rugs. It also means the furniture is made of solid wood, finished in sealants or varnishes that don't pollute. The bedding is free of anti-wrinkle chemicals and perhaps the duvet is even filled with clean wool or organic cotton. In short, the room is free of dirt and the air is healthy and fresh.

Consider exposure

We know that we will probably not keel over from breathing in one toxic glass cleaner or spraying a little weed killer on our garden. But it's important to think in terms of 'exposure'. We're not just spraying one chemical cleaner or one pesticide on any given day. In fact, the average person is exposed to 100 different chemicals a day – and that's just in personal care products. That average person hasn't even started to clean yet.

Although it's easy to believe that if a product is on the supermarket shelf it must be safe, studies show that this is not necessarily the case. Unfortunately, only a very few of the 85,000 chemicals in use today have even been tested for safety. Many that have been tested and found to cause health problems are still used in the products we buy. In addition, many scientists believe that household toxins are one of the main reasons why asthma and allergies are on the rise.

While there is clearly a lot we don't know, there is also enough that we do know about these toxins for us to limit our exposure. With that in mind, one of the goals of this book is to provide information you need to know to help reduce your exposure to these chemicals as you create your clean green home.

Breaking Down the Terms

- Carcinogens can cause cancer or worsen it by stimulating the spread of cancer cells.
- Neurotoxins can attack the nervous system and can cause brain damage with prolonged exposure.
- Endocrine disruptors can disrupt the body's hormonal and reproductive system.
- Teratogens can affect foetal development, causing birth defects.
- Mutagens can permanently alter genetic code in a cell.
- Immunotoxins can damage the immune system, either making it underactive and leaving you vulnerable to illness, or overactive, as in an autoimmune disorder.

The importance of dusting

Far from being rocket science, you'll find that one of the most important green-cleaning steps you can take is really just dusting. This is because the dust gives toxins something to stick to, so our exposure is prolonged. Breathing in all this dust means toxins may now linger in your body, where some attach to fat and build up for decades. Eventually we may transfer these toxins to our children in breast milk. Studies have found that controlling dust reduces our exposure to household toxins. That's why consistent dusting and using a vacuum cleaner with a quality filter designed to capture these particles might be the best ways you have to detox your home.

2. Green cleaning is about reducing

The green-cleaning mindset also finds ways of cleaning that help reduce energy, water and other resource consumption. Rather than buying a separate cleaner for every job, you'll have just a few, and even some you make yourself from a short list of basic ingredients such as vinegar and vegetable-based soap. You might fill the sink instead of letting the water run to hand-wash dishes, or you could buy an energy-efficient dishwasher when your old one dies.

Maintaining what you already own

You are also looking to extend the life of things you already have and keep appliances running as efficiently as possible. For example, dust build-up on a ceiling fan can cause unnecessary wear and could ultimately break it. Mineral deposits in your dishwasher can interfere with the water flow, so that you need to use either a harsher detergent or more water to rinse the dishes to get the level of cleaning you desire. Dusty lightbulbs get hotter, so they need to be replaced faster. They also give less light, so you need to turn on more lamps and use more electricity to light your home. The longer you keep these things clean and well-maintained the more efficiently they run and the longer they stay out of landfill.

3. The self-cleaning home

While we can't claim that following the advice in this book will make your home clean itself, it will probably reduce the time it takes to clean. That's because the green-cleaning mindset is also about taking proactive steps to keep your home cleaner for longer, eliminate the need for harsh chemical products and make cleaning easy. When rooms are cluttered, preparing to clean them takes about as long as cleaning them – so you've doubled the time you need to spend on the job. Throughout the book, we suggest ways of arranging rooms to make them as easy as possible to clean. The easier it is to clean, the more often you'll be able to do it, even with a busy schedule.

For example, you might organize your hallway so it is designed to contain the dirt, jackets, shoes, bags, mail, and whatever else you bring in from the outside world so it won't spread all over your house. And each of those items get a designated bin or basket, hook or shelf that's easy to clear when you want to clean the hall.

When it comes to making your own cleaning materials, almost all the recipes in this book simply require a few of the eight or so basic cleaning ingredients, a spray bottle and a good shake. A few others require you to mix a powder like bicarbonate of soda with liquid soap to make a paste. None requires any exotic ingredients, and all can be mixed up in just a few minutes.

As you explore this book, you will no doubt find a few recipes you feel like making up and a few jobs that you'd rather tackle with a store-bought green cleaner. With that in mind, each section of the book highlights the ingredients you'll want to look for and those you want to avoid in that product category. You'll also learn how to tell a truly green cleaner from a purely 'green-washed' product (see page 10), so your shopping will be easier.

This book is meant to be a guide to help you explore green cleaning. It can be read from front to back, or you can just flip to the room you want to clean. Go at your own pace. Each step you take to green your cleaning will reduce your exposure to toxins. Even if you just replace three branded cleaners with homemade recipes, you're doing something great for your family and the environment. And don't forget that one of the satisfying rewards of green cleaning is that when you've finished, you can take a deep breath of clean, fresh air and reward yourself for your green efforts!

CLEANING PRODUCT LABEL PRIMER
Crack the code to recognize toxins at a glance

A big part of making the shift to green cleaning is to redefine how we understand 'clean'. Sure, a spotless kitchen worktop and polished bath taps are visual signals that a home is clean. But what about what we don't see? What chemicals are we exposing ourselves to through inhalation, skin absorption or even ingestion? Green cleaning starts with the great news that you can have your spotless worktop and polished taps

without dirtying your air, your body or the environment.

Reading labels can seem daunting – sodium laureth what? But once you know what you're looking for – and what you're not – you'll be able to choose with confidence the products you want in your home. Thanks to British and European Union consumer protection legislation, you can usually tell how toxic a product is by a glance at the label. Manufacturers

Extreme Hazard

TOXIC HAZARD

POISON: MAY BE FATAL IF SWALLOWED OR INHALED.

- 'Poison' is the strongest signal word you'll find on household products, and it is not common on cleaners.

- Meaning: highly toxic.

- Found on: some car products such as antifreeze as

well as paint or varnish removers and insecticides.

- To use this product safely you would need major ventilation and safety gear. Better still, find something less toxic to do the job.

Highly Toxic

DANGER: CAUSES SEVERE BURNS/CORROSIVE.

- 'Danger' is the second strongest signal word.

- Meaning: spills or ingestion could cause permanent tissue damage to the skin, mouth, throat and stomach or the product could be very flammable.

- Found on: cleaning products for tough jobs like some oven, toilet bowl or drain cleaners, and also bleach and spray adhesives.

- 'Corrosive' means the product can eat away at different types of materials, including human tissue.

of hazardous household substances use an internationally recognized code that ranges from 'poison' to 'caution' to tell consumers how dangerous a product can be to their health. These labels usually also include directions on how to use the products safely and what to do if there's an accident.

Reading labels is essential, since the average home contains 10–35 litres of hazardous products that we use for everything from cleaning our homes, cars and bodies to caring for our furniture and ridding our gardens of pests. It's not surprising that

90 per cent of all accidental poisonings happen at home. But researchers are also finding that, even when used safely, certain household chemicals are absorbed by our bodies and never leave. Instead we carry them around with us in our fat tissues or bloodstreams, where they have more time to cause damage to our cells and our health, possibly contributing to the rise in asthma rates as well as other chronic diseases.

Use the graphics in this chapter for easy reference to buy the cleanest and safest products for your home and health.

Medium hazard

WARNING: FLAMMABLE.

- 'Warning' is a common signal word on cleaning products.

- Meaning: flammable or moderately toxic, but not likely to produce permanent damage if handled properly.

- Found on: some toilet cleaners, flea sprays and other cleaning products.

- This product can catch fire easily with increased temperature or a nearby spark. Another word to look for is 'combustible'.

Low to Medium Hazard

CAUTION: IRRITANT.

- 'Caution' is the word most commonly seen on cleaning product labels.

- Meaning: slightly toxic, which tells you that you can ingest more before the product is fatal. This does not tell you about long-term risks like cancer.

- Found on: dishwasher detergent, glass cleaner, all-purpose cleaners, sealant, insecticide, rat poison and other products.

- 'Irritant' means prolonged or repeated use can cause injury to the area of the body in contact with it.

THE DIRTY EIGHT
Your crib sheet for toxins you don't want in your home

Wouldn't it be great to be able to recognize and understand all those unpronounceable words on ingredient lists so we could keep the worst of them out of our homes? Here's a great place to start. The Dirty Eight are some of the most common and toxic chemicals you'll find in your home.

The first four of these ingredients are very common in household products, so both your family's exposure and the environment's exposure to them may be high. For example, antibacterial ingredients are now found in over 700 product categories, including everything from sponges and cutting boards to mattresses and mascara. Yet soap and water have been found to be as or more effective in killing bacteria.

Fragrance is so common that we have to look harder to find unscented products than scented ones. However,

CLEAN HOME, GREEN HOME

Antibacterials

Major polluter

- Antibacterial products contain pesticides and they may be contributing to a rise in resistant bacteria.

- Studies show that the most common, triclosan, is contaminating waterways and has been linked to reproductive malformations in fish.

- When triclosan is exposed to sunlight and chlorinated water, it can convert to dioxin, a known carcinogen.

- These products have not been proven safe or effective. Regular washing with soap and water is as or more effective for killing bacteria.

Artificial Fragrance

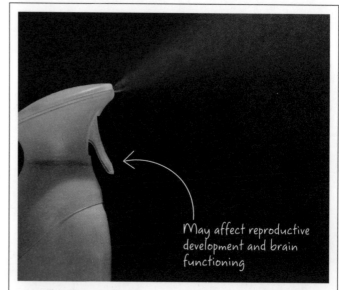

May affect reproductive development and brain functioning

- Artificial fragrance is the leading cause of irritation and allergic reaction in cosmetics.

- Most artificial fragrance ingredients are petroleum-based, a non-renewable resource, and they do not readily biodegrade in the environment.

- Phthalates, a common fragrance ingredient, are thought to be a reproductive toxin and are linked to the feminization of boys.

- Toluene, another common fragrance ingredient, is a neurotoxin that can damage the liver, kidney and brain.

manufacturers are not required to list the ingredients that go into the artificial scents in their products.

Phosphates, which soften the water so detergents clean more effectively, are relatively low on the toxic scale for our immediate exposure. But because of their severe impact on the environment, most laundry detergent companies and some countries have banned them. Still, phosphates persist in almost all automatic dishwashing detergents.

Sodium hydroxide, also known as lye, is one of the reasons oven and drain cleaners are so immediately toxic. It is an extreme respiratory, skin, and eye irritant bottled in a spray container for oven cleaners, making it very difficult to avoid body contact.

Buying products that are free of these ingredients requires a little extra label scrutiny, but the benefits of not using them far outweigh the costs of using them. Once you find a few brands you trust, you'll have no problem making greener choices for your home and family.

Phosphates

Polluting waterways and killing off fish

- Phosphates are found in almost all automatic dish-washing detergents and some all-purpose cleaners.

- They soften water and help detergents clean.

- But they are also fertilizers and can cause excessive algal bloom, polluting waterways and killing off fish and vegetation.

- The problem is so wide-spread that phosphates have been mostly phased out in laundry detergents and some governments have banned them completely.

Sodium Hydroxide

Extreme irritant

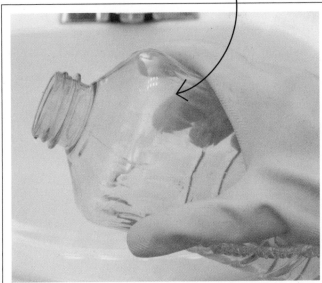

- Sodium hydroxide is found in drain, metal and oven cleaners. It is also known as lye, caustic soda, white caustic and soda lye.

- Sodium hydroxide's toxic effects are immediate. It can cause severe damage to eyes, skin, and mucous membranes, as well as to the digestive system.

- Tests on people showed respiratory irritation with only 2–15 minutes of exposure.

- Animals have gone blind with very minimal exposure.

THE DIRTY EIGHT (CONTINUED)
Four more toxins to avoid

The last four of the Dirty Eight include chemicals that are called synthetic surfactants and solvents. Surfactants are also called 'surface active agents': they reduce water surface tension and basically make the water wetter. This enables detergents to lather, spread out, penetrate stains and wash them away. Surfactants are not always specified on product labels but are usually petroleum-based. One surfactant to look for is alkyl polyglycoside. It is plant-based, which makes it a greener surfactant. Petroleum-based surfactants can be contaminated with known carcinogens, and they are not well regulated by governments.

APEs (alkylphenol ethoxylates), DEAs (diethanolamines), and SLS (sodium lauryl sulphate) are all surfactants that are commonly used in household products. SLS and its cousin

Alkylphenol Ethoxylates

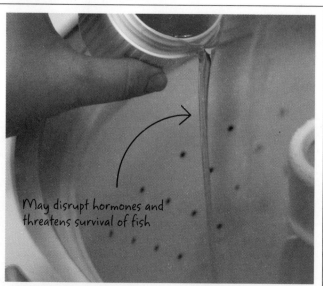

May disrupt hormones and threatens survival of fish

- APEs are a family of synthetic surfactants found in laundry detergents, disinfectants, all-purpose cleaners and hard surface cleaners.

- Though APEs do not have severe immediate toxic effects, they are suspected long-term endocrine disruptors that have been linked to the stimulation of breast cancer cell growth.

- They are commonly found in waterways, where they may be reducing the reproduction and survival rates of salmon and other types of fish.

Diethanolamines and Triethanolamines

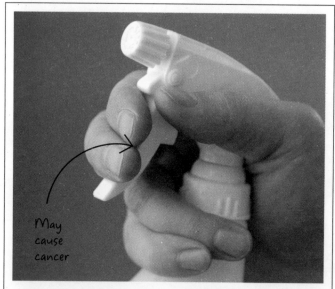

May cause cancer

- DEA and TEA are synthetic surfactants that also work to neutralize acids to make products less irritating to the skin.

- They are found in all-purpose cleaners, hand dishwashing liquids, detergents, stain removers and personal care products.

- They are carcinogenic, skin, eye and respiratory irritants, and very slow to biodegrade in the environment.

- DEA and TEA react with nitrites, which are often used as preservatives but not listed on labels, to form nitrosamines, a family of known carcinogens.

SLES (sodium laureth sulphate) are especially pervasive in personal care products, such as body washes, shampoos and soaps. Yet workers who interact with these two chemicals are told to avoid body contact because they are toxic. They have also been found to be contaminated with 1,4-dioxane, strongly suspected to be a carcinogen.

Solvents are also important toxins to be aware of. Solvents are common ingredients in many household cleaning and paint products, because they keep other ingredients from separating and keep the product in its liquid state. They also dissolve dirt without leaving a film or other residue. However, because they're soluble in fat, they are easily absorbed by the body and can enter the brain, where they may cause damage. Solvents also contaminate waterways and soil.

Butyl cellosolve is just one of the many toxic solvents you'll find in everyday household use. A few of the others to look for and avoid are: ethyl cellosolve, ethylene glycol, petroleum distillates, petroleum hydrocarbons, hexane, toluene, benzene, xylene and perchloroethylene (PERC).

Sodium Lauryl/Laureth Sulphate

Irritants that may cause cancer

Butyl Cellosolve

Can cause damage to brain and nervous system

- These related surfactants are found in any type of product that produces lather.

- They can cause severe skin and eye irritation and have been linked to abnormal eye development in children.

- Studies show they can react with other ingredients in these products to produce carcinogenic nitrosamines and dioxin.

- They have also been found to be lethal to fish at low levels of exposure.

- Butyl cellosolve is a synthetic solvent found in all-purpose, glass and abrasive cleaners.

- It's also found in auto products, floor polish, inks, leather goods, paint thinners, pesticides and home furnishings.

- Butyl cellosolve is a known neurotoxin.

- It is also a suspected blood, kidney, and liver toxin, and an endocrine disruptor.

- Its immediate toxic effects include eye, nose, throat and lung-tissue irritation.

GREEN LABEL PRIMER
Know the label claims you can trust and those you can't

Products can look green, smell green, and have a line-up of good-looking seals of approval telling us they don't support animal abuse, contain toxins or harm the environment. But not all of these seals are created equally. This does not mean that the companies who use them aren't being truthful, but that the most reliable seals are those that are well-defined and well-regulated by third-party organizations.

Knowing how a claim term such as 'organic' is actually defined can make a big difference in your purchasing decisions. Does it mean that all the ingredients are organic, or just a few? What if the ingredients are organic but synthetic chemicals are part of the processing? 'Non-toxic' is another slippery term. One manufacturer's toxin is another's 'safe' food additive.

Soil Association

- The Soil Association sets standards for organic production of food and drink, health and beauty products, textiles and the production of wood.

- Health and beauty products can use the logo if they contain 95 per cent organic ingredients.

- The association also sets standards for packaging, recycling and ethical trade that businesses seeking certification have to meet.

- Every stage of production, from raw materials to processing to distribution, is licensed.

Fairtrade

- Fairtrade means producer organisations receive an agreed and stable price for their products that covers the cost of sustainable production.

- Producers farm to internationally agreed environmental standards, working towards organic certification.

- Fairtrade benefits 7.5M people in developing countries.

- To carry the Mark, products like coffee must be 100% Fairtrade, and to widen the benefits to producers all the ingredients that can be Fairtrade are Fairtrade in multi-ingredient products.

Currently, Soil Association certification is the most specific measure of organic products in Britain. Products that carry its logo have met its standards for organic and sustainable production, which are recognized as exceeding the standards set by British and EU environment agencies.

For animal testing, the major grey area is that companies that don't test on animals themselves may subcontract to laboratories or suppliers that do. The international Coalition for Consumer Information on Cosmetics (CCIC) is working to standardize and regulate what 'not tested on animals' means, with their 'Leaping Bunny' programme. CCIC consists of the Humane Society and Beauty without Cruelty, along with other animal protection groups from around the world.

Wood is another murky topic in the green world. Wood products are thought of as more natural and green than, say, plastics. But unregulated harvesting of wood can mean a host of environmental woes, including clear-felling and illegally felling endangered woods like teak. The Forest Stewardship Council helps to identify wood from forests that are managed in line with strict environmental and social standards.

Leaping Bunny

- The Leaping Bunny logo is found on cleaners as well as skin care products, oral hygiene products, sun care products, and cosmetics.

- It certifies that the product was produced in compliance with the Corporate Standard of Compassion for Animals developed by CCIC.

- Certified manufacturers do not conduct animal testing for their products or for the individual ingredients that go into those products.

- They also do not subcontract any firms to perform animal testing of ingredients, formulations or finished products on their behalf.

Forest Stewardship Council

- FSC certifies that wood is harvested from 'well-managed' forests.

- That means the wood is harvested in a way that is environmentally responsible in terms of the type of wood harvested and the rate of harvest, among other factors.

- FSC forests must also be socially responsible with respect to protecting workers' rights, indigenous land rights, and the rights of people who live in surrounding areas.

- Genetically engineered wood is not FSC wood.

ANATOMY OF A GREEN PRODUCT
Judging a green product by its packaging

You can tell a lot about a product by its packaging, and even its lack of packaging.

Here are some telltale signs of a not-so-green product: it's double- or triple-wrapped, packaged in non-renewable materials such as vinyl with brightly coloured glossy labels, and the packaging is neither made of recycled materials nor recyclable in most locations. Currently in Britain, about 100 million tons of waste is generated each year, much of which ends up in fast-diminishing landfill sites.

The 'chasing arrows' logo, or Möbius loop, means that the packaging can be recycled. If a percentage is stated in the centre of the logo, this indicates the amount of recycled material that was used in its manufacture. The greenest packaging is made from 100 per cent recycled materials and is

Post–Consumer Recycled Waste

- Packaging made from recycled materials should mean that it uses paper or metal that was used by consumers and then recycled.

- Material labelled as 'recycled' is often the waste material generated from manufacturing new products.

- Choose products with the highest percentage of recycled materials you can find.

- Ideally recycled paper will also be chlorine free, meaning the paper was not bleached with chlorine, a process that pollutes both air and waterways.

Recyclable

- Packaging for green products should also be easily recyclable.

- That means it will be made of paper or either type 1 or type 2 plastics, which are the easiest to recycle no matter where you live.

- Green products should also have only minimal or no packaging.

- Think twice before buying a blanket made of organic cotton packaged in cardboard and then wrapped in PVC, which is rarely recyclable.

also recyclable. Ideally, recycled materials have already been used and placed in a recycling bin by consumers, then transformed into this new material.

However, the definition of recycled material also includes waste from the manufacturing process itself – scraps of unused materials left over from creating new products. Buying post-consumer waste recycled goods is an important step in closing the recycling loop. The existence of recycling programmes depends on there being a market for genuinely recycled materials. Without that market, those programmes would disappear.

Green packaging also uses non-toxic colouring. Since conventional inks and dyes are petroleum-based and give off volatile organic compounds (VOCs) that pollute the air, green manufacturers are turning to plant- and especially soy-based inks and dyes that give off far fewer VOCs.

Inks and Dyes

- Conventional inks and dyes are typically petroleum-based, a non-renewable resource. They also have high levels of VOCs that can mix with other pollutants in the air to form smog.

- Inks and dyes made using soy, rapeseed or sunflower oils have substantially less VOC emissions.

- They are also easier to recycle because they can be removed from the paper much more effectively than petroleum inks. Therefore, less hazardous waste is created in the process.

Buying in Bulk

- Green products should be available in larger containers.

- Buying in bulk can save you money, and it reduces the amount of fossil fuels and energy needed to transport the products to sell and to dispose of or recycle.

- You are also reducing the amount of waste you're sending to landfill or a recycling centre.

- Hang on to your smaller shampoo bottles and other containers so you can refill them from larger bottles.

WHAT'S IN A PRODUCT'S CLAIM?

See through the 'green washing'

When you scan the shelves of green home products, typical claims include 'biodegradable', 'non-toxic', 'eco-friendly' and 'natural'. Some products use their labels to let you know that they are free from certain chemicals or that their ingredients come from plants, not petroleum sources. Unfortunately, a number of companies are capitalizing on the green wave by making claims on their labels that suggest their products are green when they aren't. This is called 'green washing'. Many of these claims are so non-specific or even contradictory that they really don't tell you anything about the product. For example, since there is no agreed and regulated definition for 'eco-friendly', the claim may identify a green product made according to strict environmental standards, or it may be a green-washing claim for a product that contains

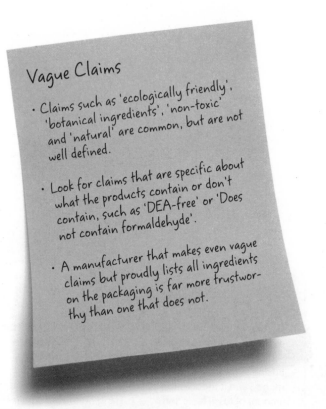

Vague Claims

- Claims such as 'ecologically friendly', 'botanical ingredients', 'non-toxic' and 'natural' are common, but are not well defined.

- Look for claims that are specific about what the products contain or don't contain, such as 'DEA-free' or 'Does not contain formaldehyde'.

- A manufacturer that makes even vague claims but proudly lists all ingredients on the packaging is far more trustworthy than one that does not.

Biodegradable

- Most products will bio-degrade eventually, give or take a hundred years, so look for claims that are time-specific.

- However, keep in mind that products like disposable nappies that go directly into landfill will generally not readily biodegrade.

- Landfill waste is not exposed to the natural conditions it needs to break down.

- Look for materials that are 'compostable'. Your compost heap will be much more effective than landfill in breaking down the material.

one organic ingredient and 40 synthetic ingredients, some of which are toxic. Since ingredient lists are hardly ever complete or understandable, we need to know how to read these claims for content.

The most specific and defined claims are the most commendable. Think 'Made from recycled materials' vs. '100 per cent post-consumer waste-recycled'. The latter tells you volumes that the former leaves out. It's important also to be educated about which chemicals have already been banned

from certain product categories. For example, aerosol cans that claim 'No CFCs' are guilty of green washing, since CFCs were banned in the 1970s. Read the entire label so you can catch conflicting claims: for instance on a cleaner that swears it is non-toxic on the front, yet bears a hazardous product warning on the back.

In general, always look for products that make very specific claims and stand by them by proudly displaying the list of their ingredients.

Stating the Obvious

Contains no Brussels sprouts!

- Be wary of products that claim to be free of chemicals that are generally not found in that product class.

- 'Phosphate-free' on automatic dishwashing detergents tells you a lot about the product, because most do contain phosphates.

- The same claim on laundry detergent is meaningless because phosphates have been largely phased out of that product class.

- Similarly, some products make claims that are not applicable to their category, such as 'organic' nail polish.

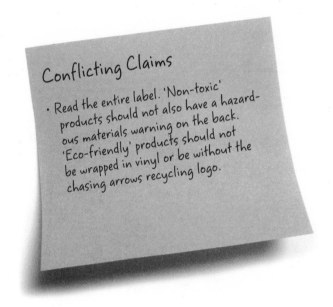

Conflicting Claims

- Read the entire label. 'Non-toxic' products should not also have a hazardous materials warning on the back. 'Eco-friendly' products should not be wrapped in vinyl or be without the chasing arrows recycling logo.

11

BACK TO BASICS

Essential inexpensive green-cleaning ingredients for your home

One of the biggest myths about 'going green' is that it costs a lot more than doing things the conventional way. When it comes to green cleaning, the exact opposite is true. In fact, it can be far less expensive to clean without toxins than it is to clean with them. Of course, you could spend the 10–30 per cent extra to replace each one of your conventional cleaners with a green one. But in fact, having so many distinct products is unnecessary; it's cheaper and just as easy to create your own cleaning products out of just a few ingredients you probably already have in your home.

As your grandmother (or hers) already knows, these basic ingredients work really well. Plus, you won't have to worry about whether a green-marketed product is actually green or wonder about ingredients that aren't listed on the label.

CLEAN HOME, GREEN HOME

White Distilled Vinegar

- Vinegar disinfects, loosens dirt and deodorizes. It also removes mineral deposits, stains and tarnish, and eliminates static cling when added to the rinse cycle.

- Look for white distilled vinegar with 5 per cent acetic acid. Dark vinegars stain.

- The alternative is lemon juice, which works to cut grease or polish metal. You can buy bottled lemon juice, but you'll use more than if you squeeze.

- Do not use on acid-sensitive surfaces such as marble.

Bicarbonate of Soda

- Bicarbonate of soda is just abrasive enough to make a great scourer that won't damage most surfaces.

- It also eats odours and works as a deodorizer for carpets, refrigerators and drains. Add it to the wash cycle to soften fabric.

- Mixing this alkaline powder with acidic vinegar will make it fizz and speed up your cleaning. This is great for toilets and to clear blocked drains.

- Look for bicarbonate of soda that is 'pure' or '100 per cent sodium bicarbonate'.

The recipes you'll find throughout this book are all based on these essential ingredients, so you can buy in bulk to save money and packaging.

As you get started, there may be some products you choose to buy for convenience or because you like the way they work. In each section, this book will note what to look for when buying green so you can choose the best products with ease and confidence.

· · · · · · · · · · GREEN● LIGHT · · · · · · · · · · · · · · ·

Split your bulk containers into smaller, recycled jars or bottles so you can keep them handy under bathroom and kitchen sinks, in the laundry room, or wherever you use them regularly.

GREEN TOOLS

Castile Soap

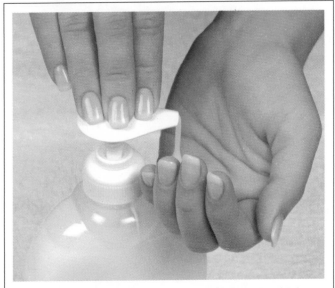

- Castile soap is soap made only from vegetable oil instead of animal fat. It's available in liquid form.

- Diluted castile soap can be used as an all-purpose cleaner, laundry soap or washing up liquid, spot remover and body washer.

- Look for 'Pure Castile' that is non-petroleum-based and does not contain detergents. The greenest choices use organic ingredients and come in 100 per cent recycled packaging.

- Buying in bulk is a great idea because castile soap is so versatile.

Borax and Washing Soda

- These alkaline minerals are like bicarbonate of soda but stronger and more caustic, so wear gloves and store out of reach of children.

- Add either borax or washing soda to your wash for extra cleaning and brightening or use to scrub extra-stubborn stains on worktops or bathtubs.

- Use borax to disinfect and whiten cloth nappies or as a highly effective mould killer and toilet bowl cleaner.

- Mix washing soda and bicarbonate of soda to clean dirty (non-self-cleaning) ovens.

13

ANTIBACTERIAL ARSENAL
Healthy, safe ingredients to combat germs

An easy way to save money and do something great for your health and the environment is to avoid antibacterial cleaning products and replace them with regular use of non-toxic soap and water, vinegar and essential oils. Research shows that antibacterial products don't work any better than regular soap and water in eliminating germs. Yet their cost to the environment and our health can be great.

Most antibacterial products contain antimicrobial pesticides, of which triclosan is the most common. In the USA it has been found in 57.6 per cent of waterways, making it one of the most prevalent environmental contaminants. Even more compelling, researchers have found a strong link between triclosan and dioxin, considered by many to be one of the most dangerous chemicals ever tested, and highly

Soap and Water

- Experts agree that soap and water are just as effective as, but less harmful than, antibacterial products.

- Soap reduces the surface tension of water and creates a thin film around dirt molecules, bacteria and even viruses. It captures them and transports them down the drain.

- Soap and water can effectively clean everything from your table and worktops to carpet and fabric stains.

- Look for vegetable-based, non-petroleum, detergent-free and fragrance-free soaps. Use warm water for fighting germs.

Vinegar

- Studies have shown that distilled white vinegar kills 99 per cent of bacteria, 82 per cent of moulds, and 80 per cent of germs.

- For best results, soak or spray and leave vinegar on the affected area. Rinse only on delicate surfaces.

- Vinegar can be used to disinfect laundry, household filters, chopping boards and just about anything.

- Keep a spray bottle of undiluted vinegar handy to clean up any problem areas quickly and easily.

carcinogenic. Studies show that triclosan is often contaminated with dioxin and can convert to dioxin when exposed to sunlight or treated with chlorine in water treatment plants. If that's not enough, strong evidence suggests that the overuse of antibacterial products is causing an increase in allergies and the creation of drug-resistant bacteria.

For a greener approach, washing your hands and home regularly and incorporating these natural products into your cleaning regimen are all you need for a healthy home.

ZOOM

When washing your hands, use regular, non-toxic soap, such as castile or glycerine. Make sure you work up a lather for a full 15–20 seconds. The soap bubbles surround the bacteria and take them with them when they're rinsed down the drain. Rinse thoroughly. Use a clean towel to dry your hands and remove any remaining bacteria.

Tea Tree Oil

- Tea tree oil is a fungicide and antibacterial that has been used for centuries.

- Adding a few drops to soap and water can enhance antibacterial effects.

- It's potent, so a little goes a long way. Anti-mould spray needs only 1 teaspoon tea tree oil to 500 ml water.

- Look for '100 per cent pure essential oil' rather than 'fragrant', 'perfume' or 'aromatherapy' oil, which may mean synthetic. The bottle should be brown or blue glass for a longer shelf life.

Lavender Oil

- Lavender is a great choice if you don't like the smell of tea tree oil.

- Lavender-scented cleaning products give you the added benefit of calming and mood-lifting aromatherapy.

- Add a few drops to a vaporizer to fight colds and infections. Add to all-purpose or glass cleaner or dilute with water to make an antibacterial spray.

- Watch out for synthetic versions and buy only 100 per cent essential oil in dark glass containers.

SPONGES AND SCOURERS

Go natural for non-toxic cleaning tools that are better for the environment

For such a simple product, the array of sponges and scourers now available is mind-boggling. When searching for the right sponge, avoid any that are labelled 'antibacterial', 'odour free', 'fights germs', or make any other claim that suggests they might be laden with pesticides (see page 2). However, sponges can collect bad bacteria that might pose a health risk, which is why some experts suggest throwing out your sponge each week to prevent the spread of germs.

But there is a less wasteful and equally effective alternative for keeping your sponges clean: microwave your sponge for 30 seconds, and you can kill nearly all bacteria except *E. coli*. Microwave for a full minute, and you can kill the *E. coli*

Natural Cellulose Sponges

Loofahs

- Natural cellulose sponges are made from wood pulp.

- The empty spaces absorb liquids and anything in the liquid, including dirt and bacteria, and the surface tension of the water keeps it from leaking out until you squeeze the sponge.

- Microwaving or replacing often is imperative to stop bacteria growing in the sponge's empty spaces.

- Even natural sponges can be coated with pesticides: make sure you read the whole label.

- Loofah is a gourd so it's renewable, biodegradable, and not a petroleum product.

- While loofahs are more common in the bath as an exfoliating tool, a few companies are introducing them as kitchen scourers.

- Loofahs can collect bacteria like any sponge, so be sure to keep them dry and disinfect them regularly.

- Wet the sponge thoroughly and place in the microwave for a minute. Give it some time to cool before removing and squeezing.

and 99.9 per cent of all other bacteria. If you don't have a microwave oven, boil the sponge for 3–5 minutes for the same effect. Throw the sponge out when you can see rips and tears in the surface fibres, which will only encourage the growth of bacteria.

Choosing the right sponge is a great opportunity to do something positive for the environment. Choose sponges made from renewable resources like natural cellulose or loofah and make sure they are unscented and chemical-free.

······· YELLOW ● LIGHT ·······

A word of caution: to minimize fire risk, be careful to dampen the sponge before microwaving. To save your fingers, wait a few seconds for the sponge to cool before picking it up.

Multi-Use Wood-Pulp Cloth

- Look for cloths made from natural wood pulp, which are odour-resistant and more absorbent than cotton cloth.

- Layers of fibre hold in dirt and water until you rinse them with clean water.

- Wood-pulp cloths feel like silk, but they do a great job scouring delicate surfaces without scratching.

- To clean, rinse, wring out and hang up to dry after use. Put them in the washing machine weekly and add 50 ml vinegar to the rinse cycle to disinfect.

Hemp Abrasive Scourers

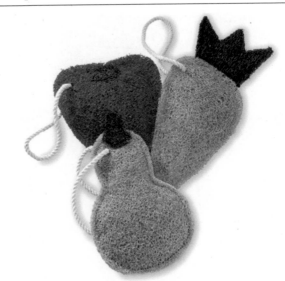

- Hemp is naturally coarse so it's perfect for scouring tough pots and pans or cleaning grouting.

- The plant is fast-growing and requires very little water and pest control.

- Hemp is naturally antibacterial, which means the scourers will outlast your sponges and cloths and need less maintenance cleaning – although it's still important to wring them out and let them dry between uses.

- Hemp is also machine-washable.

SOFT CLOTHS
Find the perfect cloth for the job and help the environment along the way

Paper towels have long been many people's cleaning cloth of choice. They're convenient and disposable so you don't have to deal with the muck. However, substantially reducing the use of paper towels can help in the fight to stop deforestation and reduce the chemical pollution resulting from the bleaching process. If you must continue to use paper towels for some tasks, look for a brand that is recycled and bleached without the use of chlorine.

Other types of cloths perform as well or better on any household cleaning job, and many of these can be recycled out of old clothes – saving both the discarded paper towels and the old clothing from the dustbin.

Old T-Shirts

- Use cotton T-shirts to dust, polish, and wipe any surface.

- The more they've been worn and washed the better, because all the finishes will have worn off and they'll be softer and more absorbent.

- Extend the life of rags by starting with the cleanest job, such as the mirror, and progressing to the dirtier job, such as the toilet.

- Throw dirty rags in the washing machine and add vinegar to the rinse cycle or washing soda to the wash cycle to disinfect them.

Wool Socks

- Old wool socks make excellent dusting tools, especially if you're delegating the job to children.

- Rotate the sock around your hand as each side gets filled up with dust.

- To make sure the dust stays on the socks instead of being pushed around, keep them slightly damp or use a damp dusting spray (see page 39).

- Dusting socks can be washed with the rest of your rags and reused indefinitely.

18

Using the right cloth can also improve the efficiency and quality of your cleaning experience. It can mean the difference between scattering the dust and actually removing the dust, or managing only a semi-clean window and achieving a spotless window. The key is to find the cloth that has the right properties for the job.

ZOOM

In the last 40 years the 'non-wovens industry' has devised specific single-use wipes for use on everything from babies' bottoms to car windscreens. Most are synthetic and not readily biodegradable. If you must have the convenience of a wipe, look for brands that are non-toxic, fragrance-free and biodegradable.

Flannel

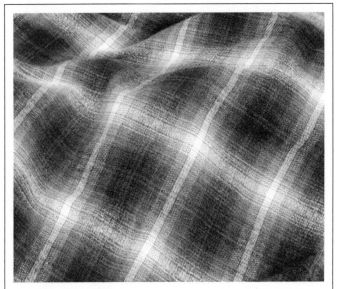

- Cotton flannel attracts dust and holds it to the fabric.

- It also makes a great polishing cloth for metal or wood because it's soft and won't scratch surfaces.

- To create dusting or polishing cloths, remove buttons and cut your old shirts into 15 x 25-cm rectangles and fold in half. As one section fills up with dust, flip or refold to a clean section.

- Throw in the washing machine with other rags and reuse indefinitely.

Microfibre

- Microfibre has become the duster of choice for the 21st century.

- Made from polyester and nylon, it is a petroleum-based product, but its ability to trap dust and bacteria without using a cleaning solution, and its reusability, make it worthy of consideration even for a green household.

- Microfibre is particularly good for dusting where using any kind of moisture or cleaning solution would cause damage, such as electronics or art.

VACUUM CLEANERS
Look for high-quality vacuum cleaners to improve indoor air quality

Studies show that indoor air is four times dirtier than outside air, and dust is a big contributor to the problem. Your vacuum cleaner is your most important tool for controlling dust in your home. But make sure the cleaner itself has low emissions or you may be counteracting its air-cleaning benefits.

Besides cleaning the air, regular vacuuming can make rugs and floors last longer. With the right attachments, vacuum cleaners can also be used to speed cleaning and reduce the need for cleaning products on upholstery, blinds and curtains, mattresses and bookshelves.

If someone in your family suffers from allergies, you'll want to stick to the models that use disposable bags to minimize your contact with dust. A HEPA filter is also crucial. If allergies are not a problem, you can reduce waste by buying a bagless

Types of Vacuum Cleaner

- Upright cleaners used to be for carpets and cylinder models for hard floors, but the distinction has blurred.

- Many upright models now allow you to turn the brush off and have attachments that make it easier to clean hard floors.

- Cylinders generally do better for upholstery and curtains. They're easier to manoeuvre on stairs and under furniture.

- Choose a cleaner that's not too heavy, doesn't require you to hunch over to use it, and has an accessible attachment compartment.

Bags

- Bagless vacuum cleaners collect dust and dirt in a container, which you then empty into your dustbin.

- This helps you reduce waste and costs because there are no special bags to buy.

- However, bagless cleaners can be hard on people with allergies, because emptying them can stir up a lot of dust and allergens.

- Most bagged models lose suction when the bag is only partially full, which means you change the bags more often.

20

vacuum. Some other types of filters work as well or almost as well as HEPA filters and mean that the cleaners cost less, so do your homework and compare the ratings published in consumer magazines.

Poor-quality vacuum cleaners can break easily and be expensive to repair. If you're buying a new cleaner, make sure the one you choose will last as long as possible. Look for models with washable lifetime filters and long-term warranties.

ZOOM

What's in that dust you're vacuuming? Unhealthy particles in the air can include tobacco smoke, dirt, pet dander, pollen and dust mite waste. But HEPA filters can also trap some of the chemical offgassing from household products. These include neurotoxic flame retardants and endocrine disrupting phthalates, as well as toxic pesticides.

Attachments

- Most cleaners come with a crevice tool, small brush, upholstery tool and floor tool.

- Other options can include motorized pet hair removal heads, car kit attachments, stair tools and different-sized brushes and floor tools.

- Extra attachments may add to the price of your vacuum cleaner. Consider which ones will be useful and which will be clutter.

- Store the most-used attachments in a mesh bag tied to the handle of an upright vacuum cleaner so they're readily accessible.

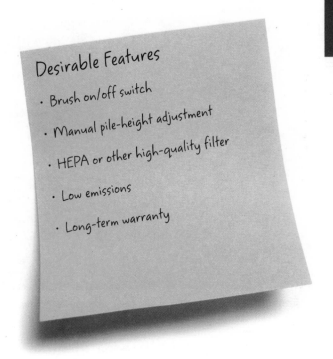

Desirable Features

- Brush on/off switch
- Manual pile-height adjustment
- HEPA or other high-quality filter
- Low emissions
- Long-term warranty

CLEAN GREEN SMELLS
Natural ways to make your home smell clean

We all know a clean home when we smell it. But just how clean is that smell? The smell of conventional cleaning products can be overpowering and make you feel queasy or give you a colossal headache – and those are just the effects you notice right away.

What smells 'clean' often truly isn't, and toxic cleaners – and especially air fresheners – can leave behind more trouble than they're worth. Rather than clean out the smells you're trying to eliminate from your home, most air fresheners simply mask unpleasant smells, which may include lingering dirty house smells or even ammonia from your cleaning products, with something even stronger. It's no wonder that the air inside a building is generally so much more polluted than outdoor air.

Lavender

- Considering that the word 'lavender' comes from the Latin *lavare,* which means 'to wash,' lavender is a natural choice for a clean home smell.

- A vase of fresh or dried lavender on the table or positioned in front of a window on a breezy day can make your entire home smell clean.

- Lavender sachets can do wonders for a stuffy wardrobe.

- As aromatherapy, lavender is considered a natural anti-depressant and can help you fall asleep.

Eucalyptus

- A few sprigs of eucalyptus in a vase can give your home an energizing, uplifting scent.

- The smell of eucalyptus also has medicinal properties that can help with colds, congestion and allergies.

- Fresh eucalyptus will last for three weeks or more if you rinse and then cut the stems under water.

- To dry eucalyptus, bind stems of a few sprigs and hang upside down in a dry and well-ventilated area.

But nature has no shortage of sweetly-scented offerings that can leave a house smelling, well, clean. Here are just a few natural products that can create the smell of the new green clean in your home.

············ RED ● LIGHT ············

Scented paraffin wax candles seem like a great way to make your home smell sweet, but these common candles are made from petroleum and pollute the air. If you see soot behind the candle, you get a glimpse of what you are breathing.

Non-toxic Candles

- Non-petroleum candle options include beeswax, soy and other vegetable-based waxes.

- Aromatherapy candles should be made with 100 per cent pure essential oils. Synthetic fragrances can emit toxic VOCs like neurotoxic toluene and benzene.

- Metal wicks may contain neurotoxic lead. Look for all-cotton wicks instead.

- To get the most out of pillar candles, make sure the first burn is long enough to establish a wide pool of melted wax – at least 2 hours for a 5-cm and 4–5 hours for a 7.5-cm diameter candle.

Essential Oils

- Essential oils can create a subtle clean scent for your home.

- Make a diffuser by adding a few drops of the oil to a small bowl of water placed over a night light.

- Mix up a room-freshening spray by adding 1 teaspoon of essential oil to 250 ml of water in a spray bottle.

- Make sure you buy only 100 per cent pure essential oils with no synthetic ingredients.

23

THE ART OF WASHING UP
A greener way to wash dishes by hand

When it comes to cleaning, low-tech cleaning solutions are often the greener ones, such as using vinegar instead of a product designed in a laboratory to clean your floors. But it's not always this obvious. Although automatic dishwashers require resources to build and distribute and they need electricity to clean, a widely-quoted study by researchers at the University of Bonn in 2004 found that using an automatic dishwasher is more eco-friendly than hand-washing. This is because the average dishwasher uses 13.5 litres of water per load while the sample of hand-washers the researchers studied used an average of 55–60 litres.

If you don't have a dishwasher – or if you have an old inefficient one that requires you to basically wash the dishes before putting them in the dishwasher – it's perfectly

CLEAN HOME, GREEN HOME

Wash without Waste

- Fill one side of your sink or a plastic washing-up bowl with enough clean, hot, soapy water to cover a load of dishes.

- Partially fill the other side of your sink with clean water for rinsing.

- Without turning the tap back on, wash the glassware, then cutlery, then already-scraped plates, then pots and pans.

- Rinse and place on drying rack. Change water in the sinks or bowls as needed.

Easy Dry

- Look for a rack that will fit all the dishes you use for a normal meal.

- Make sure your rack is either over the sink or on a draining board or tray that drains the water back into the sink.

- To prolong the life of your dish rack and tray, put away the dishes as soon as they are dry.

- Prevent mould and mildew by leaning the tray up against the rack to let it dry thoroughly.

possible to hand-wash without wasting all that water. The key is to set up a system that will reduce your water use without compromising cleanliness. Making or using non-toxic, natural washing-up liquid also helps and is a great alternative to automatic dishwashing detergent, which has more of an environmental impact.

Baking Dishes

- Steel wool is tempting for scouring baked-on food, but it can also ruin your dishes. Try this instead:

- Sprinkle 50 ml bicarbonate of soda into the bottom of the dish.

- Boil water in a kettle or pan and fill the dish with the boiling water so that all the baked-on food is covered.

- Leave the dish to soak overnight and then wash and dry as usual.

Pans

- There's no need to wear yourself out scrubbing burned pans with this technique:

- Pour 50 g regular table salt into the bottom of the pan.

- Add cold water so that all of the burned areas are covered. Stir the mixture.

- Leave to soak overnight, then scrub, wash and dry as usual.

KITCHEN

25

AUTOMATIC DISHWASHING
Green strategies for sparkling dishes and a clean environment

Washing dishes in the dishwasher doesn't have to be a feat of massive energy-consuming proportions. With greener detergents, energy-efficient machinery, and a good strategy that everyone in your family can use, you can make washing the dishes an eco-friendly affair.

If you have an energy efficiency–rated machine, you're already on the right path to conserving resources, but it's still important that you only wash full, well-organized loads at off-peak hours, such as at night just before going to bed.

Most dishwasher detergents contain ingredients that harm the environment and are irritating to our bodies. Powdered detergents can contain phosphates that can cause algal blooms in our waterways: these deplete the supply of oxygen in the water and subsequently kill off other aquatic life.

Detergents: What to Avoid

- Labels do not always list all ingredients, but this warning is your first clue.

- Most dish detergents are petroleum-based and contain phosphates, fragrance, colour and chlorine.

- Some contain alkyphenol ethoxylates (APEs), suspected hormone disruptors that do not readily biodegrade and can be contaminated with the carcinogen 1,4-dioxane.

- Other common ingredients are diethanolamine and triethanolamine, which can react with nitrites, used as a preservative, to form carcinogenic nitrosamines.

Detergents: What to Look for

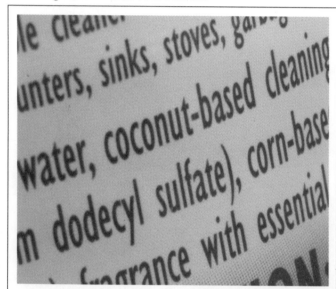

- The first indication that a detergent is a good choice is that all of the ingredients are listed on the bottle.

- Additionally, it should be a fragrance-, chlorine-, dye- and phosphate-free product.

- The ingredients should be mostly plant- and mineral-based.

- A few products are better than most, but given that all detergents are synthetic, there aren't any completely green options in this category.

Phosphates have already been banned in laundry detergents, but they are still around – and legal – in dishwashing detergents. Most detergents also contain chlorine, which is especially harsh to our lungs and skin when combined with the hot water from the dishwasher. Dyes that go into brightly coloured detergents may be contaminated with arsenic, lead or other heavy metals.

Chemicals called surfactants are another concern. These agents reduce the surface tension of the water (with the effect of making water wetter) so it can spread over a surface more easily. Almost all surfactants are derived from petroleum and have been shown to have neurotoxic and carcinogenic impact with prolonged exposure. According to some experts, even when products claim they contain plant-derived surfactants, they are still partially petroleum-based. But it is possible to find more eco-friendly detergents if you know what to look for.

Effective Loading: Top

- If you have a cutlery tray, arrange cutlery so individual pieces do not overlap or stack, and water can flow freely around them.

- Place bowls and saucers down the centre with enough space between them for cleaning.

- Place mugs and cups along the sides between prongs. Putting them over the prongs may lead to chipping.

- Hand-wash any glassware that is delicate or prone to falling over, such as stemmed wine glasses and champagne flutes.

Effective Loading: Bottom

- If you have a utensil basket, alternate between placing some cutlery pointing up and some down so they don't stack.

- Plates will be cleaner if you mix the sizes together so the water flows more freely around them.

- Place large pieces along the sides after the centre is full.

- Hand-wash wood, cast iron, painted china, nonstick pans, crystal and silver.

KITCHEN

27

SHINY SINKS
The dirt on sink cleanliness

We do more cleaning in the kitchen sink than anywhere else in the house. Yet the sink itself is often one of the more neglected areas in most people's cleaning routines. Without regular cleaning, dirt can build up on the sink, in the joints between the sink and the worktop, and around the taps. If it is neglected, the drain can start to emit odours and may become clogged.

How clean can your dishes be if the sink you washed them in is downright grimy? Even with the hottest water and soap, your sponge may be hanging out in a pool of water over a dirt-filled rim, creating the ultimate bacteria-breeding environment.

Because the kitchen sink gets so much use every day, it's a smart idea to give it a good cleaning every week. This will

Stainless Steel

- Cleaning tools: bicarbonate of soda, warm water and three soft cloths.

- Mix 50 g bicarbonate of soda with 1 litre of warm water until dissolved.

- Wash sink using this solution and a soft cloth. Use a toothbrush for rims and hard-to-reach areas of the sink.

- Rinse and wipe dry with a clean soft cloth.

- Finish by polishing with a dry cloth. If you have hard water, use a solution of half vinegar and half water to polish the surface.

Porcelain

- Cleaning tools: castile soap, warm water and a soft towel or sponge.

- Wash the entire sink with sudsy water, paying particular attention to where the sink meets the worktop and the drain opening where dirt can get caught.

- Rinse the inside of the sink with water and use a clean damp cloth to wipe the outside while minimizing drips to the floor.

- Don't use abrasive pads, wire brushes or abrasive cleaners that can scratch the surface.

ensure that the sink stays clean and that it never becomes so big a job that you feel you have to buy a toxic product to scrub it clean.

In choosing how you will clean the sink, consider its surface. Maintain its shine and avoid scratching or causing unnecessary wear with overly harsh cleaners or scourers. Also, a simple act of drain maintenance each week will keep your drains clean, clear and odour-free all year.

•••••••••••••••• GREEN ● LIGHT ••••••••••••••••
Your sink will look better and stay cleaner if you have a designated spot for your sponge, scourer and brush. Look for containers that offer drainage, such as a draining soap dish and a jar that holds your brush upright. Remember to wash the storage containers weekly to keep them clean.

Taps

- Wipe the taps daily with a clean sponge and towel dry.

- Remove mineral deposits by spraying the taps with equal parts vinegar and water and polishing with a soft cloth.

- For a weekly deeper clean, use an old toothbrush to get into all the crevices around the base, handle and spout.

- Start with mild dishwashing detergent. If crevices do not come clean, make a paste with bicarbonate of soda and water and scrub.

Clear and Clean Drain

- To clean, kill bacteria and prevent clogging, pour a kettle of boiling water down the drain each week.

- To disinfect and sharpen waste disposal blades, freeze white distilled vinegar in an ice cube tray. Grind cubes through disposal unit while running water.

- To deodorize or open up a slow-running drain, sprinkle 100 g baking soda and 120 ml vinegar down the drain.

- Cover with a wet rag and leave to fizz for 5 minutes. Flush with boiling water.

29

SPOTLESS WORKTOPS
Keep your food safe with clean worktops

Keeping worktops clean is serious business, because that's where all of your food is prepared. The most obvious danger is the spread of bad bacteria, like salmonella, which can happen when you don't clean up after slicing raw chicken or missing the bowl when you crack an egg. Daily worktop cleaning, along with frequent hand washing and the use of chopping boards, are important steps in minimizing the risk.

But in a typical busy house, worktop use is not limited to food preparation. Kitchen work surfaces can be holding zones for everything from mail to antifreeze as well as sites of art and science projects, temporary toddler holding and flower arranging.

Since each of these activities can leave its mark and contaminate food, it's important to keep the worktops as clean

Proactive Steps

- Using chopping boards for everything from carving meat to cutting lemons helps keep your worktops sanitary and in good condition.

- Use glass chopping boards that fit in the dishwasher for raw meat, or wooden ones used only for this purpose.

- Wood chopping boards are generally resistant to bacteria and are great for fruits and vegetables, but they don't go in the dishwasher.

- Choose renewable or recycled materials such as bamboo, recycled plastic or reclaimed Corian.

Chopping Board Care

Scrub with the grain

- Plastic and glass boards should be washed with soap and hot water or run through the dishwasher after every use.

- Wood and bamboo boards should be hand-washed with castile soap and a scrubbing brush after use.

- To disinfect, routinely coat with antibacterial spray and leave to dry without rinsing.

- To get deep in the crevices, periodically sprinkle coarse salt on the board and scrub with a cut lemon.

30

as possible. But how you clean them is as important as how often you clean them. Instead of trading bacteria for toxic cleaner residue, use homemade cleaning solutions to keep your worktops clean and your food safe.

Use this easy-to-make all-purpose cleaner for non-toxic daily maintenance for most surface types, and this natural antibacterial spray for extra safety.

MAKE IT EASY

Easy all-purpose solution: Combine 250 ml vinegar, 2 teaspoons borax, ½ teaspoon castile soap, 500 ml hot water in large spray bottle and shake until borax dissolves. Store and use indefinitely.

Antibacterial spray: 10–12 drops lavender or tea tree essential oil, 250 ml water. Store and use indefinitely in small spray bottle.

Easy Worktop Cleaning

- Worktops should be washed every evening.

- Most worktop surfaces, including concrete, butcher's block and stainless steel, will clean well with just castile soap and water.

- Plastic, laminate or Corian worktops can handle an

all-purpose cleaner (see above). Don't use an abrasive scourer because it may scratch.

- Don't forget to wash backsplashes as well, especially behind the sink and stove.

pH Neutral Cleaning

- Stone, marble, and tiled worktops require pH-neutral cleaners, such as mild washing-up liquid and water.

- Never use acidic cleaners like vinegar or lemon juice on these surfaces because they can be etched by the acid.

- Use a soft bristle brush to dislodge debris from grouting. Avoid abrasive pads or cleaners. Studies have found elevated radon emissions from a limited number of granite worktops. If you have granite, it's a good idea to have them tested (see page 150).

31

APPLIANCES
Eco-friendly cleaning for the long haul

Regular cleaning of your major kitchen appliances can extend their life spans, because dirt and grime don't have a chance to build up and cause damage.

As with everything else, there seems to be a product for every job and every type of appliance in the kitchen, and many are extremely toxic. In fact, oven cleaners are one of the top three most corrosive household products on the market and should be avoided. These corrosive substances can cause severe burning to your eyes, skin and throat if they are ingested. Many oven cleaners also contain the known carcinogen benzene, as well as sodium hydroxide, which can cause scarring and blindness. Luckily, with the self-cleaning function in today's ovens, there is little need to use such harsh products.

Refrigerator

Shelves slide out

Removable drawers

- Remove all food from your refrigerator and all shelves and drawers.

- Wipe down interior with a sponge dipped in castile soap and water. Use a scourer for problem spots.

- Wash each component in the sink and dry before reassembling. Add an open box of bicarbonate of soda to absorb odours and change the box every three months.

- Use soap or all-purpose cleaner (see page 31) to wipe down external doors and handles.

Dishwasher

- If your dishwasher smells or loses efficiency, it's time to clean it.

- Use warm, soapy water and a sponge to scrub the door and inside cavity. A toothbrush works well in dirty crevices.

- Remove the bottom rack and clean around the drain area.

- Place a cup of vinegar in the top rack and run the dishwasher through a rinse cycle. This will help disinfect, cut grease and eliminate hard-water deposits that can clog the drain.

Stainless-steel appliances look sleek but need to be cleaned often to battle fingerprints. Many stainless-steel-specific cleaners are extreme irritants to the eyes, skin and lungs, and quite a few of them come in spray bottles that seem to invite contact with these areas.

You can cut the risk involved with appliance cleaning by using the cleaning features built into the appliance and the most basic, non-toxic cleaning solutions.

• • • • • • • • • • • GREEN ● LIGHT • • • • • • • • • • •

For cleaner coffee, first soak the removable parts of the filter machine, and the jug, for a few hours in 2 teaspoons bicarbonate of soda dissolved in water. Wash and dry them normally. Then, fill the reservoir with white vinegar and run the vinegar through the machine. Repeat twice with vinegar and then do the same with water to rinse.

KITCHEN

Oven

- If your oven smokes, clean it immediately. Otherwise clean it every few months. Remove racks and soak in warm sudsy water for 3 hours or overnight.

- Switch a self-cleaning oven to 'clean' mode. When it's done and cooled, wipe interior with a damp cloth.

- For a non-self-cleaning oven, make a paste with 150 g bicarbonate of soda, 50 g salt and 50 ml water, and coat interior. Leave overnight then scrape with a plastic spatula. Wipe clean with a damp cloth. Replace salt with washing soda for extra dirty ovens.

Stove

- Most stove surfaces need only all-purpose cleaner (see page 31) and a sponge or cloth.

- Glass hobs often have a protective coating, so use castile soap and water or equal parts vinegar and water to cut grease.

- Electric burners have removable plates that need to be soaked and washed by hand monthly to keep them safe and sparkling.

- Wash grates or pans for gas burners by hand as well, and clean off any spills as soon as they are cool.

CUPBOARDS
Keep storage areas sanitized for a healthy kitchen

Along with a shiny sink, clean cupboard doors go a long way towards making a kitchen appear sparkling clean. Sticky fingers leave behind dirt and bacteria, especially around the door handles.

Routine wiping helps ensure that food and grime don't build up and damage the surface of the door. Make this a part of your daily kitchen maintenance routine.

But there is more to cleaning the cupboards than just the doors. Keeping the insides clean is crucial. Food and liquid spills can attract insects and rodents and even encourage the growth of mould, which contaminates stored food and dishes, as well as the air.

Under the kitchen sink, where you may store cleaning products along with rubbish and compost pails, is another area

Clean Doors

This area gets the dirtiest

- Wash cupboard doors with warm soapy water and dry with a towel to avoid streaking.

- Pay particular attention to fingerprints in the area around the handle.

- Open the door and wipe down the other side.

- Handles and hinges can collect grime, so once a season it's a good idea to unscrew them and soak them in warm water and washing-up liquid for 30 minutes. Use a brush to scrub lightly, dry and reattach.

Shelf Liners

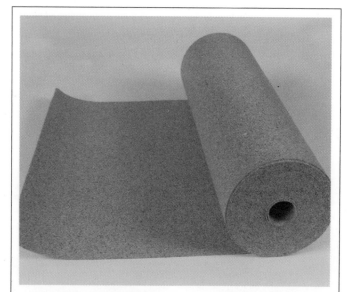

- Removable shelf liners help speed your cupboard cleaning. Take them out carefully and shake crumbs and dust into the sink.

- Avoid adhesive vinyl liners, which will pollute the air in the cupboards, and thus your food and dishes, with toxic VOCs.

- Cork is a great option because it provides some cushioning to minimize breakages.

- Other natural fabrics that are machine washable are also good choices.

that needs at least an occasional thorough cleaning. Because of the plumbing here, this is a good place to check for leaks. If you notice dampness, take care of the problem right away. Leaks account for an average of 14 per cent of household water use, and dark, wet cupboards can get mouldy fast. Lining the floor of this cupboard with old baking trays or non-vinyl shelf liner paper can make the job easier because these surfaces are washable. If you're switching to green cleaning, you'll want to dispose of old toxic cleaners appropriately and give the cupboard under the sink a deep detox.

Moths and other pests hang out here

Deep Clean

- Deep-clean once a season, or more if you have problems with pests or mould.

- Empty cupboards and place items away from your work area. Remove shelf liners to wash or wipe down with warm sudsy water.

- Use a handheld vacuum cleaner or a damp sponge to remove crumbs and dirt.

- Wash shelves and walls with soap and water. Leave to dry thoroughly before replacing shelf liners and other items.

Under the Sink Detox

- Empty the cupboard and pour flour, cat litter or sand to soak up any liquid that remains from your old cleaners. Leave for 5 minutes.

- Using a piece of cardboard, scrape mixture into an old plastic bag.

- Use washing-up liquid or laundry detergent, water and a brush to scrub the interior of the cupboard. Leave doors open to dry.

- To control spills, place old baking sheets under your new green cleaners and wash sheets as needed.

TOXIC PLASTICS
Your crib sheet for choosing the safest plastics

Plastics are under scrutiny for leaching unhealthy chemicals into our food and water and for the mountains of waste they create in our landfill sites, oceans and roadsides. Yet there's no doubt that many daily tasks, such as packing a lunch or quenching our thirst when we're out of the house, would be much less convenient without plastic. Knowing how to sort by number empowers you to know which to cut and which to keep.

Although plastic is the poster child for the green mantra 'Reduce, reuse, recycle,' it is also where the cycle most obviously breaks down. Plastic made from recycled materials uses 70 per cent less energy than when made from scratch, and recycling reduces the plastic content of landfill sites. But not all plastics are recyclable everywhere, and some are not recyclable at all. It's estimated that nearly 3 million tonnes

CLEAN HOME, GREEN HOME

Bad Plastic Type 3

- Some cling films and soft bottles are type 3 PVC (polyvinyl chloride).

- PVC contains endocrine-disrupting phthalates, to make it pliable, and vinyl chloride, which is a known carcinogen.

- PVC leaches toxins into food, especially when used to heat fatty foods.

- Use glass containers with covers instead of cling film and avoid buying products in plastic containers marked as type 3. Or, look for safer plastic: type 4 LDPE (low-density polyethylene).

Bad Plastic Type 6

- Type 6 PS (polystyrene) includes Styrofoam take-away containers and meat packaging. In its hard clear form, it's used for take-aways and plastic cups and utensils.

- Type 6 is made with carcinogenic benzene and leaches endocrine-disrupting

styrene, another possible carcinogen, into food.

- This plastic is generally not recyclable, so it's best to avoid it all together.

- If your favourite take-away place uses it, bring your own container and ask them to find a safer plastic.

of plastic is thrown away annually in the UK, but only about 7 per cent of the plastic used in British cities makes it into the recycling stream.

Reuse is also problematic because many plastics are designed for just a single use. Any good environmentalist will want to reuse that container at least a few times before finally recycling it or throwing it out.

Microwaving single-use plastic is a big risk, because studies show that chemicals from the plastic can leach into your food. Single-use containers labelled 'microwave safe' are generally misleading, because the label simply means that the container won't melt in the microwave. It's safe for the container and for your microwave to reuse these plastics, but it might not be safe for you. To be extra careful, it's best to do all your microwaving in non-plastic containers.

Of all the '3Rs', reducing is the most important. To support the planet and your health, minimize the amount of plastic you buy. This crib sheet will help you do it.

Bad Plastic Type 7

- Type 7 is usually polycarbonate, which is found in most baby bottles as well as large water bottles, reusable food storage containers and liners in food cans.

- Polycarbonate plastic leaches bisphenol A (BPA), thought to be a reproductive and hormonal toxin.

- Studies show that leaching increases with heat, yet heating is common with baby bottles and storage containers.

- Switch to glass containers and bottles or find bottles that are polycarbonate- and BPA-free.

Safer Plastics

- Type 1 PET or PETE (polyethylene terephthalate) is used for fizzy drinks bottles and plastic containers for ketchup, salad dressing and other foods.

- It is not known to leach toxins and is widely recyclable.

- Type 2 HDPE (high-density polyethylene) is used for milk, water and juice bottles along with yogurt and other tubs, cereal box liners and shopping bags.

- It is not known to leach toxins and is widely recyclable.

LIGHT FITTINGS
For a clean eating area, start at the top

Overhead light fittings are often neglected because, when we sit at the table and look up, we don't see all the dust and grime that has accumulated on top or in the crevices. A coating of dust on a lightbulb can diminish the quality and amount of light coming from the fitting by up to 25 per cent. If that bulb is under a shade that is also dusty, the reduction in light is even more dramatic. Routine dusting and cleaning

also gives you the opportunity to inspect your fittings regularly, drastically reducing the chance that they become a fire hazard due to frayed wiring or other damage.

Like it or not, another reason for regularly dusting the light fitting over the table is to minimize the amount of dust you eat. Think about those nice warm sunny days when you feel a fresh breeze coming in through your window or door. It

Dust

- Feather dusters get into hard-to-reach places, but they can disperse more dust than they grab.

- Use wool, flannel or an old cotton T-shirt sprayed lightly with damp dusting spray (see page 39). Or use a microfibre cloth to capture the dust.

- Dust all parts of the light from the base to each individual bulb and shade.

- Sturdy shades can be vacuumed with a small brush attachment. For delicate shades try microfibre or a soft paintbrush.

Deeper Clean

- Turn off light, place cloth over table below to catch drips, and remove shades and bulbs.

- For metal fittings, wipe with a cloth dampened with castile soap and water. Follow with a clean damp cloth and then a dry cloth.

- For crystal or glass, dampen a cotton cloth with equal parts hot water and vinegar. Rinse as needed.

- Some glass drops can be removed and hand-washed with warm soapy water and dried with a soft cloth.

38

doesn't seem so fresh when you consider that it's no doubt scattering the dust from your light fitting all over your grilled sweetcorn and potato salad.

Light fittings are the first task to tackle in your eating area because they are at the top of the room and any dirt or dust you do scatter will be picked up by the time you get down to washing the floors.

Polish: Stainless Steel and Chrome

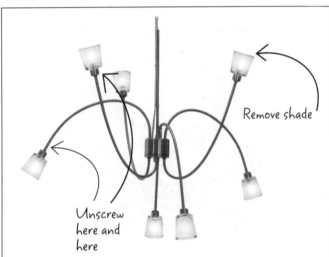

Remove shade

Unscrew here and here

- Turn off and, if possible, dismantle the light fitting for easy cleaning.

- Create a paste from bicarbonate of soda and water and apply using a soft, cotton flannel cloth. Gently rub paste into metal following the metal grain direction.

- Rinse thoroughly and dry with another clean, dry, soft flannel cloth.

- Be sure all parts are completely dry before reassembling light fitting.

Polish: Copper and Brass

Remove shade

- Turn off light, remove shade and dismantle fitting.

- Create a paste from salt, flour and vinegar.

- Apply with a soft cotton flannel cloth, wiping in the direction of the metal grain.

- Rinse each piece thoroughly and dry with another clean, soft, flannel cloth. Make sure the fitting is completely dry before reassembling light.

EATING AREAS

39

WOOD TABLES AND CHAIRS
Toxic tables make for dirty eating, so watch where you sit and eat

You may spend extra to buy your family the healthiest food available, but if your table is toxic, your eating experience is too. Wooden tables can be varnished, stained or sealed with products that contain VOCs, and unfortunately these harmful chemicals don't just stay on the table. VOCs are released as gases into the air you breathe. They can have short-term effects like irritation in the eyes, nose and throat, or headaches and nausea. They also can cause severe, long-term damage to the central nervous system, liver and kidneys. Some VOCs are suspected or known carcinogens.

If you're thinking of buying a new table, it's a good idea to look for low- or no-VOC tables, or buy an unfinished piece and stain and seal it yourself using low- or no-VOC products. While you're at it, look for a table that is certified by the Forest

Green and Clean Table

- Wood tables are perfect for a green home – but not all wood tables are green.

- Seek out this logo, which notes that the wood is harvested responsibly and respectfully both to the environment and the people doing the work.

- Luckily, wood tables are fairly low maintenance and will be fine with routine dusting and damp wiping to remove dust and crumbs.

- An occasional polish and wax will help protect the wood and ensure a long life.

Wood Polish: What to Avoid

WARNING: May be harmful if swallowed.

- Most furniture polishes can irritate the skin and eyes. Yet, because they are usually sprayed either by aerosol or spray bottle, skin and eyes are vulnerable.

- Many polishes contain petroleum distillates, which are neurotoxic and flammable.

- Polish can also contain carcinogenic formaldehyde.

- If you buy, look for a plant-based product that does not contain solvents. Otherwise, try the simple recipe on page 41 and do it yourself.

Stewardship Council, so you know the wood comes from responsibly managed forests.

But don't stop there. Keep your clean table clean by avoiding toxic cleaners. Chemicals in furniture polish can irritate eyes, skin and lungs, and they can contain carcinogens. You can get great results with this do-it-yourself recipe and enjoy your meals knowing that your table is truly clean.

Polish Technique

Polish with the grain

- For natural and unfinished wood, first dust and then wash the table with a sponge dampened with mild washing-up liquid and water.

- Put a small amount – the size of a 10 pence piece to start with – of polish on soft, cotton flannel cloth.

- Apply to the table, using long strokes that follow the direction of the wood grain.

- Varnished or shellacked wood finishes do not need polish.

Easy Fix

To get rid of water or heat rings on your table:

- Wipe the area with a damp sponge.

- Mix mayonnaise and wood ash to a paste. The ash grit buffs the finish and the mayonnaise lubricates the wood.

- Dip soft cotton or flannel cloth in the mixture and rub on to area.

- Wipe the paste off with cloth. Polish the table to even out the appearance.

EATING AREAS

41

WAXING WOOD FURNITURE
Protect your furniture without polluting the air

Waxing is key to prolonging the life of your wood furniture. Besides making it look practically new, wax protects wood by creating a slick surface that an object can slide across without scratching. Wax also creates an antistatic layer, so dust doesn't stick.

Yet most furniture wax contains toxic solvents, which are chemicals such as toluene, that keep products moist. Because they are fat-soluble, experts believe that, when we inhale them, they can go straight to the brain where they can cause damage. Many commercially available wax products also contain the known carcinogen benzene.

A safer alternative is to make your own furniture wax or find a brand that is vegetable-based. The homemade wax recipe you see here is one of the more involved recipes in this book

What to Avoid

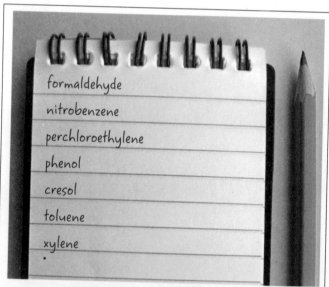

formaldehyde

nitrobenzene

perchloroethylene

phenol

cresol

toluene

xylene

- Formaldehyde and nitrobenzene are carcinogens.

- Perchloroethylene (PERC) is a toxic organochlorine solvent and probable carcinogen; it's used most commonly in dry cleaning.

- Phenol and cresol are caustic respiratory irritants that can have immediate effects like diarrhoea, fainting and dizziness, and cause long-term damage to the kidney and liver. Phenol is a suspected carcinogen, neurotoxin and mutagen.

- Toluene and xylene are neurotoxic solvents.

What to Look For

- In addition to the chemicals used as solvents and emulsifiers and more, most furniture wax uses a petroleum-based wax such as paraffin.

- Look for paste wax made from natural ingredients like beeswax and plants like carnauba or linseed.

- Beeswax is recognized by furniture conservators as water resistant, gentle on the finish and long-lasting.

- It will give wood furniture a soft, satiny look that resists scratches as well as water damage.

partly because it requires that you actually heat and mix ingredients together instead of just pouring and shaking. However, because you only need to wax your furniture every 6 months to a year, I encourage you to give it a try.

Beeswax is a great substitute for the more usual petroleum-based waxes. Beeswax is produced naturally by bees to make their honeycombs and has been used for centuries by humans, in everything from candles to lip balms.

Homemade furniture wax:
115 g jojoba oil
25 g beeswax
25 g carnauba wax
120 ml water
Melt the oil and waxes in a double boiler over medium heat. Take it off the heat and add the water. Blend with a hand mixer until creamy.

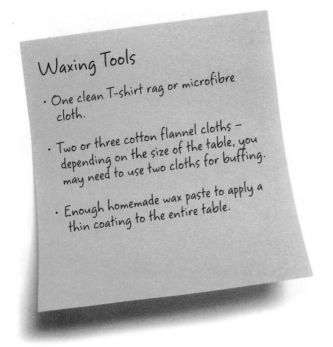

Waxing Tools

- One clean T-shirt rag or microfibre cloth.

- Two or three cotton flannel cloths – depending on the size of the table, you may need to use two cloths for buffing.

- Enough homemade wax paste to apply a thin coating to the entire table.

Wax Technique

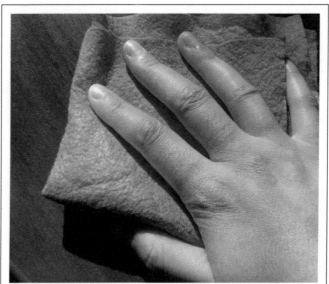

- Dust surface with a dry T-shirt or microfibre cloth.

- Dip flannel rag in wax paste. Start small. Too much wax clouds the finish.

- Coat the surface by rubbing in the direction of the grain until you've spread a thin layer evenly across the wood. On non-flat surfaces, use a toothbrush and a circular motion to apply wax. Leave to dry.

- Use a clean cloth to buff table to a shine. When the cloth starts sliding across the surface, the job's done.

EATING AREAS

43

NON-WOOD TABLES
Keep them clean enough to eat off of with plain old soap and water

While wood is the most common material for tables, there are many other types of tables to choose from. Most non-wood tables require less maintenance than those made of wood, but you need to pay attention to the surface and choose your cleaning solution accordingly.

For almost all surfaces, maintenance cleaning requires only a natural sponge with just a dab of washing-up liquid and water. It's essential to wipe down the table after every meal to get rid of any food particles. This is especially important if you have a tiled top with grouted joints, where food can become embedded, making cleaning difficult. Beyond that, routinely wiping the dry table with a microfibre or flannel dusting rag will keep it dust-free. Don't forget to wipe down the table legs and the chairs as well.

Glass

- Wipe the table free of crumbs with a sponge after every meal.

- Dust the table and base once a week so it looks clean and the dust doesn't have a chance to build up.

- For sparkling clean glass, mix one part white vinegar to two parts water with a dash of castile soap.

- Spray the solution on the table and wipe with newspaper or a clean T-shirt.

Tile or Stone

Scrub the lines of grouting

Dust c[an] build u[p] here

- Wiping the table after meals helps keep the crumbs from getting embedded between the tiles.

- Wash the table with mild soapy water and a sponge, and use a toothbrush to really scrub the grouting.

- With a wood-framed tile or stone table, avoid soaking the wood as you clean. Wring the sponge out and just wipe clean.

- Remember to dust the legs and pay careful attention to crevices where dust collects.

While tiled tables have the drawback of dirt-catching grouting, glass tables show dirt and fingerprints easily. Glass tables look best when they're wiped free of food and then washed like a window, with a vinegar and water mixture (see page 51). With clear glass tables, keeping the frame and legs clean and free of dust is even more important, since they are visible from every angle.

Tables made from plastics are definitely the easiest to clean and require only the mildest of soap and water. Like all plastics, these products are petroleum-based and should be avoided where possible.

If you're looking for a new non-wood table to buy, choose one that is low maintenance and doesn't require special toxic cleaners. It's a great idea to buy second-hand furniture and save all the energy and materials that go into manufacturing new pieces. This is an especially good choice if you want the retro look of a plastic product. Another option is to buy a table made of recycled glass, plastic, steel or tile.

Plastic or Formica

- The only real way to damage a table like this one when cleaning it is by using too abrasive a scourer or cleaner.

- Instead, wipe it clean after meals and wash with soapy water once a week.

- For tougher stains, sprinkle on bicarbonate of soda and scrub with an ordinary sponge. This will give you the grit you need to remove the stain without scratching.

- Don't forget to wash the base of the table.

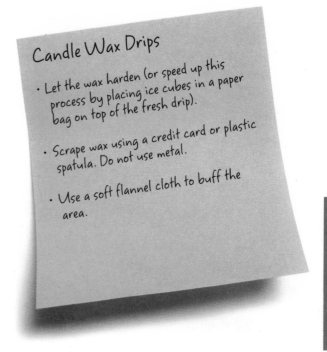

Candle Wax Drips

- Let the wax harden (or speed up this process by placing ice cubes in a paper bag on top of the fresh drip).

- Scrape wax using a credit card or plastic spatula. Do not use metal.

- Use a soft flannel cloth to buff the area.

CLEANING SILVER
Best defence against tarnish on silver? Use it regularly

If you have good silver, try polishing it without the use of toxic cleaners. Most metal polishes contain neurotoxic petroleum distillates, carcinogenic formaldehyde or respiratory-irritant ammonia. One proactive step you can take to avoid these toxins is to use your silver more often and hand-wash your pieces after each use. By using your silver more often, you will reduce the amount of polishing you need to do. Be wary of putting good silver in the dishwasher. When silver comes into contact with stainless steel, as it might in a dishwasher, a chemical reaction could damage the silver.

A method that your grandparents probably used, and that is often recommended as a green alternative to polish, is simple and doesn't require any elbow grease. Fill a large pan with aluminium foil, salt, bicarbonate of soda and warm

Silver Polish to Avoid

Metal cleaners and polishes can contain:

- Petroleum distillates – neurotoxin

- Formaldehyde – carcinogen

- Ammonia – respiratory irritant

- Phenol – respiratory irritant and suspected carcinogen

- Phosphoric acid – eye, skin and respiratory irritant

Silver-Polishing Toothpastes to Look For

- The most basic white toothpaste you can find is ideal for polishing silver.

- Gel toothpastes are not effective for polishing silver.

- The toothpaste should contain no bicarbonate of soda and no fluoride.

- It should have nothing but natural ingredients, including flavouring.

water. Then submerge your tarnished silver for an hour and rinse it. However, use caution and do this in a well-ventilated area, as some experts warn that this technique emits hydrogen sulphide gas, which can irritate your eyes and throat and may cause coughing or shortness of breath.

Using toothpaste is a gentler method that works easily and effectively. If you choose to use toothpaste, find one without bicarbonate of soda and colouring, as some experts warn that abrasive bicarbonate of soda can damage silver.

Since most recommended green methods of polishing silver involve bicarbonate of soda, this is important information to consider, especially if the silver you're polishing is a family heirloom or has significant value. That said, the limited number of non-toxic polish options means that using a mild toothpaste to polish may be the best method.

Polishing Step 1: Scrub

- For quick, small jobs like necklaces or one tarnished fork, using your finger as an applicator is fine.

- Squeeze the toothpaste on to your finger and rub into the piece until covered.

- For bigger jobs, squeeze the toothpaste on to a toothbrush.

- Rub in a circular motion until the entire piece is covered with paste.

Polishing Step 2: Rinse

- Toothpaste polishing means instant gratification. No need to wait unless the piece is badly tarnished.

- Rinse each piece thoroughly in the sink. Use a cloth to carefully remove all toothpaste, working it out of nooks and crannies.

- Dry silver completely with a towel.

- Shine with a clean flannel cloth.

EATING CLEAN
Non-toxic food crib sheets to help you navigate the supermarket

You've cleaned everything from your cupboards to your refrigerator, your light fitting to your table. The last thing you want to do is sit down in your clean kitchen or dining room to dine on dirty food.

While buying clean foods is not as easy as one would think, there are just a few things you need to know to sort the green from the green-washed.

If you're lucky enough to have a regular farmers' market that sells locally grown organic produce, this option is by far your best bet. You not only avoid the pesticides, but you also bypass all the energy and fossil fuels that go into the long distribution channels from farm to supermarket.

If you buy organic at your local supermarket, you are definitely ahead of the game, but there is some controversy

CLEAN HOME, GREEN HOME

Vegetable Dirty Dozen

- Fruits and vegetables with thick, removable skin, like oranges and bananas, contain fewer pesticides so buying organic is not so important.

- Some fruits and vegetables absorb more pesticides, so it's more important to buy organic versions of these.

- Fruit to buy organic: apples, cherries, grapes, nectarines, peaches, pears, raspberries and strawberries.

- Vegetables to buy organic: peppers, celery, potatoes and spinach.

Safest Fish and Seafood

Oily fish — herring, mackerel, sardines, wild trout, farmed carp
Cold water prawns and mussels
Alaskan wild salmon
Alaskan and Pacific halibut
Dover sole
Red mullet
Pollack

- Some fish are off the list because of high mercury levels. Mercury is neurotoxic and can have a severe impact on a child's development.

- Other fish are off because overfishing or unsustainable farming have wreaked havoc on the environment and reduced fish populations.

- Look for fish bearing the Marine Stewardship Council (MSC) label, which guarantees that the fish comes from a sustainable fishery.

- If buying farmed fish, organic is preferable.

over whether the mainstreaming of organic is making the label less meaningful and the food less healthy. The organic movement historically championed small, pesticide-free, family-owned farms as a healthier and greener alternative to industrial farming. Yet, these days, there is an entire sector of large-scale organic farming that looks just like industrial farming, but without the pesticides. The upshot is that this food is still better for you and the environment, even if the growing process has a long way to go to be truly earth-friendly.

In the meat world, label claims can be misleading. Words like 'natural', 'free-range', and even 'antibiotic-free' should not alway be taken at face value. However, there are many good producers who maintain high levels of animal welfare and produce excellent meat and dairy products. Check out local suppliers and be prepared to pay a fair price for carefully raised, delicious meat – consider eating less meat but of higher quality, and explore cheaper cuts that respond to long, slow cooking.

Dairy Products

- Revised EU legislation on organic food production came into force in January 2009, and the EU plans to introduce a new logo to be displayed on all organic produce from July 2010.

- 'Organic' means free from hormones, antibiotics, genetic engineering, radiation, synthetic pesticides and fertilizers.

- Organically reared cows eat a more natural diet with higher levels of fresh pasture, which gives their milk additional health benefits such as raised levels of omega-3 essential fatty acids and vitamins E and A.

Meat and Poultry Labels

- In the UK, free-range chickens have daytime access to outside runs for at least half their life, whether they are bred for meat or eggs.

- 'Free-range pork' has no legal definition. On the best farms, sows and piglets are kept outside for most of their lives.

- 'Outdoor bred' piglets are taken indoors after weaning, and may then be raised intensively. 'Outdoor reared' piglets spend part of their lives outside.

- Beef labelled 'grass-fed' means the animals have grazed mostly outside on natural grass.

WASH BASIN AREA
Match the type of cleaner to your wash basin to avoid scratching

It's easy to damage your bathroom fittings by using too harsh a cleanser, especially for delicate surfaces like vitreous china or copper. The key to finding the right cleaner for your wash basin is to start with as mild a solution as possible and add ingredients as needed.

Many glass cleaners contain dioxane, a known carcinogen, and ammonia, a respiratory irritant. Cleaning with ammonia in the bathroom is particularly dangerous since it is usually a smaller space with inadequate ventilation and because ammonia creates toxic gases when mixed with chlorine, a common ingredient in other bathroom cleaners.

Luckily, vinegar and water work really well on mirrors. There are two drawbacks – the smell and the streaks – but they are easily overcome. The vinegar smell is an easy one because it

Ceramic, Vitreous China or Fireclay

- These are the most common basin materials and the most durable. However, overly abrasive cleaners can do a lot more harm than good.

- Daily or at least weekly cleaning can be done with warm soapy water and a soft cloth.

- For deeper cleaning or to eliminate a stain, gently scrub with a mildly abrasive cleaner (see page 55) applied with a sponge or soft rag.

- If soap scum is a problem, use the advanced glass cleaner recipe (see page 51) and wipe clean.

Glass

- Wipe the basin dry after every use to reduce spotting.

- To clean, scrub the drain and any seams around the basin with mild soap and water and rinse.

- Then use glass cleaner recipe (see page 51) with a T-shirt rag or newspaper to wash the basin as you would a window or mirror.

- Abrasive cleaners will scratch the surface and make the glass appear dull.

50

goes away in a matter of minutes, not hours like ammonia or other cleaning chemicals. If you've previously used chemical glass cleaners, you will get streaking when you first use vinegar and water. This is not the vinegar – it's the film left from your old glass cleaner that causes the streaking. Add some castile soap to the mix for the first few cleanings to avoid streaking. After that, vinegar and water will work perfectly.

Tough Surfaces

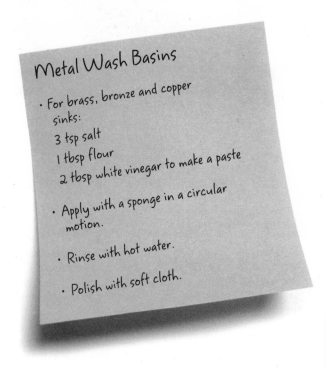

Metal Wash Basins

- For brass, bronze and copper sinks:
  3 tsp salt
  1 tbsp flour
  2 tbsp white vinegar to make a paste

- Apply with a sponge in a circular motion.

- Rinse with hot water.

- Polish with soft cloth.

- Older homes may have porcelain enamel on cast iron or steel bathroom fittings, which need some special treatment.

- Do not use acidic cleaners like vinegar and lemon juice to clean these surfaces, as they can cause damage.

- Instead, wash routinely with mild washing-up liquid and warm water applied with a soft cloth or sponge.

- A mild abrasive cleaner (see page 55) can be used gently to remove stains.

BATHROOM

51

BATHROOM TAPS AND DRAINS
Know where the bacteria hide to hone your cleaning strategy

Studies show that the wash basin can harbour about 1,000 bacteria per square centimetre on the tap handles and almost 500 bacteria per square centimetre in the drain. Compare that to a rubbish bin, with just over 60 bacteria per square centimetre, and you get the idea of what you're up against here. For lightly used wash basins that are used primarily for hand washing, wipe down the tap handles and

do some drain maintenance before guests arrive, and you're all set. The wash basin in a family bathroom, however, can become the setting for a strange tableau composed of the soap scum, toothpaste, makeup, shaving cream and, oh yes, hair discarded from everyday living. And of this, whatever is not sticking to the porcelain and taps eventually makes its way down the drain.

Taps

Don't forget to scrub here

- Wipe taps and handles dry with a towel after each use. This will reduce mineral spotting and soap scum build-up.

- When you want a shine, use glass cleaner (page 51). Spray and wipe with a T-shirt rag.

- Scrub joints around basin with mild soap and hot water to prevent mould growth and remove grime.

- Avoid abrasive cleaners in general and use soap and water instead of vinegar-based glass cleaner for porcelain fixtures or handles.

Low-Flow Clean

- Unscrew the spout of your tap and remove screens, aerator, and low-flow disc. Pay attention to the order and orientation for easy reassembly.

- Use a pin to clean out holes in disc as well as screens if they need cleaning.

- Soak the pieces in vinegar for a few hours.

- Reassemble.

Heavily used bathroom sinks need cleaning weekly at least. Most taps can be wiped with just a spray of vinegar and water, which will shine and disinfect them. Brass taps can be polished easily with bicarbonate of soda and lemon or vinegar and salt on a soft cloth.

If you notice a change in the flow coming from your tap, it's probably time to clean the low-flow attachment or screens. Hard-water deposits can build up and obstruct the flow, but they'll disappear using the technique described here.

Clearing the Drain

- Since this is one of the most germ-filled spots in the house, it's important to keep drains as clean and clear as possible.

- If it's slow to empty or you want to disinfect, pour 100 g bicarbonate of soda down the drain.

- Follow with 250 ml of vinegar and cover plughole with a rag. Leave to fizz for 5 minutes.

- Pour in boiling water unless your sink is glass or vitreous china, in which case use hot water.

•••••••••••• GREEN ● LIGHT ••••••••••••

Do you have yellow rings or unattractive stains around the plughole of your basin? Try this technique: mix either salt and vinegar or bicarbonate of soda and lemon into a paste and apply liberally to the stain. Leave on all day. Wipe off and rinse. (Do not try this if your basin is marble.)

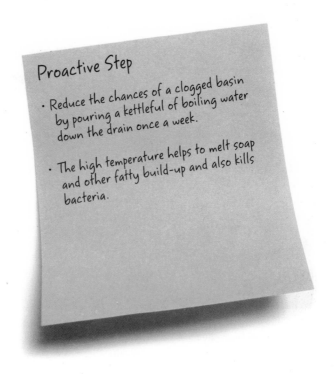

Proactive Step

- Reduce the chances of a clogged basin by pouring a kettleful of boiling water down the drain once a week.

- The high temperature helps to melt soap and other fatty build-up and also kills bacteria.

BATHROOM

BATHTUBS AND SHOWERS
Simple ingredients for a natural clean

Admittedly, cleaning the shower isn't the first thing people want to do with their spare time. That's why there's a chemical-laden 'do it more easily' product for everything – from mould and mildew to soap scum and marble – and many of them claim to work 'automatically'. But these cleaners are labelled as hazards, irritating to skin and eyes, containing known carcinogens, and more. Many are spray products, yet their labels say to avoid contact with eyes, skin and clothing. The good news is, you don't need all these pricey, unhealthy cleaners. Non-toxic ingredients like bicarbonate of soda and castile soap work just as well.

One of the biggest cleaning challenges in the bath and shower is the persistent growth of mould. Conventional wisdom is that bleach kills mould, but contractors who specialize

Oily Rings

- Oily rings are usually residue left from oily bath products, which can also make your bath slippery.

- Wash the bath with a mildly abrasive cleaner (see page 55) with warm water, using a rag or sponge, whenever you use the products.

- If you have tiling around your bath and find oily residue there as well, clean it off immediately.

- Oil can penetrate grouting and encourage mildew growth. Consider switching to less oily bath products.

Mildewed Grouting

- If you have mouldy grouting, consider installing a fan, open the window every time you shower and towel dry the tiled bath surround after use.

- Spray affected areas with tea tree oil antibacterial spray (see page 15) or straight vinegar.

- Do not rinse. Repeat daily for a week while also keeping the entire area as dry and well ventilated as possible.

- Scrub the mildewed area with a soft bristled brush and mild abrasive cleaner (see page 55).

in eliminating mould will tell you that it is the wrong product for the job. If you've ever used bleach to treat mould, you probably noticed that it went away for a while and then returned in exactly the same spot. That's because you only bleached the mould – you didn't kill it.

Instead of using bleach, the most important thing you can do to battle mould is to keep your bathroom and shower as dry as possible between uses. Open a window or install an extractor fan and ventilate the area after each use.

Soap Scum

Look for soap scum here

- Minerals from your water mix with soap to form soap scum, which shows up as a cloudy, gritty film.

- To reduce soap scum, wipe the bath dry after each use.

- To clean, skip the bicarbonate of soda recipe above, which is mineral and alkaline – possibly contributing to the problem. Use a more acidic cleaner, such as equal parts vinegar and water.

- Use vinegar sparingly and never if you are cleaning porous stone like marble or limestone.

Cleaning Marble and Limestone

- To clean, use castile soap and water with a sponge.

- Fight soap scum by using a towel to wipe down bath and shower after use.

- For oily rings or film, cover area with cornflour and leave overnight, brush it off and repeat. Then clean with warm sudsy water.

BATHROOM

55

BATH TAPS AND SHOWERHEADS
Finish off a deep clean with a healthy shine

The most common taps and showerheads, made of shiny chrome or stainless steel, don't hide their dirt and spots very well. A good way to keep them shiny is to wipe them dry after each use and occasionally clean them with washing-up liquid or the same vinegar mixture you use on the mirror (see page 51). If the handles of your taps are made of porcelain, be sure to avoid abrasive cleaners and minimize your use of acids like vinegar, which can cause damage to the surface and make it dull.

How frequently you need to deep-clean your bathroom fittings depends on your water. Hard water can leave mineral deposits that can obstruct the water flow and appears as a white film or spots on your tap and showerhead. Both are easy to clean naturally and with minimal effort.

Bath Taps

Scrub here

Porcelain handles need milder cleaner

- Dry taps after use to keep them shiny and reduce hard-water spotting.

- For chrome and other shiny metal, use a glass-cleaning mixture of vinegar, water and a touch of castile soap; polish with a dry cloth for the best shine.

- If your tap or part of it is porcelain, use mild washing-up liquid and water. Vinegar may cause damage.

- Scrub round edges and details with a toothbrush to prevent dirt build-up and mould growth.

Bath Drain

- Clean hair out of the bath plughole to prevent dirt and bacteria build-up and a clogged drain.

- Pour a kettle of boiling water down the drain once a week to melt away any build-up and inhibit bacteria growth.

- Then scrub the strainer with warm soapy water and a toothbrush.

- For a deeper clean, sprinkle 100 g bicarbonate of soda and pour 250 ml vinegar down the drain. Cover for 5 minutes with a rag. Follow with boiling water.

Pay attention to leaks while you clean. A leaking tap can lose up to 75 litres a day, which can add up to a huge waste of water over time. Fix leaks immediately.

If your showerhead was installed before the 1990s, it most probably has a high flow rate. To conserve water, consider installing a low-flow or energy-saving showerhead, which aerates the water so you still get a powerful shower, and adopt good habits such as taking shorter showers and not letting the water run unnecessarily.

Clogged Showerhead: Step 1

- Hard-water mineral deposits can clog showerheads and obstruct the flow of water.

- Fill a polythene freezer bag with 500 ml undiluted white distilled vinegar.

- Slip bag over showerhead and secure with a rubber band so showerhead is completely submerged in vinegar.

- Leave on overnight. In the morning, scrub the showerhead with a toothbrush and warm soapy water.

Stubborn Clogs: Step 2

- Unscrew showerhead. An older showerhead may be rusted, so wrap it in a towel and use a wrench to unscrew it gently.

- It's a good idea to turn off the water at the stopcock in case the pipe breaks.

- Remove any low-flow disc and clean it and the showerhead perforations with a pin; rinse. Soak in vinegar for 4 hours then scrub again with a toothbrush and soapy water.

- Before reattaching, scrub any rust off the pipe. You may need to remove and replace old sealant tape to prevent leaking. Screw on showerhead.

BATHROOM

SHOWER DOORS AND CURTAINS
Eliminate mould problems and go PVC-free

It's hard to feel clean when your shower is surrounded by grime and mould. It's also not the best situation for your respiratory system, as you breathe in the mould spores. Therefore, it's important to take some quick measures to decrease your health risks and maintain an overall clean shower.

Ventilation, in the form of opening bathroom windows and turning on extractor fans, is crucial to fighting the growth of mould. Ventilation is especially effective when you also squeegee the shower door dry or shake the water from the curtain and spread it open after each use.

Washable shower curtain liners make cleaning easier, but the most widely available shower curtain liners are made from PVC (see page 36), which contains a known human carcinogen, endocrine disruptor and mutagen. To avoid the

Proactive Step

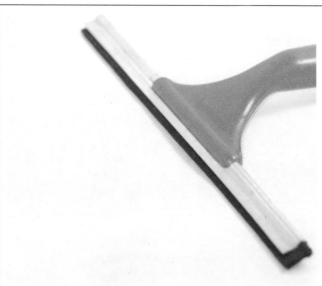

- To keep your shower door clean and clear, you don't need a daily dose of toxic, 'automatic' shower cleaners.

- Get a squeegee that fits the type of door you have, in terms of size and whether it's flat or curved.

- Each time you use the shower, drag the squeegee in straight lines from top to bottom of the door to wipe away soap scum and thoroughly dry the glass.

- Overlap each pass so you don't end up with streaks or lines.

Door Track

Mould and grime build up here

- If you use a squeegee on your shower door, water may pool in your door track, creating optimal conditions for mould growth.

- Use a towel to absorb water after use and leave the door open for further drying.

- To clean, use mild washing-up liquid and a toothbrush to get into hard-to-reach places.

- Wipe down the entire door-frame with soapy water and rinse. Dry and polish with a towel and clean soft cloth.

58

use of PVC, you can forego the liner altogether and buy a mildew-resistant and water-repelling hemp shower curtain, or a tightly woven cotton curtain. If you must have a liner, try nylon. It's a better option than PVC, but it is one that is made from non-renewable resources. Or consider replacing the curtain with a glass shower screen, which is easier to keep clean and dry.

Proactive Step

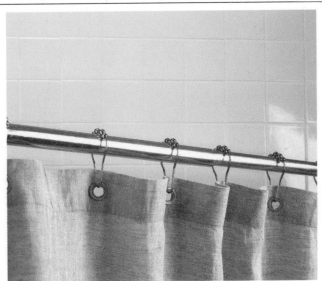

- If your bathroom tends to stay damp, and mould is a problem, invest in a hemp shower curtain.

- Hemp is a hardy fibre that does not need pesticides or much water to grow.

- A hemp curtain can be used without a liner. It will get wet as you shower, but the water won't leak through to the floor.

- Unlike vinyl liners and curtains, hemp dries quickly and is naturally resistant to mould and bacteria.

Clean Liner

Detach here

- Vinyl liners keep water in the bath, but their tendency to stick to the bath means the shower and the bath stay wet longer.

- Although petroleum-based, nylon liners dry faster and contribute to a mould-free shower without polluting the air.

- After each use, shake out and spread the liner to help it dry faster.

- To wash, remove the liner from hooks and put in the washing machine. Wash in hot water if mould is present.

BATHROOM

TOILETS

You don't need a toxic hazard to get the toilet clean

Because we think of toilets as the dirtiest spots in the house, highly toxic toilet cleaners are an easy sell. Acid-based toilet bowl cleaners are in the top three of the most toxic household products available, because they contain caustic ingredients that easily burn eyes, skin and internal tissues.

Bad bacteria like *E. coli* and salmonella may be lurking in your toilet, but the majority of the bacteria you have there are harmless. Harmless bacteria live on your skin, in your gut, in your garden and all over your home. In fact, there is increasing evidence that exposure to some bacteria may actually be good for us early in life because it helps strengthen our immune systems. This is not to say we should not clean toilets and bathrooms, but that we don't need the 275 registered pesticides found in antimicrobial products to do it.

What to Avoid

- Toilet bowl cleaners are corrosive and can cause damage and scarring if they come in contact with eyes, skin and respiratory system.

- Many contain either bleach or ammonia.

- Products containing ammonia shouldn't be mixed with other cleaners containing bleach. Products with chlorine don't mix with acidic cleaning ingredients. The reaction creates chlorine gas that damages your lungs.

- They also contain synthetic fragrances and toxic surfactants like sodium laureth sulphate, which may be contaminated with carcinogenic 1,4-dioxane.

Toilet Bowl

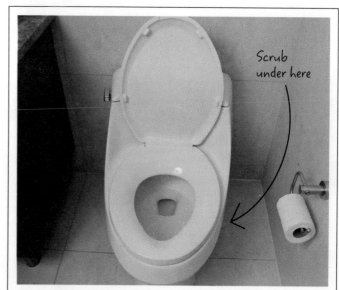

Scrub under here

- Toilet bowls should be cleaned every week, but not with toxic cleaners.

- Castile soap and bicarbonate of soda work well because the bicarbonate of soda provides enough grit for effective scrubbing, and the soap and water does the cleaning.

- To kill bacteria, use bicarbonate of soda and vinegar. Leave to fizz for 5–10 minutes.

- Scrub the bowl thoroughly with a toilet brush. Get as far down the opening and as close up under the rim as possible. Then flush.

60

To kill even the worst of the bacteria, including *E. coli*, you need hot soapy water and consistency. It's also a good idea to flush the cistern with the toilet seat down: this helps to make sure that whatever bacteria you do have in your toilet do not get scattered around on other surfaces, such as towels and toothbrushes. And, of course, you should wash your hands often and thoroughly.

·········· **GREEN ● LIGHT** ··············

Scrubbing and then putting the toilet brush back in its holder wet can create a breeding ground for not-so-nice bacteria. To combat these, soak the brush in hot water, castile soap and a dash of vinegar once a month. Replace it when it stops coming clean in the soak.

Surface

Dust accumulates here

Dust and grime accumulate here

Hard-Water Rings

- Pour a cup of white vinegar into your toilet bowl and scrub.

- Leave for an hour.

- Scrub again and flush.

- Do not use vinegar with any product containing chlorine, including bleach.

- Use all-purpose cleaner (see page 31) and a rag to wipe the exterior of the toilet.

- Start at the top to remove dust on the back and sides of the cistern. Next, wipe the lid and seat and then the exterior of the bowl and pedestal.

- Dirt and grime can collect on the pedestal, so make sure you wipe it clean all the way around.

- To clean wooden seats, use mild soap and water and wipe dry.

CLEAN SLEEP
Insomnia? Switch to cleaner sheets

If you're having trouble sleeping, or you just want to do something great for the environment and your indoor air quality, consider a complete bedding makeover. At the top of the list: invest in some organic cotton sheets, and not simply because they're trendy. Non-organic sheets are usually treated with large amounts of formaldehyde, a known carcinogen that makes them resist stains and wrinkles. Formaldehyde has also been linked to insomnia, of all things, and never completely washes out of your sheets.

Skyrocketing demand for organic cotton has led to an increase in production of about 76 per cent a year since 2000. Organic cotton is now being grown in 18 countries. The Global Organic Textile Standard, set up by the Soil Association in the UK and equivalent bodies from the USA, Germany and

CLEAN HOME, GREEN HOME

Cleaner Mattresses

Organic cotton and wool stuffing

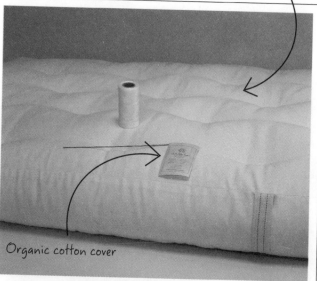

Organic cotton cover

- Stuffing: organic cotton and wool or natural rubber are sustainable non-toxic choices.

- Flame retardants: avoid the chemical treatments and look for wool, a natural flame retardant.

- Extras: to reduce chemical exposure even further, look for unbleached and untreated cotton and wool. Avoid pesticide-laden 'anti-bacterial' mattresses.

- Vacuum mattress regularly to rid it of allergens like dust mites and their faeces.

Organic Futons

- Futons can be a great alternative to conventional mattresses and are often less expensive.

- Stuffing: look for 100 per cent organic cotton, surrounded by fire-resistant wool.

- Fabric: organic cotton, wool or hemp fabrics make healthy natural covers.

- Cleaning: it's a good idea to have a removable futon cover for easy cleaning; organic cotton is a good choice. Wash cover and vacuum futon regularly.

Japan, has established a licensing system and logo for organic textiles. Opt for undyed sheets to further reduce chemical exposure, and choose cotton with the FAIRTRADE Mark.

Until very recently, many mattresses were treated with the flame-retardant chemical PBDE. While this highly polluting and dangerous chemical no doubt stops fires, there are non-toxic alternatives that do the same thing, including wool. Some mattresses and sheets labelled 'antibacterial' are also coated in pesticides and other toxins.

Green Sheets

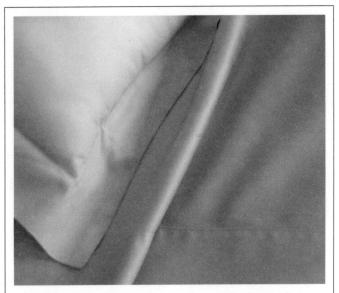

- Look for sheets that are 100 per cent organic cotton, meaning they haven't been grown using pesticides and synthetic fertilizers.

- Even with organic sheets, it's important to make sure they have not been treated with harsh chemicals in manufacturing.

- Buy unbleached and undyed sheets or look for coloured sheets with natural dyes free of heavy metals and formaldehyde.

- Avoid anything that says 'easy-care', 'wrinkle-free' or 'permanent press', which means formaldehyde. Wash all sheets before using them.

Bamboo Sheets

- Bamboo is a green option because it grows fast – reaching full height in less than 5 years – and generally without pesticides.

- Bamboo is becoming increasingly affordable, but is sometimes sold as a mixture of bamboo and conventional cotton.

- This is greener but not ideal, since conventional cotton is such a pesticide-intensive crop.

- Look for 100 per cent bamboo or bamboo and organic cotton mixes, with natural dyes and no extra chemical treatments.

DUVETS AND PILLOWS
Enjoy some clean and cozy eco-friendly options

Sleeping clean means that when you curl up with your duvet and a soft pillow, you don't breathe in harsh chemicals or mould. A simple step to combat both mould and harsh chemicals is to hang your duvets and pillows out in the sunshine for a few hours a month. This will give chemicals a chance to offgas away from you and your bedroom. Down or wool duvets are great because they absorb moisture from your body as you sleep, so you don't wake up sweaty, as you might with synthetic materials. A few hours in the sun naturally dries, whitens and sanitizes the bedding. Another simple step is to buy an untreated, organic cotton protector for your current pillow or duvet, to limit your exposure to chemicals.

If you're buying new, consider other options besides down. Most goose and duck down is a by-product of factory-farmed

Duvet Choices: Organic Wool

- Wool duvets give you the same cosy fluffiness as down and also wick moisture away from your body, so they keep you warm and dry.

- Dust mites are less attracted to wool, so it's a great choice for bedding.

- As with all bedding, check with the manufacturer to make sure the wool has not been treated with extra pesticides or other harsh chemicals.

- Avoid dry-cleaning your wool duvet. Hand-wash with a mild detergent and line-dry if possible.

Clean Down

- Down can pack a lot of allergens because it typically contains at least some feathers from geese and ducks that were raised in unsanitary conditions.

- 'Clean' down or other eco-down may be ozonated to get rid of any bacteria or mould and washed in extremely hot water or steamed to clean it.

- Look for products with organic cotton covers.

- Avoid dry cleaning. Hand-wash with a mild detergent and line-dry (see page 102).

animals killed for meat. While some organic farmers do sell their birds' feathers, it's difficult to track the sources of any given duvet. 'Clean' or 'hypoallergenic' down products are generally made up of regular down that has been steam-cleaned and sterilized to reduce allergens and toxins.

Wool is an excellent eco-choice for bedding because it naturally controls moisture, repels dust mites and resists fire. Silk floss is another natural material that is free of dust mites and naturally hypoallergenic, while being very light and warm.

Pillows are available filled with all the same materials as duvets. In addition, eco-friendly pillows are stuffed with everything from organic buckwheat and millet to recycled plastic fizzy drinks bottles. If you can get past the not-so-luxurious images associated with sleeping on plastic bottles, pillows filled with recycled materials are a great way to close the recycling loop.

Natural Pillow Choices

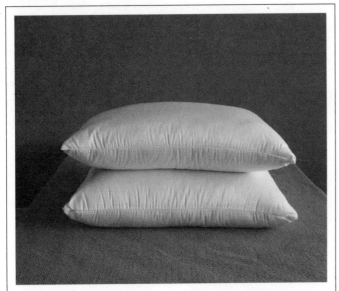

- Avoid pillows filled with synthetic petroleum-based materials such as polyester.

- Kapok pillows are filled with seedpods from the kapok tree, which feel a lot like down. They are generally free of allergens.

- Buckwheat hulls make for a supportive pillow that breathes. It is said to help with insomnia and snoring.

- The pillow is filled with about 3 kg buckwheat hulls, which move to conform to the shape of the head.

Close the Loop

- The more manufacturer demand there is for recycled materials, the wider and more extensive recycling programmes will become.

- Pillows made from 100 per cent recycled plastic bottles are hypoallergenic and as comfortable as cotton.

- Look for products that have an unbleached organic cotton cover.

- Machine-wash pillows once a month using a mild detergent. In a top-loading machine, put two pillows in at once, to balance the drum and reduce wear and tear.

65

DUST CONTROL
Reduce exposure to allergens and toxins in the home

Dust can contribute to the development and triggering of allergies and asthma, both of which are on the rise. Since we spend about a third of our lives in the bedroom, controlling dust in our bedding and furnishings is extremely important. Studies have also found that controlling dust reduces our exposure to household toxins, such as PBDE flame retardants that are probably in your mattress. The average household dust bunny consists of 70 per cent human skin; the remaining 30 per cent is a mixture of dirt, fibres, pet dander, mould, bacteria and insects such as dust mites.

Your bed is the perfect ecosystem for dust mites, because they thrive in warm, dark and moist places, and they feed on human skin. This makes them very happy to hang out in your bed, where there is no shortage of food, all day and night.

Dust Mites

- Dust mites don't bite or burrow in your skin. In fact, unless you have an allergy to them, you may not be affected at all.

- If you are allergic, symptoms include watery eyes, sneezing, itching, sinus and respiratory problems. They are caused by dust mite faeces and decaying mites.

- To fight dust mites, use a dehumidifier to dry out your bedroom and wash bedding once a week in hot water.

- Vacuum at least once a week with a filtered vacuum cleaner.

Mattress Dust

- Some experts claim that dust mite waste can double the weight of a mattress every 10 years.

- Vacuum your mattress with a filtered vacuum cleaner once a month – more if you suffer from allergies.

- Use a mattress-specific attachment, or just use a flat tool so you can cover the area efficiently. Clean the attachment if necessary before using it.

- Drag the attachment very slowly across the mattress in long, straight, overlapping lines. Don't forget to do the sides of the mattress as well.

To reduce the amount of dust in your bedroom, it's important to stop being so hospitable to dust mites. If your room tends to be damp, use a dehumidifier. It's also a good idea to get rid of wall-to-wall carpeting, which provides a desirable home for mites and hangs on to air pollutants. Regularly vacuuming or vapour steam cleaning floor rugs, mattresses and curtains will also help control the problem.

Dust here

Headboards

- Bedding isn't the only dust collector in your room.

- Before changing your sheets, use a damp T-shirt rag or microfibre cloth to dust your headboard, footboard and other visible parts of the bed frame, including legs. Vacuum any upholstered parts.

- Work your rag into decorative details or carvings, where dust can build up.

- When you've finish dusting, strip the bed, take the sheets away to wash and vacuum the floor around the bed to catch any fallen dust.

Vacuum here

Valances and Drapery

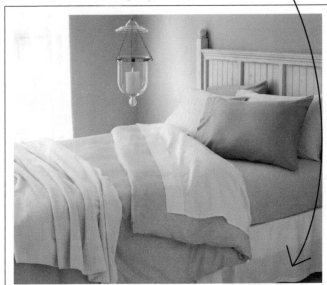

- The valance is another dust catcher in the bedroom.

- Valances are machine-washable, but because they go under the mattress removing them requires a lot of work.

- To keep them clean in between washings, use your vacuum cleaner's upholstery attachment and vacuum in overlapping vertical lines.

- Do the same for curtains or any drapery around the bed and any other fabric or upholstery that is collecting dust in your bedroom.

WINDOWS AND GLASS
Clear your view and your air and reduce your energy bills in one simple step

With their bright blue or green colouring, it's not too surprising that conventional window cleaners contain a lot of chemicals. One of the worst is ammonia, an irritant that mixes with chlorine – which is a common ingredient in cleaning products – to form toxic gases. Other chemicals in glass cleaners include butyl cellosolve, a known irritant and neurotoxin and suspected teratogen, and dioxane, a carcinogen. If you have previously used a chemical glass cleaner, these chemicals leave a coating on the glass that will streak when you wipe it with vinegar and water. Add a few squirts of castile soap to the mixture for the first few cleanings and then you can switch to vinegar and water with no streaking.

Window Frame

Dust and grime build up here

- Dust regularly with a micro-fibre cloth or damp T-shirt rag, being careful to work your cloth into tight spaces. Use a cotton swab around the lock and handles.

- For a deeper clean, wash frame with mild soapy water and a soft cloth.

- Use a toothbrush for hard-to-reach places and the junctions where the frame meets the glass.

- Dry the frame thoroughly with a clean towel.

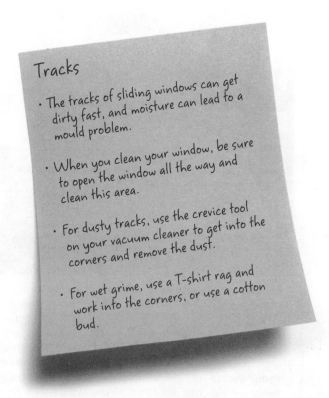

Tracks

- The tracks of sliding windows can get dirty fast, and moisture can lead to a mould problem.

- When you clean your window, be sure to open the window all the way and clean this area.

- For dusty tracks, use the crevice tool on your vacuum cleaner to get into the corners and remove the dust.

- For wet grime, use a T-shirt rag and work into the corners, or use a cotton bud.

Regularly cleaning both the inside and outside of your windows can lift your mood and lower your energy bills. Cleaner windows let in more light and sunshine, which can reduce the amount of energy you need to power lamps and your heating system. Maximizing your use of the natural light coming into your home for light and heat is called 'daylighting', and clean windows can make a big difference.

Glass Cleaning

Tools for glass cleaning:

500 ml water and 250 ml vinegar

1 teaspoon castile soap

Spray bottle

Newspaper

Gloves

- For clean glass without streaks combine vinegar, water and castile soap, and use sheets of newspaper as your rag.

- If you've already been using vinegar and water on your windows and they are not streaking, you do not need the castile soap.

- Wear gloves to keep the newsprint from blackening your hands.

- Spray the cleaner on the newspaper instead of the window, to keep it off the frame.

- Wash the window using a circular motion.

Mirror

Dust builds up here

- Use a damp T-shirt rag or microfibre cloth to dust both mirror and frame, remembering to wipe the sides. Work the cloth into any grooves or seams.

- To wash the frame, use mild soapy water to slightly dampen your cloth or sponge.

- Rinse with a clean, damp, but soapless, sponge. Dry with a clean towel.

- To wash the mirror, spray your glass cleaner mixture on a microfibre cloth or a clean T-shirt rag to protect the frame.

GREENER CLOTHING STORAGE
Reduce, reduce and ventilate

If you see small holes in your sweaters, or even catch moths fluttering out of view when you open the wardrobe door, don't reach for the mothballs. Mothballs can contain naphthalene or paradichlorobenzene, both suspected carcinogens. Naphthalene may also damage the liver, destroy red blood cells and cause brain damage in children. Mothballs certainly don't make your wardrobe smell very clean or natural.

Your clothes keep that sour mothball smell for months after you've used them, because they are designed to disintegrate and permeate the air around the clothing to keep the moths away. But that also means you easily inhale these chemicals every time you open the wardrobe or drawer or storage container where you've used them. In addition, they look edible and children may try to eat these toxic time bombs.

Declutter Technique

- Turn all of your coathangers so the open part of the hanger's hook is facing you.

- Each time you wear something, turn the hanger back around so the open hook is facing the back wall.

- After 3 months, any clothes on hangers still facing the wrong direction are fair game for the giveaway pile.

Clean Drawers

- Like wardrobes, chests of drawers can easily become overfilled and need to be decluttered once in a while.

- A drawer that is well organized and not overstuffed will save you time, and will also reduce creases and be less inviting for pests.

- At the beginning of each season, remove all the contents of your drawers and vacuum the drawers.

- Wipe down with a sponge and leave open to air-dry before replacing your clothes.

There are much safer options and some proactive steps you can take to keep your clothes clean and pest-free. Clothes moths like dark, moist places, and they are particularly drawn to clothing adorned with oils from your skin or from food or other organic spills. They don't drink water, so they need moisture to survive.

Cleaning out your wardrobe and drawers will increase ventilation and reduce moisture and thereby discourage moths. Since moths do the most damage to clothing that isn't disturbed very often, getting rid of items you rarely wear may make a big difference. Before you store clothing, be sure to launder or at least iron it, as both techniques will kill all stages of the moth life cycle.

Paring down your wardrobe will also make it much easier to vacuum and clean around your clothes; that way you can minimize the food supply – including fibres and lint – that the moths eat.

No-Pest Clothes

- Cedarwood drawer liners, coat hangers and shoe racks can help fight moth infestation.

- Look for aromatic eastern red cedar, which has oil that can kill small moth larvae.

- This oil wears off after a time so it's necessary to touch up with essential oil of cedar or replace the cedar every few years.

- Vacuuming in out-of-sight areas like the backs of drawers, under furniture and along the tops of skirting boards will also help fight clothing moths.

Out-of-Season Storage

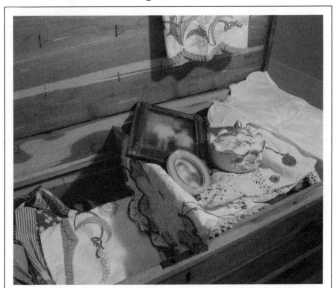

- To keep your wardrobe and drawers clean and not over-stuffed, consider storing your out-of-season clothing in a cedarwood chest.

- As the weather changes, take the opportunity to clean, and replace past-season clothes with current-season clothes.

- If you have a moth problem, placing wool sweaters in airtight plastic bags may protect them.

- Be sure not to use moth-balls, which can melt the plastic, make your clothes smell bad and pollute your indoor air.

WARDROBES
Clear the air with a cleaner clothes cupboard

Most modern wardrobes are stuffed with clothing made from both synthetic and natural fibres that have been treated with toxins aimed at keeping the fabric flameproof, water-resistant, stain-proof and wrinkle-free. But the chemicals that textile manufacturers use to achieve these conveniences are an unwelcome mix of neurotoxins, developmental toxins and endocrine disruptors.

Dry cleaning adds yet another highly toxic chemical, perchloroethylene (PERC) to the atmosphere of your wardrobe. Leaving dry-cleaned clothes in their plastic bags only prolongs your exposure to the toxin.

If everyone chose just one organic cotton T-shirt over its non-organic alternative, nearly 50,000 tons of agrochemicals would be kept from polluting our environment. Other

Clean Wardrobe

- Leaving only the clothes you wear in your wardrobe allows for air circulation and easy cleaning.

- Easy-to-remove, natural-fibre boxes keep accessories dust-free.

- Empty your wardrobe and start with the top shelf.

- Use a damp sponge to work your way down the wardrobe, wiping each shelf and rail to get rid of dust, dirt, cobwebs and any insects that may be sharing your space. Rinse the sponge frequently.

- Vacuum the floor and replace clothes.

Shoe Rack

- Storing shoes at the bottom of your wardrobe means more dirt and more time spent cleaning because you have to remove each pair individually.

- Instead, keep everyday shoes near the door so you aren't bringing outside dirt into your home.

- Store less frequently worn shoes and slippers on a shoe rack, an over-the-door hanging rack or a shoe organizer that hangs from the clothes rail.

- Simply remove the organizer when it's time to clean the wardrobe.

greener options include clothing made from organic wool, bamboo, soy and hemp. These fibres are grown without lots of pesticides, though dyes can still contain heavy metals and other toxins.

Shoe care products also tend to contain toxins that can disrupt the brain and hormonal systems. But you can easily avoid these by using the natural shoe polish recipe on this page. Keeping shoes on a rack or hanging bag in your wardrobe will keep the floor clear and make it easier to clean.

MAKE IT EASY

Natural shoe polish:
Apply a 10 pence piece-sized amount of jojoba oil and a squirt of lemon to an old T-shirt. Rub the mix into the leather using a circular motion. Buff the shoes with the clean end of the T-shirt.

Dust-Free

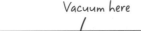

Vacuum here

- Dust will accumulate on the shelves around your clothes and may even be noticeable on your wool sweaters.

- Use your vacuum attachment for a quick clean around your clothes.

- For a seasonal clean, remove all clothing from shelves and take the opportunity to sort and store past-season clothing.

- Dust with a cloth and wash each shelf with soap and water. Dry all the shelves with a towel before replacing clothing.

Greener Shelving Options

- Avoid shelves and organizers made from engineered products such as chipboard or medium density fibreboard, which can continue to emit carcinogenic formaldehyde for years.

- Instead, look for shelving made of solid wood, such as cedar, which won't pollute the air in your wardrobe.

73

PERSONAL CARE TOXINS
Limit your exposure through educated decision making

Personal care products really are personal. We rub them into our skin and hair, paint them on our nails and lips, and even put them in our mouths and eyes. Unfortunately, many of these products contain chemicals that are known to have adverse health and environmental effects, and the industry is not required to do safety testing. Chemicals designed to preserve, mask or add scents and colour, and to sanitize personal care products are some of the most dangerous ingredients. Given that the typical adult is exposed to more than 100 different chemicals every day from personal care products, the health risks are staggering.

If you compare labels you'll find certain ingredients, such as parabens and sodium lauryl sulphate, in a good number of the products you use daily. This much exposure is alarming,

Fragrance

Could mess with your hormones

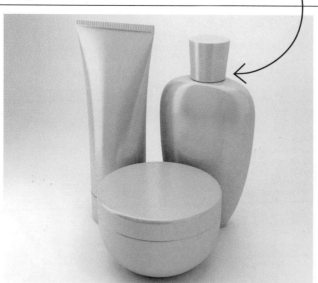

Preservatives

The most common family of preservatives:
Methylparaben
Propylparaben
Ethylparaben
Butylparaben

- Personal care product labels are required to list all ingredients except fragrance, which can include 50–100 ingredients per product.

- Studies have found phthalates in nearly 100 per cent of the fragrances tested.

- Phthalates are a family of chemical plasticizers that bioaccumulate in human tissues, leaving us vulnerable to long-term exposure.

- They have been shown to cause birth defects and liver cancer in laboratory animals, and they are suspected of disrupting the reproductive development of young boys.

- Parabens mimic oestrogen. They are potential hormone disruptors and are linked to breast cancer. Yet 99 per cent of personal care products contain them.

- Another, bronopol, can break down to produce formaldehyde or react with other chemicals to form carcinogenic nitrosamines.

- Carcinogenic formaldehyde is a preservative in eye makeup and other cosmetics.

- Although a known neurotoxin, mercury is still permitted as a preservative in eye makeup. The preservative form of mercury is called thimerosal.

because many of these products are designed to penetrate deep into the skin. As a result, scientists are finding that we store these chemicals in our tissues and fat. Parabens, in particular, have been found in breast cancer tissue, suggesting a strong link between exposure and cancer.

Chemicals that create (or mask) a product's scent are typically listed simply as 'fragrance', but can include phthalates, which make the scents last longer but are strongly suspected carcinogens and can interfere with the hormonal system.

Some personal care products also include triclosan and other antibacterial chemicals, contributing to the rise in resistant bacteria and contaminating our waterways.

Luckily there are some products available that do not contain these chemicals. The basic information below will help you read labels and make healthy decisions the next time you purchase one of these products.

Antibacterials

- Personal care product manufacturers have jumped on the antibacterial bandwagon, adding pesticides to products.

- Yet these products are designed to be applied directly to our skin, mouth and eyes.

- As in cleaning products, triclosan is a common pesticide found in personal care products. Triclosan is an environmental pollutant and is found in most waterways.

- Many experts challenge the view that triclosan is either effective or safe as an antibacterial.

Nanoparticles

- Nanoparticles are a new trend in cosmetics and especially sun care. The particles are so small they easily enter the optic nerve and go to the brain and red blood cells.

- Nanoparticles enable minerals that may be safe on the surface of the skin to penetrate the skin and possibly enter the brain.

- Because they do not behave in the same way as larger molecules of the same substance, experts believe more testing must be done to know they are safe.

- Common nanoparticles that you may see on a label: nano zinc oxide, fullersomes, fullerene (C60 hydroxide), microspheres, nanosomes, buckeye bullets, micronized minerals.

LABELS TO LOOK FOR

Chasing arrows, leaping bunnies, and other labels can distinguish natural products

Although we've been trained to think we need fancy chemicals to smell and look better, have softer skin and fewer wrinkles, there are plenty of natural ingredients that achieve the same or better results. Knowing which natural ingredients work and what else to look for on the label will make shopping for toxin-free green care products a breeze.

A typical green personal care product comes in biodegradable or recyclable packaging and features inviting claims like 'paraben-free' or 'no animal testing'. It will also be covered with an array of symbols like chasing arrows and cute bunnies.

Because there is as yet no regulatory body for green claims, we need to weigh the claims with what we know about the

Greener Cleansers

- These are some of the mildest and safest cleanser ingredients:

- Amphoteric 2, 6 or 20, cocamido betaine, cocamidopropyl betaine, sorbitan laurate, sorbitan palmitate, sorbitan stearate.

- Even better, choose cleansers that grow in nature and are not the product of a laboratory.

- Look for these natural cleanser ingredients: alfalfa extract, flaxseed, honeysuckle oil, oatmeal, quillaya bark, yucca root.

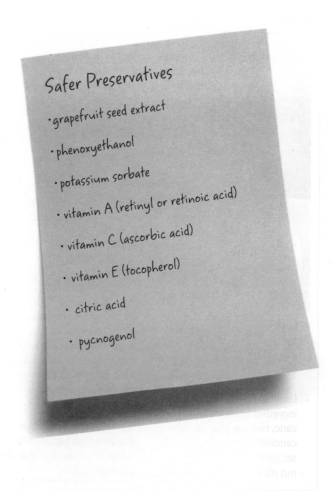

Safer Preservatives

- grapefruit seed extract

- phenoxyethanol

- potassium sorbate

- vitamin A (retinyl or retinoic acid)

- vitamin C (ascorbic acid)

- vitamin E (tocopherol)

- citric acid

- pycnogenol

brand and what other information we find on the label. When you buy products that are 'fragrance free', 'cruelty free' and 'hypoallergenic', you need to understand that these claims have not been legally defined. For example, some products that claim to be 'fragrance free' actually contain fragrance to counteract the chemical smells in the product. You smell nothing, but the toxins are still there. This does not mean you shouldn't buy products that make claims; it just means you need to look at other parts of the label before you buy.

ZOOM

Human and bovine placenta are added to some products because of their ability to condition skin and hair. Although placenta is a naturally occurring substance, it is quite dangerous in personal care products. It contains oestrogen, which is absorbed by the skin, and recent studies report that the extra hormone is enough to spur breast growth in toddlers.

Natural Moisturizers

- Luckily for us, nature is overflowing with great ingredients to moisturize our skin and hair.

- Look for these moisturizing ingredients: aloe vera, avocado, beeswax, cornflower, candelilla wax, cocoa butter, jojoba oil, macadamia nut oil, pycnogenol (pine bark extract), rice bran oil, shea butter, sunflower oil, sweet almond oil, vitamins A, C and E.

- Look for products that contain these ingredients and have as few other ingredients as possible.

Better Organics

- The Soil Association logo certifies that the product contains ingredients that have been grown, processed, and certified free of synthetic pesticides and fertilizers.

- The requirements for care products are not quite as strict as they are for food.

- Health and beauty products can use the logo if they contain 95 per cent organic ingredients.

- If a product says it is 'organic', look to see how many of the ingredients are actually organic before spending the extra money.

NATURAL HOME SPA
Be a natural beauty with these easy do-it-yourself recipes

Your skin is your biggest organ and will greedily absorb whatever you choose to lather and slather over it. A great way to be extra sure that you are putting only the most natural ingredients on and in your body is to use only natural ingredients that come directly from your own garden, refrigerator and store cupboard. The recipes here don't require a lot of time or extra shopping for exotic ingredients, and they work really well. Once you master these recipes, you'll be experimenting with others in no time. The basic ingredients for skin care recipes are herbs, vegetables and fruits, fruit and nut oils, distilled water, cider vinegar, honey and other bee products. From there the possibilities are endless.

These recipes are focused on exfoliation to support you in your efforts to detox your surroundings. Exfoliation sloughs

Easy Thyme/Fennel Cleanser

- Two sprigs fresh thyme, crumbled (or ½ teaspoon dried thyme); 2 teaspoons fennel seeds, crushed; 250 ml boiling water; juice of half a lemon.

- Mix thyme and fennel seed and cover with boiling water. Add lemon juice and steep for 15 minutes. Strain infusion and store liquid in a jar in the refrigerator. Dab on face using cotton wool. Then rinse.

- Fennel seeds are gentle cleaners and tone the skin by reducing swelling and soothing any irritation. Thyme works as a natural astringent.

Deep Cleansing Masks

- Avocado mask to exfoliate and moisturize: 1 avocado, juice of half a lemon. Skin tightening mask: 2 egg whites.

- For best results, steam your face first. Fill a bowl with boiling water and fresh herbs. With your hair tied back and a towel draped over your head, lean your face over the bowl for 5 minutes. Blot dry. Mash avocado with lemon juice and apply evenly to face and neck. Leave on for 20 minutes, then rinse with cold water. Or, beat egg whites until just stiff. Apply to face and leave on for 20 minutes. Rinse with cold water.

off the dead layer of skin cells, which helps your skin do a better job of regulating and eliminating whatever toxins are in your body.

The lemon juice in both the cleanser and mask is an alpha hydroxy acid (AHA), which works to break up the dead skin for thorough exfoliation. Yogurt and cider vinegar are also AHAs. The sea salt rub is intended for whole body exfoliation.

PERSONAL CARE

Sea Salt Exfoliator

- 500 g fine sea salt; 1 litre grapeseed or almond oil; up to 10 drops essential oil (optional).

- Mix ingredients in a recycled, clean glass jar with a lid. Shake vigorously.

- Wet body in the shower and apply salt mixture with your hand or a bristle bath brush to scrub. Use a circular motion and move from your feet up to your shoulders. Use a long-handled brush to reach your back.

- Rinse well, but it's OK to leave the oil on as it will naturally moisturize your skin.

Exfoliating Tools

- Exfoliate with just a loofah – no product or recipe is needed.

- Stand in the bath or shower without turning the water on. Rub the loofah all over your body to slough off dead skin cells.

- Shower as usual. Store your loofah in a dry place and replace regularly, because bacteria can build up.

- Sea sponges also exfoliate and are natural, but they are very slow growing and are already at risk due to water pollution as well as over-harvesting.

NO-VARNISH NAILS
Have sophisticated nails without the toxins found in varnish

If you've ever been in an enclosed space like an aeroplane or an office where someone decided they needed to touch up their manicure, you already know how toxic nail care products must be. In unventilated areas, the fumes can cause almost instant headaches or make us feel sick.

In the past, nail varnishes on the market that were less toxic just didn't measure up in terms of finish or lasting power, but now a new breed of higher-quality, less toxic nail varnishes are appearing. Unfortunately, nail varnish removers are not keeping pace and most can expose you to irritants and more. Unless you're willing to let the varnish chip its way off your nails, you might want to do without colourful nails.

If you must use nail varnish, choose a brand that lists all of its ingredients proudly. Claims should also be very specific,

Shape

- For best results, make sure your nails are completely dry before filing.

- Place the nail file at an angle under the outer edge of your nail.

- Do not seesaw – file the nail in only one direction towards the centre on each side of the nail until you've achieved your desired shape: squared-off or rounded.

- If you notice uneven results or that the grains on the file are broken or uneven, replace it.

Soak

- Cider vinegar is an alpha-hydroxy acid (AHA) that works to dislodge dead skin cells.

- By soaking your hand in the vinegar you will help remove the dead skin of your cuticles and make them much softer.

- Wash your hands first and then soak in vinegar for 5–10 minutes.

- This will also soften your nails and prepare them for the rest of this technique.

such as 'formaldehyde and toluene free'. Be wary of any varnish that claims to be organic, as this isn't a product category that is eligible for certification. If you can forego the flash of colour on your nails, pamper youself instead with this non-toxic method for achieving shiny nails, which is healthier for you and better for the environment.

PERSONAL CARE

Cuticles

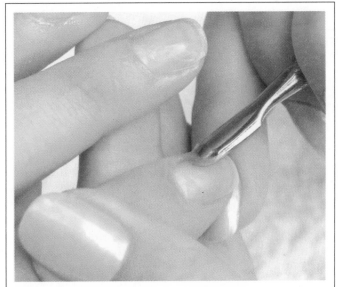

- Push the cuticles back from your nails using a manicure stick.

- If they are still not soft enough, apply a nut oil, such as almond, or a dab of lotion and rub it in.

- You can cut your cuticles, but it's best to soften them and push them back.

- Cut cuticles can become infected and may grow back thicker.

Smooth and Shine

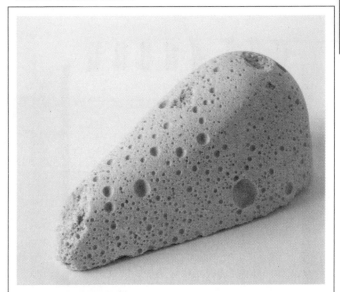

- A manicure block is a handy tool because it has different sides to file, sand and polish nails.

- First, sand the tops of your nails using the 'remove ridges' side of your tool, or a fine pumice stone.

- Then smooth the nail with the smoothing file or a buffing chamois.

- For extra soft hands and beautiful nails, use the avocado mask (see page 78) on your hands and follow with a non-toxic moisturizer.

81

OTHER PERSONAL CARE PRODUCTS
Essential products that are good for both you and the environment

Many personal care products are designed to keep us in good health and hygiene. They protect our skin from the sun, our teeth from cavities, and help to manage body odour and menstrual cycles. Because we use these products on our skin and in our most intimate body parts, they have direct access to our blood, tissues and organs. A million new cases of skin cancer are diagnosed each year, so sunscreen is not something we should be seeking to abandon. Look for products that are free of fragrance, colour and parabens. Sunscreens containing minerals such as titanium dioxide and zinc oxide are good choices, because they physically block UV rays instead of penetrating the skin. Avoid products that contain these minerals in skin-penetrating nanoparticle form (see page 75).

Sun Care

Ingredients to avoid:

benzophenone, homosalate,

octyl-methoxycinnamate (octinoxate),

padimate-O, diethanolamine (DEA)

triethanolamine (TEA), parabens,

fragrance

- These ingredients include irritants, allergens, suspected endocrine disruptors and carcinogens and should be avoided when picking sun-care products.

- SPF measures how long it will take you to burn. SPF 10 means it will take 10 times longer than usual to burn.

- But SPF represents only the product's ability to protect against UVB rays, not UVA rays, which also burn and contribute to wrinkles and cancer.

- Look for a broad spectrum sunblock that will guard against both UVA and UVB rays.

Deodorants and Antiperspirants

- Antiperspirants prohibit sweat by using astringents like aluminium to close pores. Deodorants cut the odour by reducing bacteria.

- Washing under your arms more frequently and choosing clothing that breathes and wicks away moisture can help eliminate the need for these products.

- Otherwise look for these safer ingredients: annatto, beeswax, candelilla wax, carmine, carrageenan, cornstarch, kaolin, pycnogenol (from pine trees), shea butter, jojoba, rice bran, sunflower, and sweet almond oil; and vitamins A, C and E.

82

Deodorants and antiperspirants containing aluminium have long been rumoured to cause Alzheimer's. Yet the Alzheimer's Society, World Health Organization and other bodies agree that there is no conclusive evidence to support this. There are, however, carcinogens and a whole host of irritants to motivate us to seek non-toxic products.

Toothpastes can also keep us healthy, but they are filled with synthetics, including preservatives, artificial sweeteners, colours and flavourings. The debate continues over whether fluoride should be added to dental products and municipal water systems to fight cavities. The British Dental Association and the Department of Health still say 'yes', but many natural caregivers highlight studies that link fluoride to reproductive disorders, bone cancer and poor kidney health. At this point, using fluoride toothpaste is a matter of personal choice.

Considering that women use up to 11,000 feminine products in their lifetime, they are particularly vulnerable to whatever chemicals the manufacturers put in them. Look for unbleached, certified organic cotton products that are better for your health and for the environment.

Oral Care

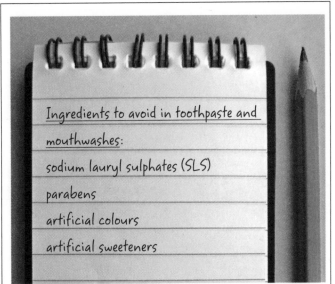

Ingredients to avoid in toothpaste and mouthwashes:

sodium lauryl sulphates (SLS)

parabens

artificial colours

artificial sweeteners

- Look for oral care products that are free of artificial colours and flavours, including artificial sweeteners.

- Some natural toothpastes are available in fluoride-free versions (see page 84).

- Look for floss products that don't contain perfluorochemicals (PFCs) and do contain vegetable waxes and essential oil flavouring.

- To close the recycling loop, look for toothbrush brands that use 100 per cent recycled plastics or that reduce waste with replaceable heads.

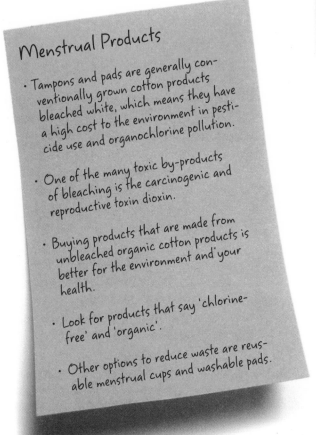

Menstrual Products

- Tampons and pads are generally conventionally grown cotton products, which means they have bleached white, which means they have a high cost to the environment in pesticide use and organochlorine pollution.

- One of the many toxic by-products of bleaching is the carcinogenic and reproductive toxin dioxin.

- Buying products that are made from unbleached organic cotton products is better for the environment and your health.

- Look for products that say 'chlorine-free' and 'organic'.

- Other options to reduce waste are reusable menstrual cups and washable pads.

BABY PERSONAL CARE
Smart choices keep babies healthy

Despite the cute pictures and marketing lullabies on the labels, baby personal care products are just as toxic as adult products. As babies can absorb proportionally more contaminants in the air and through the skin than adults, it's even more important to shop wisely.

In general, avoid products that include fragrance, dyes, harsh preservatives and antibacterial agents. Choose the mildest products available and resist the urge to over-clean your children. Most experts recommend washing newborn babies (after the umbilical cord falls off) with warm water alone. Babies don't need to be washed more often than every 2–3 days, otherwise soaps can dry out their skin. As they get older a plant-based castile or glycerine soap is really all they need to get clean.

Baby Wash

Also look for phthalate-free baby toys

- Calling a product 'baby wash' implies that it contains milder ingredients, but these products contain many of the same toxic chemicals that adult products contain.

- Look for surfactants that are milder than SLS, like cocamidopropyl betaine or cocamidopropyl hydroxysultaine.

- Check for washes that proudly list all of their ingredients on the label.

- Plain warm water is enough to keep a tiny baby clean.

Teeth

No artificial sweeteners, no artificial flavours, no artificial colours

- Toothpastes can give some carcinogenic artificial flavours and colours direct access to our kids' bodies.

- Fluoride is a controversial chemical in toothpaste. In moderation it can reduce tooth decay by 60 per cent.

- Yet when there is overexposure, it is a suspected neurotoxin and linked to reproductive disorders, cancer, and poor kidney health.

- Check to see if your water is already treated with fluoride and, if it is, consider reducing exposure with fluoride-free toothpaste.

For oral care, toothpaste does not need the artificial sweetener saccharine or carcinogenic colouring to clean a child's teeth. Many non-toxic toothpastes use appealing natural flavourings of everything from cinnamon to raspberry.

As for sun care, babies under 6 months should not use any sunscreen. Instead, floppy sun hats and long sleeves and trousers are just the right SPF. For older babies, sunscreen is important on sunny days at the beach, but covering up is still more effective and non-toxic than sunscreen.

ZOOM

To wash a baby, first fill a baby bath with 5–7.5 cm of warm water. Support the baby's neck and head, and pour water over your baby by squeezing a flannel or using a small cup. Use a wet flannel to gently wipe the baby from head to toe and rinse. When you've finished, wrap your baby in an organic towel and hug dry!

Sun Care

- Most experts recommend not putting sunscreen on babies under 6 months old.

- Sunscreens can contain toxins and are too harsh for a baby's skin.

- Covering up with hats and long sleeves is the least toxic sun-care option available.

- However, when it is time for sunscreen, look for mineral-based products, such as zinc and titanium dioxide, and make sure they are not in nanoparticle form (see page 75).

Chemicals to Avoid in Baby Products

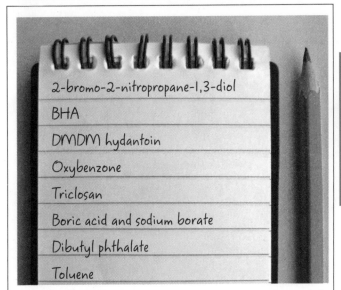

2-bromo-2-nitropropane-1,3-diol

BHA

DMDM hydantoin

Oxybenzone

Triclosan

Boric acid and sodium borate

Dibutyl phthalate

Toluene

- DMDM hydantoin and 2-bromo-2-nitropropane-1,3-diol are allergens that can form carcinogens. Both are found in baby wipes, washes and other products.

- BHA is found in nappy rash cream and affects children's skin pigmentation.

- Oxybenzone is found in sunscreen, insect spray and lip balm. It's an allergen that damages skin.

- Boric acid and sodium borate, found in nappy rash cream and baby powder, are considered unsafe for infants.

- Phthalates and toluene are endocrine disruptors and suspected carcinogens.

THE NAPPY QUESTION

What you need to know to choose the best nappies for your baby, lifestyle and the environment

The not-so-funny thing about conventional disposable nappies is that they're not disposable at all. It's estimated that nearly 3 billion single-use nappies are thrown away each year in the UK, of which about 90 per cent go into landfill. These could take hundreds of years to break down. This sounds like the makings of an environmental catastrophe.

But the damage begins in that fleeting period between the moment when you put the nappy on your baby and when it becomes rubbish. Disposables can expose your baby's skin to chlorine, plastics, glues, dyes and worse. While many parents like the fact that disposables stay 'dry' next to the baby's skin, the chemicals that create that dryness are not natural.

Disposable Nappies to Avoid

- Disposable nappies account for mountains of waste in landfill sites, along with groundwater and land contamination.

- The bleaching of the materials in disposable nappies also has a huge environmental impact.

- The bleaching process creates dioxin as a by-product, which is released into the air and water.

- Dioxin is highly toxic – a carcinogen and a persistent organic pollutant (POP) that has been found in meat, fish and dairy products, as well as breast milk.

Greener Disposables

- While studies show that no nappy is actually biodegradable in landfill, choosing chlorine-free nappies reduces the environmental impact of disposables.

- Nappies made from renewable resources like wood pulp and cotton, without fragrances or dyes, are also good choices.

- Disposable nappies wick moisture away from the baby's skin because they contain the super-absorbent gel sodium polyacrylate. However, experts still do not agree on how safe this gel is for your baby's skin.

- There are greener nappy options available, both with and without this gel.

Fortunately you have choices, but there are so many greener options that it's hard to decide which is best. They all use fewer chemicals, and some really are disposable because they do biodegrade in a reasonable amount of time or they're flushable.

The green standard, the cloth nappy, is making a comeback. Cloth nappies have the advantage of being washable and reusable. While they do have some environmental impact, especially if you use conventional cotton or when you use a nappy service, they remain the greenest choice. The key is to weigh the facts with your lifestyle and priorities to make the green choice that's right for you.

Flushable Liners

- Like cloth, flushable nappies reduce waste because most of the nappy is reusable. But like disposables, flushables relieve you of having to deal with all the mess.

- Remove the biodegradable liner and flush it down the toilet without involving the landfill at all.

- Look for flushable liners that go back into the ecosystem in a neutral or even beneficial form.

- Nappy systems based on reusable nappies with a choice of washable or disposable liners (for use when you're away from home) are also available.

Cloth Nappies

- Cloth nappies avoid landfill – and encourage earlier potty training – but require water, energy, and detergent for laundering, either at home or through a nappy service.

- A lot of pesticides go into growing conventional cotton for cloth nappies.

- Organic cotton cloth nappies, washed at home in non-toxic laundry soap and chlorine-free bleach and line-dried, are the greenest option.

- Whatever option you choose must be balanced with what is practical in your circumstances.

EASY CLOTH NAPPY CARE
The greenest nappy option for babies

Nappy services are certainly convenient. They pick up your dirty cloth nappies each week and drop off fresh clean ones. You don't even need to rinse them. But the fossil fuels used to make deliveries, and the water and detergent used to launder mass quantities of nappies, add up. Buying organic cotton nappies and laundering them at home can be the most eco-friendly option, especially if you have an efficient washing machine and line-drying is a possibility for at least part of the year.

To avoid contamination and the spread of viruses in ground-water and land, the advice is to rinse disposable nappies before throwing them away. If you're prepared to do this much, cleaning cloth nappies is very little more work, and throwing them in the wash may not seem like such a big inconvenience.

Toxic Waste

Natural Stain Removal Tricks

- Add 120 ml vinegar or lemon juice or borax to the washing cycle (as long as your detergent does not contain chlorine bleach).

- Dry nappies outside on a line in the sun for natural whitening.

- Try non-chlorine, oxygen bleach for less toxic bleaching.

- To control odour, some purpose-made nappy buckets use chemical-laden scented deodorizing discs or aerosol sprays, which affect our ability to smell.

- Deodorizing discs may emit polluting VOCs and aerosol propellants can be neuro-toxic and/or carcinogenic.

- Instead, use a covered waste bin that you will be able to go on using well beyond the nappy stage. To control odours, sprinkle the nappies with bicarbonate of soda. Wash the bin out frequently with borax and vinegar.

As with disposables, the first step in washing cloth nappies is to dispose of any solid waste in the toilet. After that some people choose to soak the soiled nappies in a bucket filled with water and bicarbonate of soda, and others store them in a dry, covered bucket. When you have enough for a load, take the nappies from a wet bucket and run them through the spin cycle to get rid of the extra water. Or take them from the dry bucket and run them through a cold cycle or a cold soak to loosen the stains.

From there the procedure is the same: wash the nappies on a hot cycle with a cold rinse. Use less detergent than you would for your own clothes, about 50 ml. Add borax to the wash cycle to whiten the nappies, and white vinegar to the rinse cycle as a fabric softener. It's recommended that you don't wash more than 24 nappies at a time to prevent unnecessary wear from friction. Dry the nappies on the line in the sunshine whenever possible, for added whitening and sanitizing benefits.

Baby Detergents to Avoid

- Baby-specific detergents can get expensive because using them means you'll be washing your baby's clothes separately from your own.

- Separate detergents also mean extra packaging that eventually hits the waste stream.

- Many baby detergents contain the same harsh irritants and environmental pollutants as ordinary detergents. The best bet is finding a less toxic option for all clothes.

- Avoid 'whitening enzymes'. These are too strong for babies and may cause severe rashes.

What to Look For in Detergents

Fragrance-free
Dye-free
Chlorine-free
No optical brighteners
No masking agents

- The truth is that what is best for baby is also best for you.

- Look for a detergent that is free of dyes, fragrances and colourings that you can use for both you and your baby, so you can wash all the laundry together.

- Look for detergents that list all their ingredients on the label.

- You'll still want to wash the dirty nappies separately to minimize wear and maximize cleanliness.

TOYS
Wood and organic cotton are the best bets for safe toys

Plastic toys have been a big hit with parents for the last 40 years, because they are easy to clean and come in bright colours that kids love. But plastics contain chemicals that may be endangering our children.

Teething rings, dolls, polymer clay and other toys made with type 3 plastic or PVC can expose children to lead and other heavy metals as well as phthalates, which studies show can cause reproductive and sexual development problems in children even with limited exposure. And exposure is not limited for most children. Phthalates are in everything from baby washes and laundry detergent to shower curtain liners and practically everything with fragrance.

Plastics aren't the only danger in toys. Choking remains the top cause of toy-related infant death and injuries and is the

Washable Toys

- Stick to simple toys that don't involve plastics.

- Look for soft toys made from organic and renewable resources that use only natural dyes and are age-appropriate.

- Organic cotton and hemp toys are soft and washable, which means they start off clean and can stay clean for your child.

- Wash toys at least once a month in unscented laundry detergent. Add vinegar to the rinse cycle to make sure they come out soft.

Wooden Toys

- Choose wooden toys that are made of solid wood obtained from sustainable sources.

- Avoid plywood or fibreboard, which can offgas formaldehyde and other toxins.

- Look for finishes that use natural oils or beeswax.

- If the label doesn't tell you what the paint or finish is, call the manufacturer for details.

basis for recalling tons of toys. These toys are found to have unsafe construction or inappropriate age designations. Lead content is another reason toys are recalled. Be vigilant with your children's toys, particularly when they are given as presents by other people, and check that they are appropriate for the child's age. British toys, and many European toys sold in Britain, carry the Lion Mark, which indicates that the supplier has followed a strict code of practice covering quality of manufacture, toy safety and ethical advertising.

To simplify your life, remember that less is more – kids don't need mountains of toys. Eliminate PVC toys and reduce plastics as much as possible in your nursery and home. Luckily other options exist, such as wood and organic cotton or hemp toys. Choose products that are easy to clean and free of heavy dyes and small pieces that can break off. Your child will have hours of fun without the risk of long-term damage.

Questions to Ask about Toys:

- How long will the toy hold the child's interest?

- Will it last for generations?

- Does the label assure you that the paint and finishes are toxin-free and safe?

- Is it imported or antique, which may mean lead paint?

- Does it smell toxic or perfumed?

- Is it made of PVC/vinyl plastic?

- Is the packaging wasteful?

- Can you get a version made locally?

Cleaner Bath Toys

- Bacteria and mildew can be a problem with bath toys – especially popular ones that tend to stay pretty wet.

- Cleaning them once a month helps reduce this problem.

- Put them in a big bowl or bucket and add 30 ml

vinegar for each litre of water.

- Leave them to soak for 10 minutes. Then rub them with a sponge to get any dirt or grime off and let them dry completely.

NURSERY
A healthy environment means a healthy baby

To reduce your baby's exposure to toxins in the nursery, focus on making changes to those elements that can have the most impact on air quality: furniture, mattresses, linens and cleaning chemicals. For example, spending a bit more for hardwood furniture instead of plywood or chipboard will reduce formaldehyde exposure. Even better, choose pieces that have been treated with low-VOC paints or coatings, or buy unfinished wood and low-VOC products to finish them yourself. Recycling is also a great option because older furniture has already offgassed most of its chemicals.

The average baby spends 10–14 hours a day either sleeping or playing in his or her cot. That's a lot of time spent breathing on or just above the mattress. Yet most mattresses have PVC surfaces to make them waterproof (see page 36), with

Cot

- Avoid non-hardwood cots, which can offgas carcinogenic formaldehyde for years.

- Look for finishes that are no-VOC or that you can finish yourself.

- Forest Stewardship Council certification tells you the wood used to make a product came from an environmentally and socially responsible source.

- A hand-me-down or used cot that is only a few years old is another good green choice, but make sure that it meets the latest standards in cot safety.

Mattress

- Avoid cots and mattresses covered in vinyl, infused with toxic fire retardants and 'antibacterial' pesticides, and stuffed with petroleum-based polyurethane foam.

- Look for organic cotton, wool, or natural rubber fillings. Wool is a natural fire retardant.

- Food-grade polyethylene makes a safer waterproof cover; less-toxic fireproofing options are also available.

toxic phthalates making up about 30 per cent of this surface's weight. The outer surface is also treated with toxic flame retardants, and the filling for most mattresses is polyurethane foam with all kinds of chemical additives, many of which are well-known toxins. Also, this foam is highly flammable so it is also treated with flame retardant.

Organic, non-toxic cot mattresses are readily available on the Internet, and some even have earth-friendly waterproof covers so you don't have to sacrifice any of the convenience of a regular mattress. These mattresses are made from natural fibres such as springy coir, organic cotton and natural wool, which provides fire resistance without chemical additives.

Once you have the basic components in place, organic cotton bedding and consistent green-cleaning practices will ensure a healthy, soothing environment for your baby.

Bedding

- Waterproof mattress pads made of wool and organic cotton are good options to top off your non-toxic mattress.

- Regular cotton sheets are hard on the environment because of pesticide use in growing the cotton and pollution from bleaching it.

- Sheets are often treated with formulas that contain formaldehyde to prevent wrinkling, as well as harsh dyes and even antibacterial toxins.

- Look for organic cotton or bamboo sheets that are not treated with synthetic dyes or anti-wrinkle formulas.

Nursery Easy Clean

- Cleaning the nursery should not add toxins or dirty the air your child is breathing.

- Wash the bedding every week or as needed if there are stains or smells.

- Vacuum the floor and any upholstery weekly to minimize dust and dust mite exposure.

- Castile soap, warm water, and a sponge will do the job for everything from cot and changing table surfaces to skirting boards and windowsills. Use vinegar and water for the windows.

BODY TOXINS
Limit your toxins to get cleaner, healthier nourishment for your baby

CLEAN HOME, GREEN HOME

There is no question that breast milk is still the healthiest food for babies. However, recent studies have revealed that we are all carrying stores of persistent toxins around with us in our bodies, and these get into breast milk. Dangerous chemicals, including DDT and PBDEs, and heavy metals such as lead and mercury, are among the chemicals found most often in breast milk worldwide.

While many chemicals simply pass through our bodies, others build up over time in our fat stores. They're in breast milk because it's full of fat. The good and bad news is that breastfeeding rids the mother's body of at least some of these chemicals, but they go directly to the baby. If a woman breastfeeds multiple children, each one will get cleaner milk than the last. By limiting the toxins you bring into your home,

Cleaner Breast Milk

- A drastic change of diet will not completely eliminate the stores of toxins we harbour in our tissues, but it can make a difference.

- Eat less animal fat and limit your intake of fish such as tuna and swordfish, which tend to contain more mercury (see page 48).

- Increase the amount of organic foods you eat to reduce your exposure to chemical pesticides and fertilizers.

- Eating more organic fruits and vegetables and whole grains is healthier generally.

Bottles

- Glass bottles are making a comeback because they don't leach any toxic chemicals and they come from a renewable resource.

- While these bottles are tough, children should not walk around with them unsupervised or sleep with their bottles.

- Other green options include BPA-free plastic bottles.

- These are generally opaque and made from safer plastics, like polypropylene (type 5 plastic) or polyethylene (types 1, 2 or 4).

you're already on the right track to giving your baby cleaner breast milk.

Once the baby graduates to bottles and training cups, new concerns arise. Most plastic bottles are polycarbonate plastic (type 7) and contain Bisphenol-A (BPA), which can cause long-term problems with normal hormonal functioning and development. BPA-free plastic as well as classic glass bottles are available for babies, and BPA-free and steel trainer cups are great options for toddlers.

Teats

- Synthetic rubber teats can be contaminated with carcinogenic nitrosamines, which can be ingested along with the contents of the bottle.

- These teats tend to be amber-coloured and don't last very long.

- Look for longer-lasting and safer natural rubber or clear silicone teats.

- Whenever you see a crack or tear in a teat or in a bottle, it's time to recycle and replace it. Cracks can be havens for bacteria; in glass bottles they lead to breakage.

Training Cups

- Avoid training cups made from polycarbonate plastic (type 7).

- If you want plastic, look for cups made from polypropylene or polyethylene plastic.

- Steel or aluminium training cups don't leach chemicals

into your child's drink. They can weigh as little as 100 g and are small enough to fit small hands.

- Make sure the spout is made from safer plastics and look for reputable brands, as some cheap versions have been found to contain lead in their paint.

WASHING
Reduce your environmental impact without sacrificing clean clothes

The simple everyday act of washing your clothes can have a far-reaching impact on the environment. After the toilet, the washing machine uses the most water, and it is one of the biggest energy consumers in the home.

Once the water leaves your home and enters the sewage system, it takes with it the chemicals from your wash. Conventional detergents may clean the spot out of that sweater, but they can pollute air and waterways near and far. Unlike soap, detergents are synthetic and most are petroleum-based. To enable them to penetrate stains and wash them away, many detergents use surfactants that belong to the chemical class alkylphenol ethoxylates (APEs), which are known to be toxic to the immune system and suspected of interfering with the hormonal system. APEs are a major

Greener Washing

- Switching to an A-rated energy-efficient washing machine could reduce your energy and water consumption by up to 40 per cent.

- Only wash full loads or adjust the water level according to the load size.

- Wash in cold water and save even more energy – 90 per cent of the energy used to wash clothes is spent heating the water. Switching from hot to warm can cut your energy use by half.

- Run the washing machine at off-peak periods.

What to Avoid

Alkylphenol ethoxylates (APEs)
Linear alkylate sulfonate (LAS)
Diethanolamine (DEA)
Triethanolamine (TEA)
Chlorine
Fragrance
Dyes

- APEs are highly toxic surfactants with long-term impact (see page 4). LAS is corrosive and can cause major damage to skin, respiratory system and eyes.

- DEA and TEA are used to cut grease but can react with some preservatives to create carcinogenic nitrosamines (see page 4).

- Chlorine is an irritant that takes a toll on the environment and is responsible for a high proportion of household poisonings.

- Fragrance usually hides a long list of chemicals, including phthalates. Dyes are unnecessary and can be carcinogenic.

contaminant in waterways and are suspected of disrupting the reproduction and threatening the survival of fish. Because they do not readily biodegrade, APEs and other petroleum-based surfactants do a lot of damage to marine life and to the soil and plant life around the water.

To reduce your environmental impact, when it's time to replace your washing machine buy an A-rated model that saves energy and water. Look for detergents that are plant-based, biodegradable and free of fragrance and dyes.

What to Look For

Fragrance-free

Dye-free

Biodegradable in 3–5 days

Plant-based

Recycled container

- Look for products that are plant-based as opposed to petroleum-based. This means they use renewable resources and do less damage to the environment.

- Pay careful attention to the packaging. Does the product come in bulk? Is the packaging recyclable, and

is it a product made from recycled materials?

- Look for concentrated formulas that you use less of and therefore have less packaging.

- Or try the recipe above to make your own laundry soap.

Easy laundry soap:
25 ml castile soap
100 g washing soda (to cut grease)
100 g borax (to remove stains)
Combine. If your clothes don't feel clean enough, increase the castile soap until you're satisfied with the results. Optional: add 50 ml vinegar to rinse cycle to soften fabrics and water.

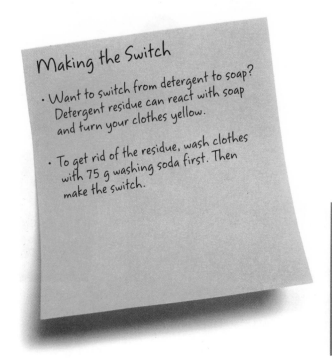

Making the Switch

- Want to switch from detergent to soap? Detergent residue can react with soap and turn your clothes yellow.

- To get rid of the residue, wash clothes with 75 g washing soda first. Then make the switch.

LAUNDRY ROOM

97

WHITENING CLOTHES
Try some green alternatives to bleach

Bleach has been around forever. It's dirt cheap and does a great job of whitening clothing. However, it is also a pesticide and can damage our health and the environment.

Chlorine bleach is highly caustic and can irritate skin, eyes, noses and airways. Worldwide, it is the most common cause of poisoning in children under the age of six. If you have children, this is not a product you want to keep under the sink or on the laundry room worktop. After the bleach has done its job of whitening your socks, it enters the sewage system and from there can eventually contaminate drinking water. Specifically, it produces organochlorines that are suspected carcinogens, neurotoxins and immunotoxins.

Using chlorine bleach in combination with other cleaners can be even more harmful. If they contain ammonia or acids,

Proactive Step

- Create a system where it's easy for everyone in the household to sort their own dirty clothes.

- This will make doing the laundry a lot faster and reduce the need for bleach.

- Sort by fabric, so that rougher, heavier and darker-coloured clothes are washed separately from lighter, more delicate clothes.

- This can prolong the life of your clothes and reduce the energy you use to dry them.

Natural Whitening

- Sunshine is the most natural whitening and sanitizing solution available.

- For maximum whitening, first add lemon juice to the rinse cycle and wash normally.

- Then hang the clothes on a line outside to dry. Choose a sunny day when the wind is not blowing too strongly. Otherwise you may find your clothes are dirtier than when you started.

- Line-drying will also save you money and the energy of using the tumble dryer.

as in many toilet and oven cleaners, the mixture can produce chloramines and chlorine gases, which are immediately and extremely toxic.

Adding borax to your wash and drying washing in the sunshine may be all you need to whiten your clothes and linens. If not, there are quite a few bleach alternatives on the market that are eco-friendly.

Vinegar or hydrogen peroxide goes here

Borax goes here

Non-Chlorine and Oxygen Bleach

- Non-chlorine bleaches generally use hydrogen peroxide to whiten clothes.

- Oxygen bleach generally uses sodium percarbonate, which is a combination of washing soda and hydrogen peroxide. It breaks down into oxygen, water and soda ash, which are harmless to the environment.

- You can find these alternative bleach products in powder or liquid form.

- It's a good idea to experiment to see what works best with your water and clothes.

Other Whiteners

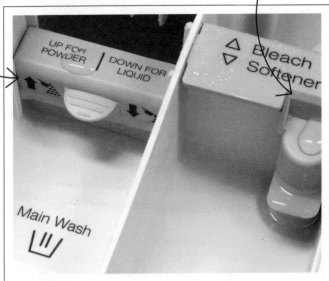

- Borax whitens clothing, helps fight mould and bacteria, and neutralizes odours.

- Add 100 g of borax to your wash cycle.

- White vinegar also whitens and helps disinfect your clothes. Add vinegar to the rinse cycle and it will also work as a fabric softener and reduce static cling.

- Alternatively, you can add 120 ml of hydrogen peroxide to the rinse cycle for extra whitening.

LAUNDRY ROOM

DRY-CLEANING ALTERNATIVES
Clean even your most delicate garments without polluting the air

Dry cleaning is not good for the environment or your health. The main culprit is the chemical perchloroethylene, or PERC, used by 90 per cent of all dry cleaners. PERC is a hazardous air pollutant, and the International Agency for Research on Cancer classifies it as a probable carcinogen. In fact, places like New York City are slowly phasing out the use of PERC in dry cleaners in residential buildings because of reports of tenants being made ill by it. But what do you do if your favourite sweater says 'DRY CLEAN ONLY'?

There are several greener alternatives beginning to sprout up, especially if you live in a progressive area or a major city. One promising option is 'wet cleaning', which uses computerized machines and non-toxic, biodegradable detergents to wash garments, which are then dried and ironed or

Dry Cleaning

- Clothing manufacturers sometimes put this label on clothes that can also be washed by hand.

- You can hand-wash unlined cotton, silk, linen, wool and even cashmere items that are not embroidered.

- Angora sweaters, as well as lined and tailored clothing, should be taken to a professional wet cleaner or very rarely dry cleaned.

- In the future, avoid buying clothes with these labels unless you are sure you can wash them by hand.

Hand-Washing Alternative

- Fill the sink with cool water and add just enough mild washing-up liquid to create suds to cover the entire surface of the water.

- Add the item you want to wash and gently work the suds into the fabric by moving it around and squeezing.

- Leave to soak for 10 minutes and remove.

- Replace the soapy water with fresh water to rinse. Repeat until the water stays clear.

steam-pressed. There is no air or water pollution, and you're not bringing home a bag full of carcinogens.

Home dry-cleaning kits are another PERC-free option. However, they do contain toxins that are very similar to those you want to watch out for in your laundry detergent. Kit manufacturers tend not to come clean with their actual ingredients, claiming it's proprietary information. However, we do know most contain detergent with petroleum-based surfactants in their stain-removal products, and mega amounts of

fragrance, which usually means phthalates, in the sheets that go in the tumble dryer with your garments. All that, and the fact that they are designed to be disposable, make these not a great choice for your health or the environment.

Many products that claim to need dry cleaning can actually be hand-washed perfectly safely. As you experiment with these techniques, keep in mind that if you ignore the manufacturer's dry-cleaning recommendation, you can't expect the store or manufacturer to be sympathetic if it backfires.

Drying

- Squeeze item carefully to release excess water.

- Lay it out on a clean, dry, neutral-coloured towel and arrange it in its proper shape. Pull gently if needed.

- Roll the towel and item up as you press down to squeeze the water out.

- Repeat with a dry towel and spread the item out on another dry towel to air-dry, or hang from a line if the fabric won't stretch.

Wool and Silk

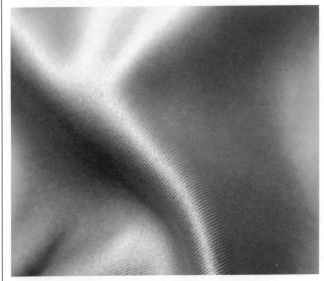

- To avoid shrinking wool, use cold water and press out water instead of rolling in a towel.

- For coloured silk, test an inside seam for colour fastness by wetting it and then dabbing the wet patch with a white towel.

- Wash colourfast silk in tepid water and add 50 ml vinegar to your first rinse water to get rid of any residue. Then rinse with clear water.

- Hang a silk garment on a padded hanger to dry.

DOWN DUVETS
Avoid the dry cleaner and safely wash your down duvet

A down duvet is another item you might expect to have to have professionally cleaned. At one time dry cleaning was recommended for down quilts, because it was feared that washing might destroy the down clusters and wash away the natural oils that protect them. Yet the ducks and geese who originally owned the feathers had no trouble getting wet and drying without losing their fluff.

In fact, down duvets are easily washed if you know how to set about it. Whether you wash by hand or in a machine, the real issues are cleaning too often, with too harsh a detergent and with too much agitation.

Professional laundering is a good way to go, but, if you have a big enough space to wash your duvets, you can save money by doing it at home. Since most household washing

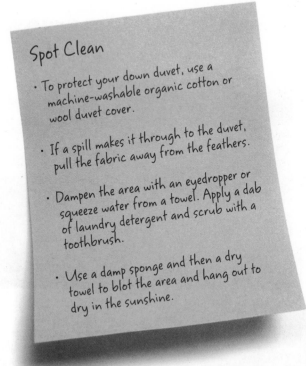

Spot Clean

- To protect your down duvet, use a machine-washable organic cotton or wool duvet cover.

- If a spill makes it through to the duvet, pull the fabric away from the feathers.

- Dampen the area with an eyedropper or squeeze water from a towel. Apply a dab of laundry detergent and scrub with a toothbrush.

- Use a damp sponge and then a dry towel to blot the area and hang out to dry in the sunshine.

Washing Down

- To wash your down duvet in a washing machine, you need to have a large front-loading machine. The central agitator in top-loading machines can damage the duvet.

- Use warm water and a small amount of very mild laundry detergent.

- Run the rinse cycle twice to ensure all the detergent is out of the duvet.

- If your own machine isn't large enough, take the duvet to a launderette or wash by hand in the bathtub.

machines are not designed for such large, heavy articles, hand-washing in the bath will yield the best results for your duvet and save your washing machine.

Hang your duvet outside in the sun for a few hours a month (see page 98) to increase the time between washes. If you do that consistently, and spot-clean when necessary, you may only need to wash your duvet every couple of years.

(see page 98)

·············· GREEN●LIGHT··············

If you're drying a duvet in your tumble dryer, throw in a couple of tennis balls. This will save you the trouble of pulling the duvet out of the dryer to refluff periodically. The tennis balls do the fluffing work for you.

Drying Down

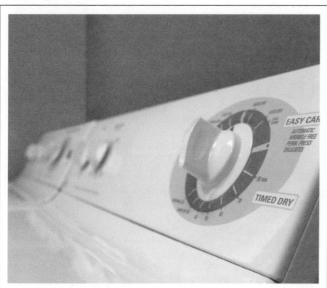

- Run the duvet through the washing machine's spin cycle a second time to remove excess water.

- As you remove it, squeeze out any remaining water without wringing or twisting the duvet.

- If you use a tumble dryer, you'll need to dry the duvet for a few hours on low heat.

- Remove periodically to fluff and add dry towels to help absorb the moisture.

Line Drying

- The best way to dry down is in the sunshine.

- Because a wet duvet is heavy, use plenty of clothes pegs to hold it on the line.

- If you have parallel washing lines, it may work better to securely attach two sides, creating a kind of hammock, to reduce the amount of weight on one line.

- Periodically remove the duvet and shake it. Then reattach to dry completely.

LAUNDRY ROOM

103

STAIN REMOVAL
Start mild for effective, non-toxic stain removal

Conventional commercial stain removers are petroleum-based and contain many of the same harsh chemicals as laundry detergents. What's more, because they are formulated to treat all kinds of stains, they are frequently ineffective. The general rule for effective and non-toxic stain removal is to treat the stain as soon as you can and start with as mild a method as possible.

The first step is to scrape off or absorb by dabbing (not rubbing) any part of the stain that hasn't yet penetrated the fabric. Use a knife or a cloth, depending on the substance. For greasy stains try cornflour to absorb the oil. For older stains, apply glycerine to loosen the stain for easier removal.

Next, hold a colourfast towel behind the stain to absorb it and use another towel to dab ice-cold water on the front of

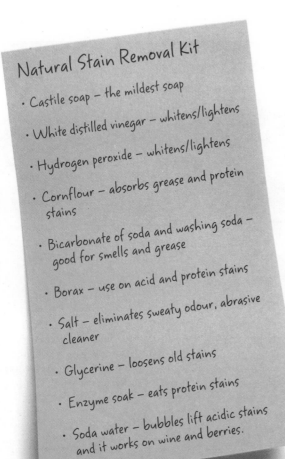

Natural Stain Removal Kit

- Castile soap – the mildest soap

- White distilled vinegar – whitens/lightens

- Hydrogen peroxide – whitens/lightens

- Cornflour – absorbs grease and protein stains

- Bicarbonate of soda and washing soda – good for smells and grease

- Borax – use on acid and protein stains

- Salt – eliminates sweaty odour, abrasive cleaner

- Glycerine – loosens old stains

- Enzyme soak – eats protein stains

- Soda water – bubbles lift acidic stains and it works on wine and berries.

Common Stains

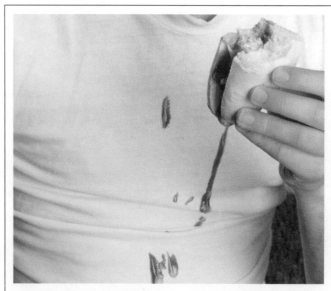

- Mustard – Flush with white vinegar. Wash with washing-up liquid and cold water.

- Tomato sauce – Scrape off solids. Dab with diluted washing-up liquid and soak in cool water.

- Soy sauce – Apply diluted washing-up liquid and use a toothbrush to work it into

the fabric. Flush with cold water. Do the same with vinegar if the stain persists.

- Sweat – Soak garment for an hour in water to cover and 50–100 g salt. Wash as normal and dry in the sun. The sun's bleaching power will prevent the sweat from yellowing the garment.

the stain. If that doesn't do it, the next step is to continue to hold the towel behind the stain and apply an ice cube to the front of the stain. For many stains, this is all it takes. If there is only a faint stain left on a white garment, apply white vinegar with a cotton swab. The vinegar is a whitener and may take care of it.

If that's not enough, you'll need to try more powerful solutions, but pretest the fabric in an inconspicuous place to make sure your chosen technique won't ruin it.

Beverage Stains

- For coffee, tea or wine stains, boil a kettle full of water.

- Ask someone else to hold the stained fabric taut over the sink.

- Stand on a chair and slowly pour boiling water from about 1 m above the fabric until the stain starts to lighten and disappear.

- Alternatively, rinse with soda water and blot the stain up with a clean, light-coloured towel.

Kid Stains

- Grass – Use an enzyme spray and wash as usual.

- Blood – Place stained clothing in the sink with cold water and 30 g salt. Soak for an hour. For tough stains, try soaking area in hydrogen peroxide. Scrub with detergent. Wash as usual.

- Chocolate/ice cream stains – Scrape off any unabsorbed food. Wet area with water and mild washing-up liquid. Scrub with a toothbrush. For tough chocolate or ice cream stains, spray with an enzyme cleaner. Launder as usual.

MACHINE AND NATURAL DRYING
Dry garments smartly to conserve energy – and save money

Tumble dryers are the second-biggest energy drain after the refrigerator (which is constantly running) in the average household. But you can save energy with your clothes dryer by making a few smart choices.

Some dryer features can help you save energy. These include controls that automatically shut off the machine when the clothes are dry and set a start-time to run during off-peak hours when energy is cheaper. Try shortening the drying time to prevent over-drying your clothes, and run only full loads. When the time comes to replace your tumble dryer, buy one that is A-rated for energy efficiency.

Drying your clothes in the machine presents you with another choice – whether to use fabric conditioner sheets. They are yet another contributor to the mountains of items

Greener Machine Drying

- Another energy-saving step includes drying heavy articles separately from lighter clothes, which take far less time to dry.

- Do consecutive loads to make use of the hot air that's already in your dryer from the previous load.

- Clean the lint filter often and make sure the outside vent on a vented model closes tightly.

- If the vent does not close tightly, repair or replace it so you can keep the cooler outside air from leaking in.

Fabric Softeners to Avoid

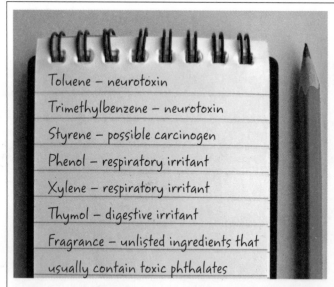

Toluene – neurotoxin
Trimethylbenzene – neurotoxin
Styrene – possible carcinogen
Phenol – respiratory irritant
Xylene – respiratory irritant
Thymol – digestive irritant
Fragrance – unlisted ingredients that
usually contain toxic phthalates

- Wash natural-fibre clothing, like cotton and linen, separately from synthetics. Synthetics are prone to static, but natural clothing by itself is not.

- Add vinegar to the rinse cycle (see above) to eliminate static and soften your clothes. Bicarbonate of soda in the wash cycle also softens clothes.

- For fragrance, add a few drops of your essential oil of choice to the rinse cycle.

- Or put the oil on a face flannel and put it in the dryer with your clothes.

building up in our landfill sites. They can contain neurotoxins, respiratory irritants and skin irritants, which are transferred to your clothes. Look for less toxic options or try adding vinegar to the rinse cycle for easy fabric softening.

Hanging your clothes out to dry in the sunshine can also save money and energy. Line-drying one load of laundry cuts 1.5 kg in carbon dioxide emissions, which can add up to hundreds of kilos over a year.

Fresh-Air Drying

- Run a washing line between your garden fence and your house, or between two poles.

- A height of about 2 m off the ground is good, but adjust it depending on what's comfortable for you.

- For small spaces, use a rotary clothes dryer because you can fit more clothes and still have air circulation between them.

- Pay attention to the weather when you're line-drying. Very windy days can kick up dirt and dust.

Crease-Free Clothing

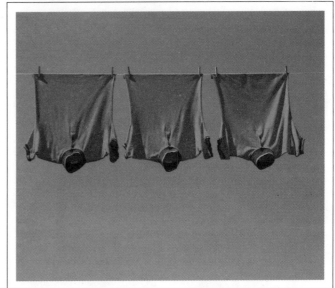

- Remove wet items from the washing machine as soon as the cycle ends and peg them out immediately.

- Shake out clothes before pegging to reduce creases.

- Attach shirts securely to the line by pegging the hem.

- Fold trousers along the desired vertical crease. Attach the hems at the bottom of each leg to the line with clothes pegs.

- For brightly coloured clothing, turn the articles inside out before hanging so they won't fade in the sun.

LAUNDRY ROOM

LEAVE THE DIRT AT THE DOOR

Take a proactive step to reduce your cleaning burden for the entire house

The simplest way to keep dirt out of your home is for everyone to leave their shoes at the door. Shoes can track in everything from mud and pet waste to pesticides, lead and tar. Although wearing shoes in the house doesn't seem like a big deal, an American study has shown that pesticide-carrying shoes are a major source of exposure for children.

This is because children are more apt to be on or closer to the floor for longer periods of time, and they constantly put their hands in their mouths. Even if you don't use any pesticides in your own garden or have lead content in your soil, you really don't know where everyone's shoes have been and what they're walking into your home.

CLEAN HOME, GREEN HOME

Provide the Tools

Make It a Rule

- A textured recycled rubber or rope mat will get the dirt off and helps close the recycling loop.

- Placing a shoe scraper on the step or porch next to your door will help with particularly muddy shoes that have deep grooves in the soles.

- Make your own scraper by placing an old rectangular, stiff-bristled broom head alongside your doormat.

- Screw both into an appropriately sized board for stability.

- For a shoes-off system to work, it has to be a habit with all household members and a clear request for guests.

- Create or buy a sign and display it prominently so guests are clear about the rule.

- Once everyone gets used to it, it will just come naturally and your home will stay cleaner longer.

Creating a designated space near the door to store shoes and contain the dirt will mean less exposure for your family. It will also support you in your efforts to reduce the amount of cleaning products you need to use and the amount of time you need to spend cleaning.

Don't forget to apply the same rule to people delivering items to your home or performing services. They may come equipped with their own overshoes, though you may need to prompt them to put them on. If not, and if they aren't lifting heavy objects or using tools, ask them to remove their shoes just like everyone else. If this is a frequent occurrence, you might consider buying your own stash of overshoes.

It may seem awkward at first to ask guests to remove their shoes when they arrive, but, as long as you make it a rule and don't cave in to every complaint, they'll get used to it. And with the right set-up, you can make it an easy and even inviting thing to do.

Shoe Storage

- Provide a space that is clean and easy for people to remove their shoes.

- Stacking shelves have room for more shoes without taking up too much space.

- These shelves will get dirty very quickly, so be sure to wash them as part of your regular hallway cleaning routine.

- Remove the shoes and vacuum the shelves or use a dustpan and brush. Then wipe clean with all-purpose cleaner and a rag.

A Cosy Touch

- Fill a basket with inexpensive, washable and comfortable slippers and place it by the front door.

- Make sure you have a basic range of sizes – small, medium and large.

- When guests enter and remove their shoes, they can grab a pair of slippers and no one will ever notice the hole in their sock.

- Remember to wash these slippers frequently, especially in the summer when guests might not be wearing socks.

HIGH-IMPACT UTILITY ROOMS
Let your utility room keep your whole house clean

It's easy to put off cleaning the house when it seems as if there just isn't enough time in the day. It's not that you don't really have the time to do a simple thing like, say, wiping down the kitchen worktops, but if in order to do that you first have to sort the mail, recycle the newspaper, move the children's homework, put away sunglasses, keys and the dog's lead, you just might not have time. The more you can do to keep all these things off the worktop, the better chance you'll have of keeping it clean.

If you're lucky enough to have a spacious utility room or boot room, using this space wisely will help control clutter throughout your home. Create specific spaces in the room to place shoes, keys, mail, pet gear and outdoor clothing. The kitchen work surfaces and table, as well as the back of the

Cleaning Station

- Put up a wall-mounted rack for long-handled brooms and mops. Mops will dry better and your cleaning tools won't be sitting in a dusty corner.

- It's also easier to clean the floor without having to move them around.

- Store cleaning materials in a cupboard near the brooms and mops.

- Keep the basics together in a carrying container so it's easy to transport everything you need with you as you clean your home.

Gardening Station

- Store gardening tools where they are most convenient to the garden.

- Place pots, watering cans, and any larger objects on shelves; spread them out enough for you to see what you have without wasting space.

- Use bins or empty pots to hold gardening gloves and other soft things, as well as any smaller tools that you can't hang up.

- Put up hooks for small garden tools that do hang, so you can see them easily.

couch, the floor and the stairs, can then stay clear of clutter. This arrangement may also save you hours of searching for the dog's lead, your keys or your umbrella. Best of all, designated stations that offer a place for everything make the usually arduous task of cleaning the utility room much easier. Boxes or baskets can be removed easily for dusting or washing shelves and worktops.

If you don't have a designated utility room, setting up a corner of a front or back hallway will help you control daily clutter and prevent it from spreading throughout your home. Small bookshelves or shelves hung in specific locations will help with this process.

Pet Station

- Place food in a storage bin that closes tightly so it won't tempt unwanted rodents or pests and will stay fresh longer.

- Set up your pet's feeding station near the food.

- Have a separate bin for leads and extra collars, and a bag or basket for the waste bags you'll need when you go for walks.

- A cookie jar for treats and bones and a bin for toys will complete the station.

Small-Space Utility Room Necessities

- A mat or shelf for shoes

- Hooks for coats with mats below to catch drips

- Hooks or a box for keys

- Slots or baskets for mail

- Baskets for seasonal gear like hats and gloves

- A container for umbrellas

111

HALLWAYS AND UTILITY ROOMS
Follow some routine tasks for dirt control

If you tend to do most of your cleaning just before guests arrive, you probably aren't focusing too much on your utility room. It is, after all, the utility room. Yet utility rooms, boot rooms and entrance halls work best at controlling dirt when they are cleaned regularly. If not, whatever dirt you're trying to contain builds up, spreads out and gets walked into the rest of the house anyway.

Main entrance halls create the first impression on your guests. Routine cleaning should include dusting and occasionally polishing any furniture you have there, as well as weekly vacuuming and occasional mopping, depending on your floor.

Even if guests never enter through the back door of your home, the area should also be dusted and vacuumed or

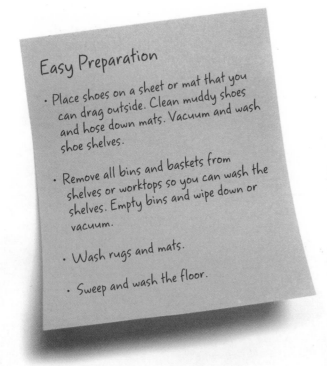

Easy Preparation

• Place shoes on a sheet or mat that you can drag outside. Clean muddy shoes and hose down mats. Vacuum and wash shoe shelves.

• Remove all bins and baskets from shelves or worktops so you can wash the shelves. Empty bins and wipe down or vacuum.

• Wash rugs and mats.

• Sweep and wash the floor.

Maintenance

• Remove coats from hooks and inspect hooks for rust and sturdiness.

• Tighten loose screws so hooks can handle the multiple coats that often get piled on them.

• Try to remove minor rust stains by applying a paste of borax and lemon juice. Leave to dry and rinse off.

• If the rust is beyond cleaning, replace the hook. The rust will stain jackets and bag handles that hang there.

swept on a fairly regular basis to keep the dirt down to a minimum. That's why organization is key. A pile of shoes in the corner makes for a lot of clearing up when you need to wash the floor. Shoes arranged on a recycled rubber utility mat are easy and quick to move. The less preparation required, the more often you'll clean and the more effective the space will be in containing dirt so it won't get walked into your home.

Even if you don't have time to remove shoe storage or bins on the floor, vacuum or sweep around them to control the dirt as much as you can. Then, schedule a periodic deep clean based on how dirty your utility room gets. If you have kids, plan to spend some time dusting and washing shelves and moving shoes, mats and bins out for a thorough floor cleaning every month or two. Better yet, delegate the job to your kids. Having the responsibility of cleaning the space might just give them the encouragement they need to keep it clean on a daily basis.

Containing Dirt: Tools for the Utility Room

- Recycled rubber utility mats

- Washable rugs

- An extra door mat between utility room and the rest of the home

- Regular cleaning

Seasonal Clutter Control

- Schedule a deep-cleaning session at the beginning of each season.

- Check bins and baskets for out-of-season gear and replace with current season necessities.

- For the transition from winter to spring, hats and gloves can be removed and stored out of the way to make room for rain hats and umbrellas or sun visors as you head into spring.

- Remove heavy coats and replace with windbreakers and raincoats.

HALLWAY DÉCOR AND STAIRS
Keep pictures and stairs dust-free for easy cleaning

Hallways and stairs can be neglected spaces when it comes to cleaning. After all, most of us don't linger long in the hall or on the stairs. Instead, we use them as a means to get from one room to another. We may not notice a build-up of dust on pictures or stairs, or fingerprints that can lessen the appearance of hallway décor and may even ruin valuable art if left unattended.

Regular cleaning can be less frequent for these places than the kitchen, bathroom or living areas. Depending on your family, once a month may keep it looking neat and clean. Start at the top for both and remove any cobwebs accumulating in the corners of the ceiling or stairs. Dust light fittings to keep them clean and in good condition. Dust furniture and banisters and periodically dust and wash the skirting

Framed Photographs

Perspex

- If your photos or art are mounted behind Perspex instead of glass, wipe them with a damp cloth only.

- Even a soft dry cloth can scratch Perspex.

- Dust accumulates in tight spaces. If your frame is delicate or has some chipped paint or detailed carving, dust gently with a clean paintbrush.

- Use a T-shirt rag or microfibre cloth to dust the sides and front of the frame and the glass.

- Dust the surfaces that immediately border the glass. Use a cotton bud if you can't get your cloth into the space.

- Dust the back of the frame.

boards where dirt can accumulate. Dampen an old, clean T-shirt with warm soapy water and wipe them down. Vacuum against the direction of traffic on carpets to slow the wearing process. Vacuum both bare and carpeted stairs.

Apart from these routine cleaning tasks, the most important job in the hall may be caring for paintings and photographs that line the walls. Keep these emotionally or financially valuable pieces clean and dust free to prolong their life and keep them looking their best. But dusting pictures is not the same as dusting a side table. Too much pressure or the wrong tool can cause damage, such as paint flaking. Framed photographs may seem straightforward, but harsh cleaning solutions or even water can ruin them.

Dust Control

Dust builds up here.

- As in any room, start your dusting at the top. That means using a vacuum attachment or long-handled broom to reach any cobwebs on the ceiling.

- Next dust any pictures or other wall hangings.

- Then tackle the banister. Dust the top and sides with a just-damp T-shirt, wool sock or dry microfibre cloth.

- Dust each baluster or post separately and work your cloth into any carved areas or details that may harbour dust.

Handheld Vacuuming

Use attachment or handheld vacuum to get in here

- For a shorter staircase, a handheld vacuum cleaner may be the easiest tool to use.

- Make sure the cylinder is empty of dust before starting this task so you'll have more suction power to do the job.

- Start at the top of the staircase and slowly drag the vacuum cleaner in strips from back to front on each stair tread.

- Line up the vacuum opening with the sides and then the back of the stair and slowly vacuum.

BOOKS
Keep your books free of dust, mould and pests

In well-ventilated and dry living areas or offices, book collections can be cosy and inspiring. However, if the room tends to be damp and humid, you may have to deal with mould and pests such as silverfish, which love to nestle up to the likes of Shakespeare and Emily Dickinson, and even Harry Potter. Running a dehumidifier may do the trick to fend off pests, but if the mould problem is already widespread, you may have to consult a professional and maybe move your books into a different room.

Silverfish pose a problem that's much easier to solve. Since they feed on the glue in bookbindings, as well as the paper, it's a good idea to get rid of any unruly stacks of magazines

Coffee-Table Books

Dust accumulates here

- Coffee-table books should be dusted every time you clean the living room. Do not use a solution for this job or you risk damaging the books.

- First use a dry microfibre cloth to dust the areas that are visible, where the most dust can accumulate.

- Then pick up each book and run the cloth over the spine, the back and the pages.

- Dust underneath the books and replace.

Spine Smudges

Look for smudges here

- When people peruse your bookshelves, they can leave oil from their fingers (or their lunch) on the spines of glossy books.

- Dampen a towel or clean T-shirt rag with lukewarm water. Do not use soap or detergent.

- Wipe the length of the spine until the smudge disappears.

- Dry immediately with a dry cloth.

or newspapers you have lying around. In her book *Home Enlightenment*, Annie Berthold Bond suggests two more direct methods for ridding your books of silverfish. The first is to wrap a jar in easy-to-climb masking tape and place it open on the shelf alongside your books. Overnight the silverfish will climb up and fall in, making it easy to flush them down the toilet the next morning. Another technique is to microwave each book for 30–60 seconds and shake out the dead insects into the bin. Do not use this technique with fragile older books, or books with gilded edges or any metallic elements that could cause a fire in the microwave.

To keep your book collections clean and pest-free, remember that while you are collecting books, the books are collecting dust. Using the right vacuum attachment can make regular dusting easy and fast. That, and an occasional deep cleaning for which you actually take the books off the shelves, will keep your books in good order and your home less dusty.

Quick Clean Bookshelf

Vacuum here

- First, remove any small objects that could be sucked up by the vacuum.

- Use the small brush attachment to gently dust the tops of books and spines as they are lined up vertically or the sides and spines for horizontal stacks.

- This can also be done for other sturdy objects like bookends that share the shelves.

- Next, use the crevice tool to dust any open spaces on the shelves around the books.

Deep Clean

- Remove everything from the shelves.

- Dampen a T-shirt rag with mild soap and warm water.

- Start at the top and wipe each shelf completely.

- Dry with a dry towel.

- Use the same damp towel to wipe down each item as you return it to the shelf.

UPHOLSTERY
Fight dust mites and stains without using toxins

While there is an impressive range of products devoted to getting your upholstery clean, a little green knowledge can completely eliminate your need for a special cleaner. It's a good thing, too, because conventional upholstery cleaners can contain the same carcinogenic chemical as that used by dry cleaners (perchloroethylene), as well as irritants, neuro-toxins and suspected teratogens like butyl cellosolve.

When cleaning, think about what makes upholstery dirty. The most visible issues are spots and stains. As with other fabrics, the faster you treat stains, the better chance you have of removing them.

Stain removal is easier if your cushion covers can be removed, soaked and washed. Look for furniture that has this feature when you are buying a new couch or chair.

Upholstery

- For routine dust removal and cleaning, vacuuming works best.

- Attach your upholstery brush tool and vacuum the seats, back and armrest of each sofa or chair.

- Vacuum scatter cushions as well.

- Switch to the crevice tool for tight spaces, such as in between the cushions. Flip cushions regularly to even up wear on each side.

Cushions

- If you notice your cushions looking a little dingy or stained, look for zips.

- Unzip and remove the covers. Soak any stains in mild washing-up liquid and water or choose another stain-removal technique (see pages 104–5).

- Look inside the covers for care instructions and wash accordingly.

- Pay particular attention to the drying instructions, because a shrunken cush-ion cover will not do you much good at all.

Upholstery also gets dirty because it is a natural magnet for dust. No matter how sophisticated the science, an upholstery cleaner won't be able to do much about dust. Instead, make the most of your vacuum attachments to remove dust and control dust mites in your furniture. Alternatively, vapour steam cleaners work really well on upholstery.

Leather furniture needs a little extra care and protection. Try this easy leather cleaner to keep your leather furniture clean and conditioned.

MAKE IT EASY

Leather cleaner:
120 ml jojoba oil
25 ml distilled white vinegar
Rub into leather with a soft cloth for cleaning and conditioning. Do not use on suede.

Emergency Clean

- Scrape off any unabsorbed spillage with a knife.

- Grab a white cloth and press it firmly into the spot.

- Repeat until you've absorbed everything you can.

- Scrub with castile soap and water.

- For oily spills, sprinkle cornflour on the spot.

- Leave for a while to absorb grease, then scrape off with a knife.

Leather

- Dust leather regularly with the dust brush attachment on the vacuum cleaner or with a microfibre cloth.

- For spills, dampen a white cloth with warm water and blot the spot until you've absorbed everything you can. Do not scrub.

- To clean, make sure the furniture is dusted and test the leather cleaner recipe (see above) on an inconspicuous spot.

- Dip a soft cloth into the mixture and apply small amounts at a time to your furniture using circular movements. Remove any extra cleaner with a dry rag.

LAMPS
Lighting the way to cleaner air and lower energy bills

A lamp can harbour loads of dust, which reduces the amount of light it gives off and can cause unnecessary wear. Dusty lamps also decrease indoor air quality, because the dust is released back into the air every time someone disturbs the lamp or turns it on or off.

It's important to dust the lamp base and lightbulb regularly, but don't forget the shade. Microfibre cloths work well, but so can an old pair of tights if you happen to have some around. Slide your hand inside the tights and wipe the shade clean. For deeper cleaning, some fabric shades can be fully submerged in water. Others, such as those made from parchment, need a different approach.

Keeping lightbulbs and shades clean can help maintain the quality of light coming from that lamp. But choosing the

Dust Control

Dust gets in here

- Fluted shades or other types of shade that do not have flat, even surfaces can get very dusty in hard-to-reach places.

- Turn off the lamp and remove the shade. Take it outside or hold it over a sink or rubbish bin as you wipe each groove with a clean paintbrush, soft brush or feather duster.

- Apply only the slightest pressure as you brush each groove and eliminate the dust.

- Dust the lightbulb with a microfibre cloth.

Washable Shades

Do not submerge the base.

- Check the care instructions on your shade. In general, hand-sewn fabric shades do best with this cleaning method.

- Fill a sink with lukewarm water and mix in a tablespoon of the mildest laundry detergent you have.

- Submerge shade and remove. Wipe gently with a clean soft cloth or sponge.

- Rinse with lukewarm water from the tap and blot dry with a towel. Blow-dry with a hair dryer on cool.

right lightbulb is crucial for setting the mood you want in the room, as well as for managing your energy bills and reducing your carbon emissions. Since it's estimated that 20 per cent of household energy use goes on lighting, choosing energy-efficient compact fluorescent lightbulbs is a great idea. These bulbs have come a long way from their glaring-white-light ancestry, and they are also becoming even more efficient. One bulb can last up to 11 years.

· · · · · · · · · · · GREEN ● LIGHT · · · · · · · · · · · ·

Compact fluorescent lightbulbs are now the most energy-efficient bulbs available. Keep in mind that CFLs generate more light with less wattage, so here's how to know if you're buying the right wattage for your space: 15-watt CFL = 60-watt incandescent bulb; 20-watt CFL = 75-watt incandescent bulb; 26–29-watt CFL = 100-watt incandescent bulb.

Non-Washable Shades

- Parchment or paper shades cannot be washed. Instead, dust frequently to keep them from showing dirt.

- Use a paintbrush or soft brush to dust all the way around the shade. Pay special attention to seams and details where dust can stick.

- A hair dryer on a cool setting can also do this job, although the dust will scatter.

- To remove marks, try a pencil eraser. Apply very light pressure to avoid leaving an eraser mark.

Bases

- Lamp bases should be dusted regularly with a microfibre cloth, just damp T-shirt rag or wool sock.

- Pay special attention to angles and detailed areas where dust can collect.

- Run your damp cloth down the flex to remove dust there as well.

- For fingerprints and other dirty residue on the base, spray all-purpose cleaner (see page 31) or castile soap and water on the cloth and wipe clean.

FIREPLACES

Keeping the fireplace clean minimizes its impact on indoor and outdoor air quality

The debate over whether a wood-fired or gas fireplace is greener continues to rage, with gas usually winning. Wood seems like the obvious green choice, since it is a renewable resource and smells so natural and pleasant. However, wood fires contribute to 'particulate matter air pollution' coming from our homes. Health experts say that the more we breathe in these particles, the more we risk developing health problems that range from asthma and bronchitis to lung and heart disease.

Part of the problem here is improper use, such as burning rubbish in the fireplace, as well as neglecting routine maintenance and cleaning. If you prefer to burn wood, there are

Wood Fire

- For occasional fireplace use, clean out your firebox (the area where you actually build the fire) after each fire to reduce the amount of ash that gets blown into your air.

- Be sure the fire is completely out and coals are cold. Sweep out the firebox into a metal bucket with a lid.

- Take bucket outside and away from the house. Leave it for one day to eliminate any fire hazard.

- Sprinkle the ashes around non-edible plants like roses or other flowers as a no-cost mulch.

Gas Fire

- Gas fires are much easier to clean than wood because there is no soot or ash to remove.

- Just wash the interior and exterior glass with vinegar and water glass cleaner (see page 51) and newspaper.

- Wipe down the exterior of the fireplace with all-purpose cleaner (see page 31). Vacuum the surrounds free of dust.

- Have your gas fire inspected once a year.

a number of things you can do to make your fireplace green. A woodburning stove that keeps the fire burning at a higher temperature has fewer emissions than lower-temperature open fires. Modern woodburners are much less polluting than older stoves. Burning wet or soft wood (like pine) creates more smoke, so always burn dry, seasoned, harder woods and avoid painted or treated wood. Regular cleaning of the fireplace is essential, to reduce both indoor and outdoor pollution.

Surrounds

Use the crevice tool to vacuum here

- Soot creates stains, so clean the fireplace surrounds regularly.

- A wet/dry vacuum is best for this dirty job. If you use your regular vacuum, clean the attachments thoroughly before putting it away.

- Vacuum the area in front of the fireplace and in the cracks and corners. Use the brush attachment on the vertical surface of the fireplace.

- Clean the glass with vinegar and water glass cleaner (see page 51) and newspaper and the frame with all-purpose cleaner and a rag or towel.

Fireplace Tools

Vacuum under here

- These tools are meant to get dirty, but to keep the dirt from spreading, periodically take them outside for cleaning.

- Vacuum or sweep the area where they sit near your fireplace.

- Wipe off each tool with a rag and all-purpose cleaner (see page 31). Use vinegar and water for shiny handles.

- Take the broom and sweep the grass to remove any ash that has collected between its fibres.

WINDOW DRESSINGS
Keep curtain and blind cleaning to a minimum

Curtains are another household essential that are often labelled 'DRY CLEAN ONLY'. To avoid coming in contact with carcinogenic PERC and other toxic chemicals (see page 100), consider hand-washing the fabric (if it can withstand this). If you don't want to risk it, locate an eco-friendly cleaner to have your curtains professionally laundered once a year. Or use a vapour steam cleaner, which may eliminate the need to ever take them off the track for cleaning. Use a vacuum cleaner with a hose extension and an upholstery attachment to prolong the time between cleanings and control the dust.

For natural wood and fibre blinds, vacuuming is also an easy method to control dust. Alternatively, blinds can be dusted with a microfibre or recycled flannel cloth and sponged clean using mild castile soap and water.

Dust-Free Curtains

Vacuum in this direction

- As an alternative to toxic dry cleaning, vacuum your curtains at least once a month.

- Use the upholstery tool and set the suction on your vacuum cleaner to low.

- Spread the curtains out flat across the window.

- Vacuum from the rail at the top to the hem at the bottom in long slow lines. Overlap lines so you don't miss any dust.

Washing Curtains

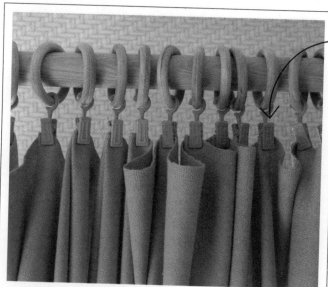

Detach here

- For washable curtains, unscrew the ends of the rails and slide the curtain off. Remove rings or other fixing devices.

- Follow the directions on the label of your curtains, but as a general guideline, wash your curtains on the gentle cycle.

- To avoid ironing, shake out wet curtains and put them in the tumble dryer on low for 10 minutes.

- They will still be damp. Remove and hang outside to dry.

Besides enhancing your décor and creating privacy, your curtains and other window coverings can help make your home more energy efficient. Heavy interlined curtains reduce drafts. Slatted and fabric blinds reduce the amount of heat coming into the home when the sun is shining.

If you're buying new window treatments, look for natural fabrics and fibre options that also help conserve energy. Matchstick-style bamboo blinds are one green choice, but they do nothing to conserve energy. Look for blinds made out of bamboo that also have an insulated lining, or choose interlined curtains. If you're feeling crafty, buy interlining to sew into your existing curtains.

If your main problem is heat in the summer, Forest Stewardship Council-certified wooden blinds are a good choice because the wood comes from consciously managed forests. Wooden Venetian blinds are fairly easy to keep clean and will help you regulate how much heat and light comes into your home.

Fabric Blinds

- Lower the blind to have as much of the fabric as possible visible.

- Use the upholstery brush on your vacuum cleaner and set the suction to low.

- Vacuum across the very top of the blind.

- Dust either from top to bottom or side to side, whichever more closely follows the weave or detail on the blind. This way you'll remove the most dust possible.

- Overlap strokes to avoid missing spots.

Venetian Blinds

Vacuum or wash horizontally

- Lower the blind all the way and flatten the slats. Use your vacuum brush attachment with the suction set to low.

- Start at the top and vacuum across the top panel. Work your way down, vacuuming each slat from side to side. If possible, flip the slats and repeat.

- If there are vertical fabric strips, finish the job by vacuuming those from top to bottom.

- Once or twice a year, use a rag or towel dampened with mild soap and water and wipe down each slat individually.

DESKS AND PHONES
An organized desk makes cleaning quick and easy

When you're in the middle of a project or have multiple family members using a desk, it's easy for mountains of clutter to pile up. The more clutter, the bigger the project it will be to actually clean the desk, and the dirtier the space will become. Contrary to the familiar image of the messy professor, dusty office air is not good brain nourishment for creating your best work. And if anyone is using the computer as their lunch- or snack-time companion, crumbs and spills are added to the dirty mix.

Dust, crumbs and spills can encourage pests and also ruin your electronics, so it's important to get this area organized for easy, regular cleaning. Creating clearly marked places for every

CLEAN HOME, GREEN HOME

Paper Clutter Control

BILLS

PENDING

FILING

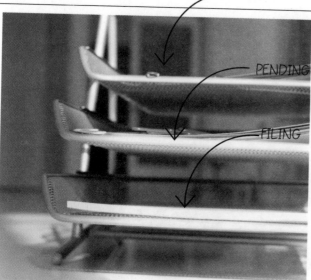

Desk Organizer

- To manage paper clutter, label three separate trays BILLS, PENDING and FILING.

- Write the due date on the outside of the envelope for each bill and arrange in chronological order.

- Place paperwork and mail that needs action in PENDING and finished business in FILING.

- Pick one day a week that you go through each tray. For example, pay bills on Monday, take action on pending matters on Wednesday, and file on Friday.

- Reject the plastic desk organizer set, and look for containers around your home.

- Use a Kilner jar or empty jam jar, washed and stripped of its label, to hold your pens and pencils.

- A dish or small tray can hold smaller objects, such as paper clips, a calculator and a stapler.

- These items will be easy to remove when it's time to clean your desk and can easily be emptied and washed periodically.

form of clutter, as well as reducing the amount of clutter coming into the space, will set you on track for a cleaner office.

Once you've got your system in place you'll find that it's much easier to clear your desk each evening or after each use so you can start fresh the next time. From there, you can dust your desk weekly and wash as needed.

Drawer Organizer

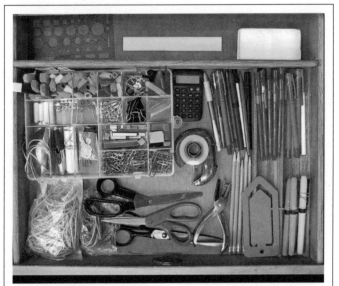

- To keep your drawers neat and easy to dust and clean, use an organizer.

- You can use a purpose-made office organizer or an old cutlery tray that fits the drawer.

- Separate the items that you use regularly, like pens and staplers, so they are visible and easy to grab.

- When you want to clean the drawer, remove the organizer. Dust or vacuum inside and then wipe down with warm soapy water. Dry and replace the organizer.

Cleaning the Phone

Use cotton bud here

- Unplug the phone and dampen a clean cloth with warm sudsy water.

- Wipe the base of the telephone and the headset.

- Use cotton buds dipped in vinegar (but just damp) to get into dirty tight spaces like between the buttons.

- Be careful not to let any liquid drip into the phone.

- To disinfect, dampen a cloth with vinegar and wipe the handset. Do the same with your headset if you use one.

COMPUTERS
Dust and dirt can ruin computers – here's how to keep them clean

The more a computer runs, the more heat it generates. And the more heat, the more risk of damage to the machine. The computer also generates static, which draws in dust from the surrounding area, and that dust acts as an insulator, causing the computer to run even hotter. Dust, along with temperature extremes, humidity, smoke and air pollution, can substantially shorten your computer's lifespan.

The first step in computer care is to position it in a well-ventilated area so that cool air flows in and the hot air can flow out. Clutter around the computer obstructs this airflow and adds to the dust that gets on and in your computer. It's important to keep the whole area as dust-free as possible.

While there are chemical products designed specifically for cleaning computers, they are unnecessary; non-toxic

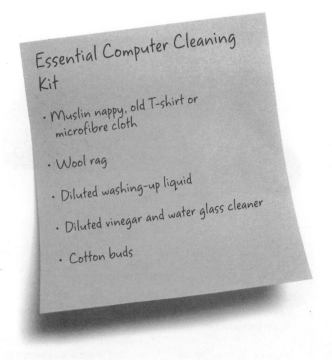

Essential Computer Cleaning Kit

• Muslin nappy, old T-shirt or microfibre cloth

• Wool rag

• Diluted washing-up liquid

• Diluted vinegar and water glass cleaner

• Cotton buds

Monitor Screen

• Flat-screened monitors have LCD or plasma screens. To clean, turn the monitor off and wait until it has cooled completely.

• Use a dry muslin nappy or microfibre cloth to remove dust from the screen. Do not press too hard or you may damage the screen.

• For a CRT monitor, dampen the cloth with plain water. It should be just damp but not wet.

• Wipe down the monitor screen, and then polish with a dry cloth.

methods can work just as well. Don't use a vacuum cleaner when cleaning out dust from a computer. Vacuums generate static that can damage the computer's components.

Check your computer manual before cleaning to make sure there are no special instructions you need to follow. Otherwise, regular dusting along with occasional cleaning with the mildest solutions possible will keep your computer clean and green and functioning for many years.

Monitor Frame

- Dampen a cloth with diluted washing-up liquid and fold over so it fits entirely into your hand with no trailing ends.

- Wipe down just the frame without touching the screen with this solution.

If you do, dry with a clean dry cloth immediately.

- As the cloth picks up dust, refold it to a clean surface.

- Use cotton buds to get into tight spaces.

Other Equipment

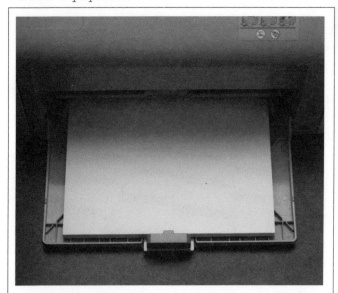

- Use the same cloth you used for the monitor frame. Spray lightly with diluted washing-up liquid so it's just barely damp.

- Wipe down the casing of your CPU, printer, scanner, fax and other equipment. Use cotton buds for vents and between keys.

- Use diluted glass cleaner on your fax and printer screen, but just dust your scanner screen with a dry cloth.

- Keep dust out of your printer by emptying and closing the paper tray if the printer is not in frequent use.

MORE COMPUTERS
Keyboards and mouse devices are magnets for dirt and crumbs

In a family with kids or someone working full-time from home, the best intentions, and even the strictest rules, may not stop the occasional computer-front meal. Crumbs can join dust in the crevices between computer keys and in the seams of your mouse. Both need to be cleaned regularly but delicately, and neither object makes that job easy. While compressed-

air cleaners seem like a good idea in theory for getting rid of dust from a keyboard or a mouse, they pose several unseen risks to both your health and the environment.

When you take a closer look at these products you'll notice that that's not air you're blasting into your breathing space. It's actually a mixture of greenhouse gases like tetrafluoroethane,

CLEAN HOME, GREEN HOME

Laptop Keyboard

Dust accumulates here

- Your computer should be off and unplugged.

- Check your manual to see if your keys are removable. If they are, remove them.

- Wipe the area under the keys with a cloth just moistened with distilled water.

- Allow to dry completely before replacing the keys.

- Wipe the casing and keys with a cloth dampened with diluted washing-up liquid. Make sure the computer is dry before plugging it in.

Detached Keyboard

- Unplug keyboard from the computer.

- Take it outside or hold it over a rubbish bin. Turn it upside down and shake gently. This will loosen the dust stuck under the keys.

- Repeat until you don't see any more dust coming out.

- Dampen a cloth with diluted washing-up liquid and wipe down keys and keyboard casing.

one of the HFCs that work as refrigerants, as CFCs did before their use was severely restricted. If inhaled in high concentrations, these gases can lead to heart trouble, unconsciousness or even death. When you spray them on the keyboard you are inhaling this gas.

But there is another big danger to consider if you have children. Recently, teenagers have been using these products as a way to get high. It's called 'dusting', and kids are dying from either heart attacks or asphyxiation as the gas replaces the air in their lungs.

There are safer and more environmentally sound ways to clean your computer keyboard, and, it turns out, they're not that difficult.

Cleaning a Mouse with a Ball

- Flip the mouse over and locate the ball that it rolls on.

- Press firmly on the disc around the ball and turn counterclockwise to release. If it doesn't turn, try using a coin to gently dislodge it so you can remove the ball.

- Clean the ball by wiping it with a cloth dampened with diluted glass cleaner.

- Use a cotton bud dampened with water to wipe the rollers. Leave to dry then replace the ball and disc.

Cleaning an Optical Mouse

- For newer mouse products that don't have a roller ball:

- Disconnect the mouse from computer.

- Dampen a microfibre cloth with diluted glass cleaner.

- Clean the entire mouse except the optical centre, which can be easily damaged by any lint or solution.

- Leave to dry completely before reconnecting to the computer.

131

ELECTRONICS AND OTHER MEDIA

Keep components working longer and out of landfill with regular cleaning and maintenance

Cleaning and maintaining your electronics and other media has become a serious environmental issue. Electronic waste is mounting up in landfill, and 70 per cent of that e-waste is toxic, with heavy metals such as lead and mercury, flame retardants, plastics and more. As with your computer, dust and dirt are attracted to these machines and create a natural insulation, making them run even hotter, which can cause more wear and tear.

Cleaning electronic equipment is important, but cleaning the wrong way can cause damage. For example, with flat-screen TVs and monitors, it's important not to touch the screen because the pressure can cause the pixels to burn out.

Flat-Screen TV

Look for dust here.

Look for smudges here

- Never use a glass cleaner or detergent on LCD or plasma screens, and apply only minimal pressure while cleaning.

- There are special cleaners you can buy for these types of screens, but they are generally unnecessary.

- Use a dry microfibre cloth to dust and a clean soft flannel rag to polish the screen.

- Use a just-damp cloth with diluted washing-up liquid on the frame, base, and back of the television.

Speakers

- Refer to your manual for specific cleaning instructions.

- Generally, dusting with a microfibre or lamb's wool duster is the most important step towards clean speakers.

- Dampen a cloth with diluted washing-up liquid and wipe down all plastic or wood surfaces. Use a dampened cotton bud to get into tight places.

- Some speakers have removable cloth covers that can be rinsed in the sink. Be sure to let them dry completely before replacing.

Spray a cleaner on the screen, and you'll regret it every time you try to view something through the cloudy surface.

Another consideration here is upgrading your technology when it's not really necessary. Every year the latest and greatest product hits the market, making your current model seem woefully inadequate. Yet, constantly upgrading computers, MP3 players and phones means you're contributing to the e-waste stream. A simple solution is to resist upgrades and keep your current equipment running for the long term.

But sometimes upgrading is actually good for the environment. With 1.8 billion CDs sold annually worldwide, you can imagine the number of discs and plastic cases that end up in landfills. Going digital with an MP3 player can lessen your contribution to this waste in the long run.

If it really is time to upgrade, first check with the manufacturer of your old equipment to see if it recycles the products. If your old machine is not too old, you may be able to sell or donate it.

Media

- Store CDs and DVDs away from direct sunlight.

- Use your dust brush attachment to vacuum the tops, sides, and shelf area around your media as you would your books (see page 117).

- To clean the discs, use a cotton T-shirt rag and wipe from the centre to the edge all the way around. If necessary, use vinegar and water glass cleaner (see page 51).

- Once or twice a year, remove all media from shelves and dust and wash the shelves.

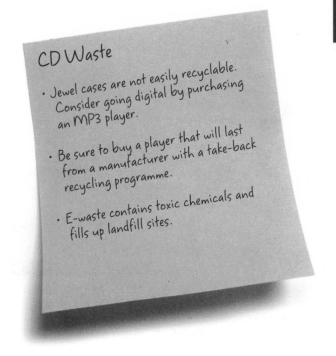

CD Waste

- Jewel cases are not easily recyclable. Consider going digital by purchasing an MP3 player.

- Be sure to buy a player that will last from a manufacturer with a take-back recycling programme.

- E-waste contains toxic chemicals and fills up landfill sites.

133

MANAGING OFFICE WASTE
How to create a practically no-waste office

A home office or family computer can generate a lot of waste, with botched print jobs as well as junk mail, discarded envelopes and worn-out office supplies. It's important to set up the office to encourage and simplify recycling. By creating designated and clearly labelled spaces for things like reusable printer paper or scrap paper for phone messages, you can make it easier to minimize office waste.

When you're ready to buy new paper, look for a source of paper made from post-consumer waste. Otherwise, you may be buying paper that is just made from paper scraps left over from making new paper. The National Association of Paper Merchants (NAPM) awards its Approved Recycled Mark to recycled paper made from a minimum of 75 per cent genuine waste fibres.

Reuse

Recycle

- Not all the documents you print from your computer need to be on pristine paper. Before printing, ask yourself if you even need a hard copy at all.

- Use unwanted documents that are only printed on one side to print new documents.

- Place used paper, printed side down, in a clearly marked tray and load the printer with it.

- Get yourself and anyone else who uses your computer into the habit of using this paper first, and only grabbing new paper when it's absolutely necessary.

- If you print a lot, buy printer cartridges where you can also recycle them.

- Your local authority may collect empty printer ink cartridges for recycling.

- Royal Mail's Simply Drop scheme and some manufacturers provide postage paid envelopes in which you can send cartridges and other electronic equipment for recycling.

- Some printers won't recognize a refilled cartridge they have already recognized as empty. Test this on your printer before refilling more than one cartridge.

Dead batteries need special treatment. They contain hazardous materials such as cadmium, lead and potassium hydroxide, which can affect the reproductive system, kidney, liver and brain functions, as well as polluting the environment. Regular household alkaline batteries contain 97 per cent less mercury than they did 10 years ago, but they are still dangerous if not handled properly. In some places, it's harder to find a way to recycle these single-use batteries than it is rechargeable NiCd or NiMH batteries. Some local authorities collect batteries for recycling: the current UK target is for 25 per cent of batteries to be collected by 2012 and 45 per cent by 2016. Producers are to be given responsibility for recycling their products, and from 2010 there will be a requirement on some retailers to collect exhausted batteries.

Rechargeable batteries are more eco-friendly because they can last for 10 years and 500–1,000 charge cycles. They can also be collected by recycling centres. To extend their life, remove batteries from devices when they're not in use.

Safe Storage

- Certain office supplies contain toxins that are emitted into the air you breathe as you work.

- These include ink and toner cartridges, non-water-based permanent markers, adhesives, correction fluid and some craft supplies.

- If you have these supplies, store them in a closed cabinet.

- As you begin to run out of each item, look for replacement products that are less toxic, such as water-based markers.

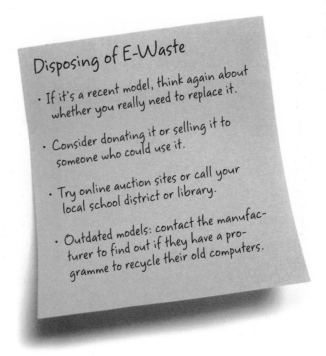

Disposing of E-Waste

- If it's a recent model, think again about whether you really need to replace it.

- Consider donating it or selling it to someone who could use it.

- Try online auction sites or call your local school district or library.

- Outdated models: contact the manufacturer to find out if they have a programme to recycle their old computers.

135

VACUUMING
Follow these green strategies for more effective floor care

Experts recommend that homes of allergy sufferers need daily vacuuming to reduce dust, pollen and other particulates that trigger symptoms. But even homes without allergy sufferers need vacuuming once or twice a week to control dust and improve indoor air quality.

How you vacuum is as important as how often you vacuum. If the vacuum bag or cylinder is full, the machine will have less sucking power. Vacuum too fast and you can miss a lot of the dust and debris embedded in the carpet fibres or in the joints of wood floors.

If you vacuum without moving the furniture, the room will look better, but you'll miss tons of dust building up behind the furniture. Moving furniture is also a good strategy for combating the tendency of carpeting to permanently flatten

Vacuum Inspection and Maintenance Checklist

Before every use: Empty bag if more than three-quarters full; cut strings or hair wrapped around the brush roll.

After every use: Use the crevice tool attachment to vacuum clean the brush attachments and roll brush under the vacuum. Wipe down the casing with a damp rag to remove dust and debris.

- To keep your vacuum in top shape there are a few more things you should do every month:

- Clean and lubricate the bearings on the brush roll.

- Check the belt and wipe it clean with a dry rag.

- Check the filter. Some filters can be easily removed, rinsed, and replaced. Follow specific instructions for your vacuum cleaner.

High-Traffic Areas

- High-traffic carpeted areas show wear quickly because there is only one path of travel.

- To combat this wear and tear, vacuum against the flow of traffic. This will make the fibres stand up in a different direction so they don't stay matted down.

- These areas also tend to get dirtier faster because they receive so much use.

- Vacuum at least twice a week in these areas and your carpet will last longer.

out under the weight of furniture. For hard floors, make sure you can shut off the vacuum's roller brush or use a different head, otherwise you'll be scattering the dust away from the vacuum instead of picking it up.

It's important to make your vacuum cleaner last as long as possible. Routine inspection and maintenance are key to optimal performance and a long life.

The most common thing to break on a vacuum cleaner is usually the belt. You know it's broken because the roller brush is no longer spinning, but you might be able to catch it before that happens. If the machine is hard to push or there is a smell of burnt rubber when it's running, it could mean that the belt is slipping. Refer to your instruction manual and try adjusting the belt; but you may need to replace it to get it operating smoothly again. As long as replacement belts for your machine are available, this can be a cheap and easy thing to repair yourself.

Strategy

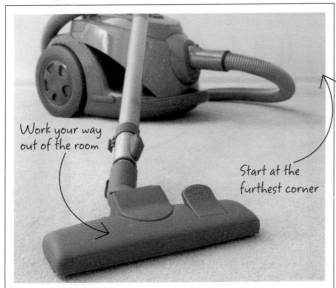

Work your way out of the room

Start at the furthest corner

- Dust the room before vacuuming so you pick up anything that has fallen to the floor.

- Start at the furthest corner away from the door. Vacuum yourself out of the room – that way you won't leave footprints on your newly vacuumed carpet.

- Move the furniture as you go. This keeps the carpet under the furniture from getting matted and controls the dust build-up in areas that don't get used so often.

Long Overlapping Strokes

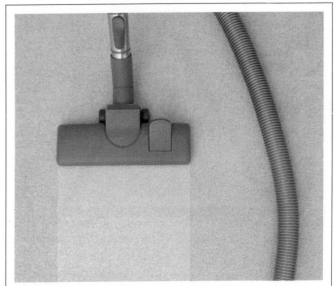

- Survey the floor before you begin and pick up any plant leaves, pins or paper clips that could cause damage to your vacuum cleaner.

- To vacuum, pull back in a long slow stroke.

- Push the vacuum forward right next to where you pulled it and overlap the line. This is easy to see on carpeting, but try to overlap lines on hard floors as well.

- The key is to go slowly and pay attention to your lines so you don't miss any spots.

CARPETS AND RUGS
Spot-clean and shop wisely for cleaner carpets

A great deal of fitted carpet includes petroleum-based synthetic fibres, which can contribute VOCs, formaldehyde and xylene to your indoor air pollution. Carpeting also traps dust and provides an appealing home for dust mites. If you have the choice, opt for other types of flooring and use natural fibre rugs wherever you want to tread on softer ground. If you need to get rid of a carpet, look for recycling programmes in your area, then help close the loop by buying rugs made out of recycled materials.

To keep your carpet free of toxins, avoid conventional carpet cleaning solutions. Carpet-protective treatments, cleaners and deodorizers are loaded with artficial fragrances and other toxins such as perchloroethylene, which are known or suspected carcinogens and can cause immediate irritation as well as

Carpet Cleaner: What to Avoid

Eyes: corrosive, severe irritation. May cause chemical burns with permanent corneal injury & sensitization. Skin: severe irritation.

- Watch for this ingredient on the label: perchloroethylene. PERC is a known human carcinogen and suspected neurotoxin, which can induce nausea, dizziness, fatigue, and long-term kidney and liver damage.

- Other ingredients to avoid: napthalene (neurotoxic and suspected carcinogen),

butyl cellosolve (neurotoxin), propylene glycol methyl ether (irritant), aliphatic petroleum solvent (neurotoxic), isopropyl alcohol (carcinogenic), fragrance.

- Carpet cleaners can also include 1,4-dioxane (carcinogenic), ethanol and ammonia.

Carpet Cleaner: What to Look For

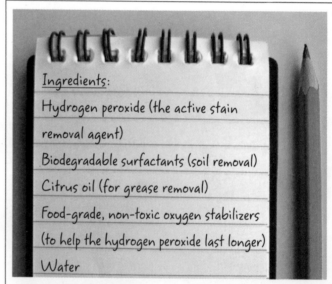

Ingredients:
Hydrogen peroxide (the active stain removal agent)
Biodegradable surfactants (soil removal)
Citrus oil (for grease removal)
Food-grade, non-toxic oxygen stabilizers (to help the hydrogen peroxide last longer)
Water

- Look for products that provide a complete list of their ingredients.

- Choose plant-derived ingredients and look for specifics on how long the product takes to biodegrade.

- The more words you recognize in the ingredients list the better.

- Look for packaging that is made from recycled materials and is recyclable.

long-term organ and nervous system damage. Regular vacuuming, deodorizing and non-toxic spot treatment will reduce your need to have your carpets cleaned. When it is time for cleaning, it's a great idea to hire a steam cleaner. To keep it green, rinse the machine to rid it of any toxic residue, and use your own choice of mild detergent to clean the carpet.

MAKE IT EASY

Carpet deodorizer:
Liberally sprinkle bicarbonate of soda on carpet or rug and leave overnight. If your vacuum is temperamental, sweep up powder and then vacuum. Otherwise, just vacuum.

Dust, dirt, soot, animal dander, mould, fungi and VOCs build up here

Routine Cleaning

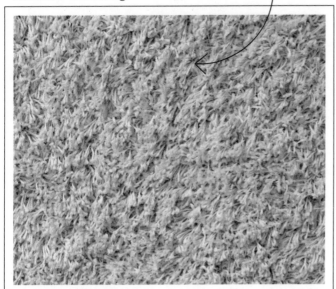

Spot Cleaning

FLOORS

- Carpets can be home to a lot of different allergens and unwanted guests. A filtered vacuum cleaner and bicarbonate of soda are your best defence.

- First, vacuum the carpet thoroughly to get up as much dirt as possible.

- Next, sprinkle bicabonate of soda to thinly cover the carpet. Leave on overnight.

- If your vacuum cleaner is likely to become clogged, sweep the carpet and then vacuum. Otherwise, just vacuum: you'll have a clean and deodorized carpet.

- Coffee, wine, tomato, fruit juice and other acid stains are extremely common but they shouldn't mean the end of your carpeting.

- All you need is a bottle of soda water and a clean white towel.

- First, pour 50–120 ml soda water on to the stain, then blot with a clean white towel.

- Repeat the procedure until the stain has gone.

MOPPING
One job where less is more

We've been trained to use sudsy products every time we clean the floors, but the truth is, you're better off dry or damp-mopping and vacuuming more and washing less. This is especially true for wood and bamboo floors, which wear better when they stay dry. Using a dry microfibre or damp sponge mop instead of a broom for sweeping keeps the dust on the mop instead of scattering it into the air.

Microfibre mops are made from polyester and nylon, and thus are petroleum-based, but their usefulness in cutting the need for cleaners and their long life make them a good choice for floor care. They work by trapping or 'hooking' dirt in their fibres in the same way that pieces of Velcro fasten together. Microfibre mops are designed to trap the dirt without needing any solutions or moisture.

Dust Mop

Slide off here for washing

- Use a dry microfibre or dampened looped cotton dust mop.

- Start in the far corner of the room and mop in long strokes that overlap as you work your way out of the room.

- Avoid picking the mop up off the floor and scattering the dirt you just picked up; use the swivel function instead.

- When the head is saturated with dirt, remove the cover and put it in the washing machine. Replace with a clean cover and continue.

Damp Mop

Squeeze here for a drier mop

- For larger areas, damp mopping with a squeezable sponge mop may be easier.

- Fill a bucket with clean, plain water. Dip sponge head and squeeze as much water out as possible.

- Mop in overlapping strokes from the furthest corner of the room to the door.

- Rinse and squeeze your mop every few strokes to ensure you aren't spreading the dirt around.

Using microfibre is ideal for dry-mopping in smaller spaces. As soon as the mop is filled with dirt, you can just throw it in the washing machine ready for the next use. For cleaning larger areas you need several mop heads so you can keep working after the first one fills up with dirt.

Damp mopping is also a great alternative for larger areas. Damp mopping can be done with any type of mop head, but one of the greener options is a cellulose sponge head made from wood pulp. The key is to have a mop with an effective system to wring the sponge out thoroughly after every dip in the bucket, so you don't soak the area you're cleaning. It's also important to change the water in your bucket when it looks murky, so you aren't just reapplying the dirt to the floor. Damp mopping absorbs the dust without detergent and leaves the floor looking great.

Homemade Washable Mop Head

- To transform your disposable sponge mop head into one that is washable and reusable, cover your dry sponge mop head with an old, thick hand towel and clamp it down.

- When it's dirty, rinse and wring it out or replace with a clean towel.

Wet-Mopping Strategy

- Vacuum or sweep the room. Then fill a bucket with warm water (tepid if floors are waxed) and a tablespoon or two of cleaning solution or castile soap (see page 31).

- Work your way out of the room from the furthest corner, moving the bucket to an unwashed area of floor as you go.

- Work across the room in overlapping back-and-forth strokes.

- Rinse and squeeze mop head every few minutes. Replace water in the bucket when it looks dirty.

WOOD, CORK OR BAMBOO FLOORS
The drier the better for clean wood floors

To give your wood, cork or bamboo flooring a long life, it's crucial that you know the appropriate care for your specific product, so check with the manufacturer to be extra sure. That said, the most important thing to know about any wood floor is that water can cause major damage. Clean up any spills as quickly and thoroughly as possible and cover wood flooring with a rug in areas near a sink or other water source.

In general, vacuuming and dry- or damp-mopping are the best way to do regular cleaning for all types of wood floors. Spot cleaning with a damp cloth and mild washing-up liquid is much better than wet mopping, which risks dulling the finish or ruining the floor completely. Oil soaps are also not a great idea because they can leave behind a residue that damages the floor.

What to Avoid

May be hazardous to your health

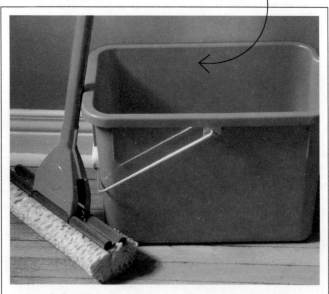

What to Look for

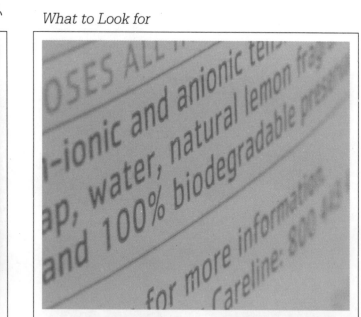

- Most floor polish and cleaners contain skin and eye irritants as well as carcinogenic formaldehyde.

- Petroleum distillates, another common ingredient, can be toxic to the nervous and digestive systems.

- To eliminate the need for such harsh cleaners, vacuum regularly with a machine that lets you turn off the rotating brush so you don't scatter the dirt.

- Mop up spills as soon as they happen so crumbs don't get ground in and liquids don't damage wood.

- Look for cleaners that have more plant- and mineral-based ingredients than synthetic ones – the more names you can pronounce the better.

- Choose products that are either fragrance free or scented with natural essential oils.

- Look for brands that list all of their ingredients on the label.

- Or try the simple recipe (see opposite page) and do it yourself.

Even floors with wax seals do not completely block out water. For occasional deep cleaning of sealed floors, you can damp-mop using the solution on this page. The vinegar cuts grease but also helps the solution evaporate quickly so the floor is not affected.

Unsealed as well as varnished or shellacked floors all do better with a damp mop and a solution of just equal parts vinegar and water.

FLOORS

Strategy

- Although your floor looks smooth and impenetrable, the grain of the wood and the joints between the boards create perfect hiding places for dirt.

- Follow the direction of the grain when you vacuum, sweep, or mop to be sure that you get as much of this dust as possible.

- Sealed wood floors can be cleaned with the damp-mop solution (above).

- Waxed wood floors should be cleaned with a sponge mop only slightly dampened with clean tepid water.

Drier Mopping

- Wood, cork and bamboo floors will look better for longer if you don't get them wet.

- Instead of using a bucket to wash the floors, put the wood floor solution (above) in a spray bottle.

- Squirt an area of about 1 m square in front of you and mop. Continue that way across your whole floor.

- Use only what you need, to reduce the risk of getting your floors too wet.

OTHER FLOORS
Start mild for long-lasting flooring

You could probably buy a special cleaner for every floor surface there is, but you'd be wasting a lot of money and introducing a lot of toxic chemicals into your home. Many of these products contain mineral spirits and petroleum-based solvents, both of which are eye, skin and respiratory irritants and known neurotoxins. Petroleum-based solvents can also contain small quantities of benzene, a known carcinogen.

As with wood floors, less wet-mopping and more vacuuming and dry- and damp-mopping is best, especially for the most natural types of flooring like linoleum and cork. It's also important to start out with as mild a solution as possible, and vinegar and water often does the trick. Then if you still have blemishes, stains or spots, you can target those directly with castile soap and water.

Ceramic Tiles and Slate/Grout

- Vacuum or sweep often to remove dust. Damp- or dry-mop to clean. Wet-mop with a sponge, warm water and a few squirts of castile soap.

- For grimy residue, spray on diluted vinegar, but avoid getting the vinegar into grouting. Too much can etch glazed surfaces.

- For neutral-coloured grouting, spray a 50/50 solution of hydrogen peroxide and water on the stain every 15 minutes until you see it lighten. For stubborn stains, create a paste of bicarbonate of soda and hydrogen peroxide. Let it bubble and then apply.

Concrete

- Vacuum or sweep often to control dust and catch debris before it damages the seal on concrete.

- Catch spills immediately. Mop up and dry with a clean towel.

- Damp and dry mopping are your best choices for cleaning concrete floors.

- Spot clean if you see dirt or spots with castile soap and water.

If you're planning to buy new flooring, consider natural linoleum, which is made of solidified linseed oil on a canvas backing. It's an ideal flooring choice for green homes because it's a renewable resource, low maintenance and durable. To keep your linoleum floor as green and clean as possible, be sure to use low-VOC sealants that don't contain formaldehyde.

Marble

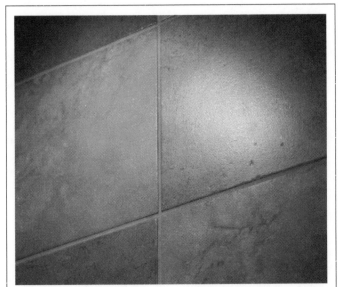

- Be sure your vacuum wheels are clean and the vacuum itself will not scratch your flooring. Vacuum often to remove dirt and grime that can damage the marble.

- Damp mopping with just plain water is the best cleaning solution.

- For tough spots, use castile soap and water, and dry the area when you've finished.

- Do not use acid cleaners like vinegar on marble because they will etch the stone.

Sheet Flooring

- Sheet vinyl floors can be wet-mopped. Mix 3–4 squirts of castile soap in warm water or 750 ml vinegar in a bucket of water.

- Squeeze mop slightly. Wash once with a wet mop. Then go over same area with a fully squeezed mop to dry.

- For vinyl floor tiles, stick to damp-mopping to avoid swelling and cupping, which could happen if you get them too wet.

- To shine dull spots, make a paste of cornflour and water. Apply with a rag and rub into the floor. Remove paste with a damp cloth and buff with a dry cloth.

FLOORS

145

VENTILATION

Cleaning the air in your home can be as simple as opening the right windows

Your indoor air quality can be four times worse than the air just outside your home. In fact, indoor air pollution has been ranked in the top five biggest threats to our health. Part of the problem is that in our efforts to build more energy-efficient homes, we've done everything we can to seal ourselves inside. In the past, indoor air quality (IAQ) concerns centred on cigarette smoke, radon, lead and asbestos. But more recent studies show that pollution sources include household products such as cleaners, pesticides and air fresheners, as well as furnishings and building materials. Sealed houses mean these chemicals stay put and pollute the air we breathe. This may be why reported cases of allergies have

Ventilation Strategy

- Breezes and temperature differences inside and outside the building move air in and out of your home.

- Cross-ventilate using two windows directly opposite each other to clean the air in one room. Experiment with more complex airflow patterns to ventilate a larger space.

- Open a small window on the shady side of your home and a large window or door on the sunnier side. Keep all windows between these two shut.

- The air will enter through the small window and ventilate a larger space on its way to the larger opening.

Fans

- Use circulating fans to increase the effectiveness of window ventilation.

- Place a fan in front of your open shady window so its back is facing the window and the fan is blowing into your room.

- Place another fan, this time blowing out of your house, in front of the larger window or door where the air exits your home. This can also be effective when the intake window is on the ground floor and the outlet is on a higher floor.

doubled in the past 30 years, and the incidence of asthma has gone up by almost 75 per cent in the same period.

By following the suggestions throughout this book you can improve your IAQ. Another easy step is to develop a strategy for increased and effective ventilation. Simply opening a few windows can help, but be strategic about which windows you open. Cross-ventilation is key, and can be even more beneficial when coordinated with fans that help guide the indoor air circulation and effectively clean the air.

Whole-House Ventilation

- Whole-house ventilation consist of a series of ducts and vents running from the ground floor up to the roof.

- An extractor fan pulls air up through the house so there is a constant inflow of fresh air at the bottom.

- More energy-efficient passive systems use the pressure difference caused by air flow over roof vents to draw out stale air.

- The movement of air draws cooler air into your home through windows or vents on the lower floors.

Extractor Fans

- Extractor fans are important in humid rooms such as the bathroom, laundry room and kitchen.

- These fans will help clear out moisture and warm air generated by your appliances and shower and effectively cool the room.

- Exhaust fans are key to fighting mould and mildew, which can't survive without excess moisture.

- Turn the fan on when you're using the appliances or shower and leave running for 20 minutes afterwards. Open windows to speed up the drying process.

INDOOR AIR QUALITY

PLANTS
Make use of the most natural air cleaners available

Common houseplants are a simple, attractive and effective way to clean the air in your home. One cleansing plant for every 10 square metres of space in your home or office can improve your indoor air quality (IAQ), besides adding to the natural look and feel of your home.

While there are some pollutants that plants cannot absorb, such as asbestos or soot, they do absorb many of the chemicals from common household products. In fact, if you have a specific concern like formaldehyde from chipboard furniture, or toluene and xylene from paints and adhesives, you can choose the plants that are particularly good at eliminating those chemicals.

Researchers found that as these plants absorbed carbon dioxide in the process of photosynthesis, they also absorbed

Aloe Vera

- Aloe is one of the most effective plants for the removal of low-level concentration formaldehyde.

- It will do best in or near a window that gets full sun.

- Place aloe anywhere you think formaldehyde is a problem, such as near very

new engineered wood or MDF furniture, emulsion paint or wallpaper, or newly finished wood flooring.

- Each time you water, soak the plant thoroughly, but allow enough time between waterings for it to dry out.

Peace Lily

- Peace lilies help to remove formaldehyde, benzene and carbon monoxide from the air.

- They also remove 'bioeffluents', which are the gases, including ethyl alcohol and acetone, as well as odours, bacteria and viruses that we exhale.

- Keep peace lilies away from direct sunlight to avoid burning their leaves.

- Water at least once a week. Check the soil and water before it dries out completely.

other chemicals and rendered them harmless in the process. As the roots and microbes in the soil also play a role in air cleaning, cutting off the bottom leaves that touch the soil helps to make the plants even more effective.

Plants absorb both light and pollutants through the pores in their leaves, so it's important to keep them dust-free. Clean your plants regularly by wiping the leaves with a microfibre or damp cloth to remove dust.

Philodendron

- Philodendrons are one of the best plants for removing formaldehyde from the air at high concentrations.

- It's a good idea to put one anywhere you have MDF or laminated wood furniture, cupboards or other sources of formaldehyde.

- Both vines and large floor plants are effective.

- Keep the plant out of direct sunlight.

- Let the soil dry out between waterings and don't soak it.

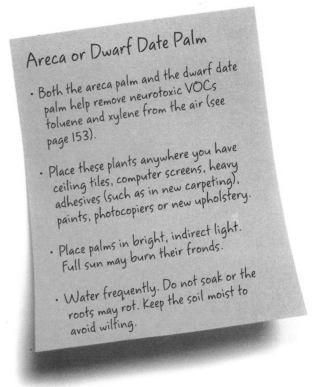

Areca or Dwarf Date Palm

- Both the areca palm and the dwarf date palm help remove neurotoxic VOCs toluene and xylene from the air (see page 153).

- Place these plants anywhere you have ceiling tiles, computer screens, heavy adhesives (such as in new carpeting), paints, photocopiers or new upholstery.

- Place palms in bright, indirect light. Full sun may burn their fronds.

- Water frequently. Do not soak or the roots may rot. Keep the soil moist to avoid wilting.

INDOOR AIR QUALITY

149

SPECIAL AIR QUALITY CONCERNS

How to identify and eradicate the most threatening pollution problems in your home

Carbon monoxide, radon, lead and mould can make your home unsafe, but they can also be detected and dealt with before they become a problem. The key is being proactive and knowing the signs.

Carbon monoxide can cause severe health problems before you can actually smell it in your home. At low levels, carbon monoxide poisoning is easily mistaken for the flu. As the level rises, health effects become severe, ranging from angina, reduced vision and neurological effects to death. The likely poisoning suspects are combustion appliances or equipment including non-electric, poorly vented space heaters, gas fires, car exhaust and gas appliances.

Carbon Monoxide

- Install at least one carbon monoxide sensor on each floor of your home. One of these should be near the bedrooms.

- Place the sensor further than 5 metres away from kitchen and heating appliances and not in humid places like the bathroom.

- For safety, use single-use batteries, which hold their charge longer than rechargeables. Replace the batteries twice a year and the whole sensor every two years.

- Schedule routine inspections of your boiler and other gas appliances.

Radon

- Every home should get a home radon detector kit, which needs to stay in place for an extended period, usually 3 months, to detect radon levels.

- Detectors can be ordered from the Health Protection Agency (hpa.org.uk).

- The follow-up report includes advice on what to do if your radon level is high.

- Typically, this involves sealing floors and walls, improving ventilation in the house and under the floor, and installing a radon sump under the foundation, vented to above the roof.

Even sneakier and more difficult to detect than carbon monoxide is radon. A dangerously high radon level indoors is the second leading cause of lung cancer. Radon gas is produced when uranium in the soil breaks down, and it enters the home through cracks in concrete, drains and sumps.

Lead can pollute air and drinking water, contaminate soil and linger in dust. But the most dangerous threat is from old lead-based paint that is chipped, sanded or scraped. If your home was built before 1978 you may have lead in your home, and in a house built before 1960, you can assume you do. Lead affects foetuses and children more severely than adults and can result in developmental impairments, from behavioural problems to lower IQs.

Most mould is visible in damp places like showers or under leaky sinks, but some is hidden. It can grow behind wallpaper or other places that you don't see. Mould can severely affect those who are allergic or who have asthma, but it can act as an eye, skin and respiratory irritant to anyone. Some moulds produce 'mycotoxins' that can cause liver and nervous system damage, affect the endocrine system and cause cancer.

Lead

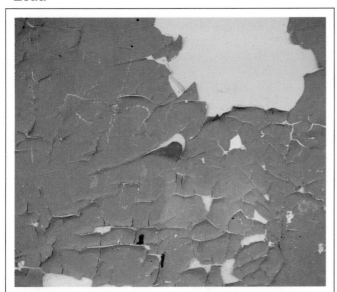

- Pre-1978 chipped paint is a clear sign that you should get the paint tested for lead. In children the ingestion of flaking lead-based paint is the major source of exposure.

- You can also have your drinking water and your children tested for lead.

- If you do have lead paint, have it professionally removed. Do not do this yourself.

- For cleaning up, any all-purpose cleaner is recommended for the job.

Mould

- Mould likes damp, dark environments and may grow in places that you don't normally see, like air ducts.

- Musky smells or mould growing on the visible parts of air ducts or insulation are signs of a larger mould problem.

- Mould can trigger unexplained allergic reactions.

- With all mould, focus first on eliminating moisture and improving ventilation.

- If you have a serious problem, find an environmental specialist who will send samples to a lab for testing.

VOCS
Low- or no-VOC is the way to go

Volatile organic compounds, or VOCs, are chemicals that leach out of sealants, paints, wood preservatives, engineered wood, carpets, moth repellents, air fresheners, dry-cleaned clothing, cleaners and other products. Health effects include eye and respiratory irritation, headaches, dizziness, trouble seeing, and memory problems. Some VOCs are suspected of affecting the nervous and respiratory systems and causing cancer.

There are a few things you can do to limit your exposure. First, reduce the amount of VOC-emitting products you bring into your home. Avoid having clothes dry cleaned and switch to green and no-VOC cleaners, air fresheners, paint and sealing products.

Fortunately, several companies specialize in these no-VOC products, which are regularly available at some of the big DIY

Formaldehyde

Symptoms of formaldehyde exposure:

joint pain	dizziness
depression	loss of sleep
headaches	
chest pains	
ear infections	
chronic fatigue	

- Formaldehyde is a known human carcinogen, according to the International Agency for Research on Cancer.

- It is also a suspected neurotoxin and a sensitizer that can cause asthma.

- To reduce exposure, look for formaldehyde-free alternatives.

- Store products that contain formaldehyde where you won't breathe their fumes. Increase the ventilation when you use them. Use aloe vera and philodendron plants to help clean the air.

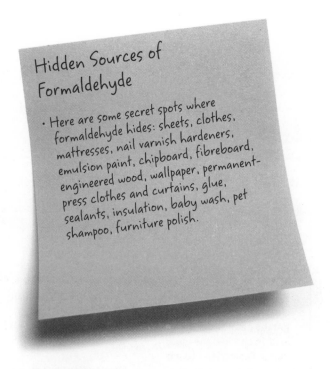

Hidden Sources of Formaldehyde

- Here are some secret spots where formaldehyde hides: sheets, clothes, mattresses, nail varnish hardeners, emulsion paint, chipboard, fibreboard, engineered wood, wallpaper, permanent-press clothes and curtains, glue, sealants, insulation, baby wash, pet shampoo, furniture polish.

stores. If you already have furniture and fittings made of chip-board and MDF in your home, apply non-toxic sealants to seal in the VOCs and keep them out of your air space.

If you do need to use or already have products that emit VOCs, focus on ventilation and proper disposal when you're finished with them. If you are storing any of these products, make sure they are stored properly and well out of the way of normal home traffic.

Toluene

- Toluene is a common solvent found in many household products.

- These include nail products, engine cleaner, auto paint, rust remover, adhesive, bathroom cleaner, house paint, metal polish, fillers, wood finish, paint thinners and lawn products.

- Symptoms of toluene overexposure: headaches, fatigue, eye, nose and throat irritation.

- Long-term effects: liver and kidney damage, damage to foetuses.

Xylene

- Xylene is also a very common solvent that is a severe eye irritant and a skin irritant.

- Xylene is found in floor wax, automotive products including cleaners and paints, home paints, varnishes and sealants, markers, herbicides and other garden products.

- It is a strong neurotoxin that can cause memory loss, and high exposure can cause loss of consciousness or death.

- Xylene can also cause damage to liver and kidneys as well as birth defects.

INDOOR AIR QUALITY

AIR FRESHENERS
To truly freshen the air, go natural

Despite the name, air fresheners don't actually freshen the air. Instead, most of these products work either to neutralize our sense of smell or mask one odour with a different one. Given what we know about synthetic fragrance (see page 2), it's no surprise that products that are almost completely made up of fragrance can pollute our indoor air. These fragrances are generally petroleum-based and can contain neurotoxic phthalates as well as suspected carcinogenic naphthalene and neurotoxic xylene. It's also not surprising that fragrance is a huge allergy and asthma trigger for many people.

But air fresheners can be dangerous in another way. Your nose is one of your best tools for knowing what's going on in

What to Look For

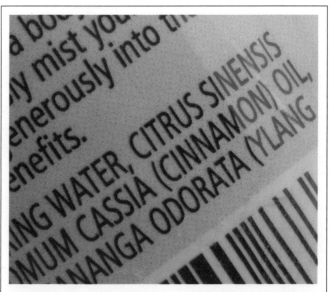

- A green air freshener comes in a recyclable and recycled pump sprayer rather than an aerosol can or other more plastic-intensive dispenser.

- It is completely plant derived and biodegradable.

- Its fragrance comes only from natural (not synthetic) essential oils.

- Natural beeswax candles scented with essential oils also make great air fresheners.

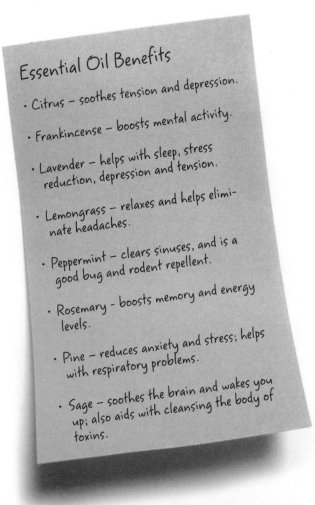

Essential Oil Benefits

- Citrus – soothes tension and depression.

- Frankincense – boosts mental activity.

- Lavender – helps with sleep, stress reduction, depression and tension.

- Lemongrass – relaxes and helps eliminate headaches.

- Peppermint – clears sinuses, and is a good bug and rodent repellent.

- Rosemary – boosts memory and energy levels.

- Pine – reduces anxiety and stress; helps with respiratory problems.

- Sage – soothes the brain and wakes you up; also aids with cleansing the body of toxins.

your home, and foul odours are a great alarm system, letting you know that something serious may be present. When you mask odours, you take away your ability to find the source and take care of the larger issue through cleaning, ventilating and fixing any problems that contribute to the smell.

If you do want scent, essential oils can help your home smell fresh and also change your mood, soothe your nerves or make you feel more alert.

····· GREEN ● LIGHT ·····

You've identified a foul smell in your home, found the cause, and planned how to eliminate it. But it may take a while to get the smell out. In the meantime, place an open container of bicarbonate of soda or zeolite in the smelly room to absorb the odour.

Make Your Own

- Choose the appropriate essential oil for your mood or desired mood.

- Add 5–10 drops of the oil to a spray bottle.

- Add 500 ml water and shake well.

- Spray into the air or on sheets and pillows as needed.

Easy Diffuser

- Take two or three cotton wool balls (preferably organic) and soak them in your preferred essential oil.

- Place cotton wool balls wherever air can pass through them and carry the scent into the home.

- Possibilities include vacuum cleaner bags, wall vents, air conditioner units, dehumidifiers or humidifiers, air purifiers.

- Do not place them on or near any heat source that would make them a fire hazard.

INDOOR AIR QUALITY

BATHING YOUR PET
Keep it simple and plant-based for a healthy pooch

Every year, pet lovers spend millions of pounds on dogs and cats, buying everything from chaise lounge-style doggy beds to rhinestone-studded collars. A better way to focus our efforts and money would be on reducing their exposure to toxins.

Like children, the animals' smaller size, closeness to the ground and desire to sniff everything make them more vulnerable to toxins, such as pesticides, than full-sized adult humans. On top of that, pet bathing products contain similar or worse toxins than adult products. Many of them contain harsh detergents as well as antibacterial chemicals. Pay particular attention if a product that is designed for washing or treating your pet has a label advising you to wash your hands after use.

What to Look For

Dog Bathing Preparation

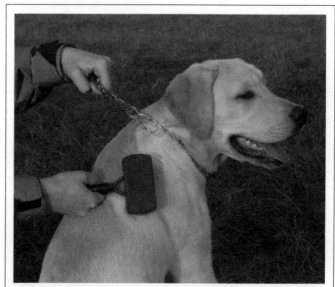

- Green pet shampoos contain plant-derived ingredients, non-toxic preservatives, and natural oil fragrances.

- Look for recycled containers that are also recyclable and don't have excess packaging. Some come in bar form, which further reduces packaging.

- Choose products that proudly declare all of their ingredients.

- Look for something that is 100 per cent biodegradable.

- Bath your dog every 3 months unless the animal is really dirty.

- Bathing too often can reduce the natural oils in the dog's coat and lead to itchy, flaking skin.

- To save your drain getting blocked with hair, start by taking the dog outside and brushing the coat thoroughly.

- Then, line the bath with a bath mat or towel so the dog doesn't slip, and fill it with 7.5–10 cm of luke-warm water.

Reducing toxins on your pet is important, especially if you and your children enjoy stroking, hugging and cuddling the animal. Bathing dogs every 3 months (as recommended by the RSPCA), using a mild, non-toxic shampoo, can help wash off any chemicals they've come into contact with that can put them – and you – at risk. If you bathe them more frequently or use harsh detergents or strong chemicals, you risk removing the natural protective oils on the animals' fur and drying out their skin.

Dog Bath

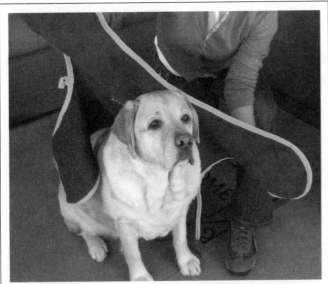

Safe Eyes

• To prevent soap from getting in your dog's eyes, try this: create a half circle of suds around the back of the dog's head. This will create a barrier to deter soapy water from dripping into the dog's face.

• Use a spray hose or jug to wet the dog.

• Use quarter-size squirts of shampoo and massage it into the coat. Add more shampoo as needed but don't overdo it. Avoid eyes, nose and ears.

• Rinse from head to tail. This needs to be very thorough. Leaving any shampoo on the dog will result in dry itchy skin.

• Dry with a big fluffy towel, and let the dog shake off outside.

PETS

PET BEDS
Control pet dander at the source

Providing your dog or cat with a comfortable, safe place to sleep can help keep him off the couch and other furniture. That means you also reduce your cleaning burden and need for cleaning products. But it's important to clean the pet's bedding regularly: it can get dirty fast, with accumulated dander and dirt that can spread to the rest of the house if it is allowed to build up. Dirty bedding can also harbour pests like fleas and dust mites. There are about a million choices when it comes to pet bedding, but one key consideration is that it's easy to clean. Look for beds with durable covers that can be unzipped and washed in the washing machine. Shaking the bed outside periodically can lengthen the amount of time between washings. Crates can and should be regularly hosed down and washed with mild castile soap.

Beds

- Conventional pet beds are often filled with petroleum-based polyurethane foam, which is flammable and can contain formaldehyde and PBDE flame retardants.

- In animal studies, PBDE has been found to damage the thyroid and reproductive systems, and suppress the immune system.

- Other beds are filled with polyester fibrefill or PET plastic, which contains carcinogenic dioxane.

- Look for bedding that is filled and covered with natural fibres like hemp, wool and organic cotton. Other natural fillings include kapok, buckwheat and recycled plastic bottles.

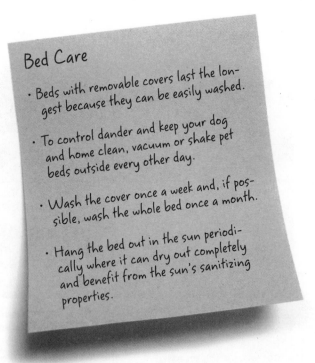

Bed Care

- Beds with removable covers last the longest because they can be easily washed.

- To control dander and keep your dog and home clean, vacuum or shake pet beds outside every other day.

- Wash the cover once a week and, if possible, wash the whole bed once a month.

- Hang the bed out in the sun periodically where it can dry out completely and benefit from the sun's sanitizing properties.

The same considerations apply to pet bedding as to human bedding (see pages 62–63), and it's a good idea to avoid products that are treated with toxic flame retardants or antibacterial chemicals. Look for natural fillers, such as buckwheat. Some natural bedding materials can even make the job of caring for your pet easier. For example, cedar chips are a popular filling because they deter fleas and naturally absorb odours.

Blankets and Mats

- Blankets and mats for your pets can help preserve your car, furniture and home, and save you some cleaning time.

- Look for fitted blankets for the car that can't be balled up when your pet decides to nest.

- Spread out blankets on furniture wherever your pets tend to luxuriate.

- Shake the blankets out every other day and wash them once a week.

Crates and Houses

- Wash crate and house bedding with the rest of your pet's blankets and bed covers once a week.

- Wash the structure once a month.

- For plastic, hose it down first. Then, scrub with hot soapy water and rinse.

- Leave outside to dry in the sun before replacing clean bedding.

- For wicker, use a wet, soapy sponge to wipe down the entire structure. Follow with a wet, plain water sponge and towel-dry. Let it dry fully in the sun.

PETS

TOYS ETC
Look for earth-friendly pet accessories

For some dogs or cats, stuffed toys – no matter how tough or expensive – are disposable items. They are fun for a while, but then the moment comes when, without warning, the toy gets ripped to shreds in a matter of minutes. Of course, this is wasteful, gets expensive, and may make you want to skip the toys altogether. Yet toys can be crucial to help your pet fight boredom and behave. But be wary when picking out the right toy for Fido: some toys have been known to contain carcinogens, neurotoxins and endocrine disruptors.

If your pet likes to rip open his toys, filled soft toys are a bad idea in general because the fillings and squeakers are unsafe. Some fillings can include things like nutshells or polystyrene

CLEAN HOME, GREEN HOME

Scratching Posts

- Carpet-covered scratching posts emit toxic VOCs, which worsen the more your cat scratches.

- The carpet also becomes a sticking place for dander, dust and other allergens.

- Vacuum the post once a week. For a deeper and deodorizing clean, get it out of the cat's reach and sprinkle with bicarbonate of soda. Leave it on overnight and vacuum in the morning.

- Vacuum rope scratching posts. For deeper clean, wipe the rope down with a soapy sponge followed by a plain water sponge, then leave to dry in the sun.

Toys

- In choosing safe toys, it's important to determine whether your pet tends to destroy every toy or keep them around for years.

- For the chewers, look for non-toxic recycled plastic toys that can be washed in the sink.

- For non-chewers, look for stuffed toys that are washable and made with recycled materials, organic cotton or hemp.

- All toys should be washed frequently, especially if they move between outdoors and indoors.

beads, which are hazardous if your pet ingests them. No stuffing is truly digestible and, as with children, choking is a big hazard, especially with stuffed squeaking toys, small chips and ropes.

Since the purpose of toys is to entertain your dog or cat, the best toys are the most interactive ones. Tug or fetch toys are great, but you can also help your pet play hide-and-seek with any toy.

Choose materials that are non-toxic, recyclable and easy to clean. Cats will scratch on natural hemp rope as easily as they will on toxic carpeted posts, and dogs will go fetch recycled denim or hemp as fast as they will the plastic ball.

Collars and Leads

- Many collars and leads are made from petroleum-based nylon and other synthetic materials.

- Look for natural fibre products that are sustainable. Hemp makes an excellent choice because it is tough and naturally antibacterial.

- Collars and leads should not be machine washed because plastic and metal parts can damage the machine or melt in the dryer. Instead, soak and scrub them with mild washing-up liquid and warm water. Dry in the sun before returning them to your animal.

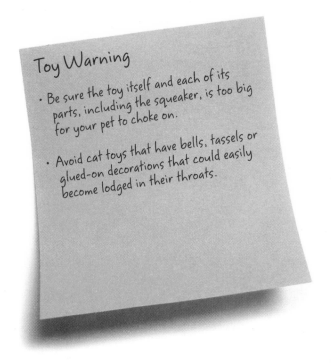

Toy Warning
- Be sure the toy itself and each of its parts, including the squeaker, is too big for your pet to choke on.

- Avoid cat toys that have bells, tassels or glued-on decorations that could easily become lodged in their throats.

PETS

161

PET WASTE MANAGEMENT

Greener alternatives for cleaning up after your pet without hurting the earth or your community

Pet dogs and cats contribute millions of tons of waste annually. And most of that clearly biodegradable matter is preserved forever in neat plastic bags in landfill sites. But there are greener options available.

Biodegradable bags are a step in the right direction, because both the bag and the waste will break down in the short term. But the problem remains that pet waste is a threat to our soil and water supplies. That's because it's full of bacteria, parasites and pathogens that can spread to other animals and to humans.

Children playing in the dirt – or eating it as they tend to do – are particularly vulnerable. Cat waste is of particular

Bags

- Biodegradable waste bags offer a greener alternative to preserving waste in regular plastic bags that don't break down.

- They work best if you empty the bag in the toilet and then compost the bag.

- For non-composters, a better option is to reuse any plastic bag that comes into your home rather than buying new products just for this purpose.

Natural, Non-Toxic Litter

- Most cat litter is made of clay that is strip-mined at a high environmental cost.

- Cat litter can also contain chemicals to make it clump and to mask smells. These are toxic to your cat, who breathes them and may ingest them in her morning grooming session.

- Other options include renewable, fragrance-free, chemical-free, and naturally clumping wheat-, pine- or maize-based litter.

- Dump the waste clumps into the toilet and compost the litter or use as mulch in a non-vegetable garden.

concern because of toxoplasmosis, which is caused by a parasite. Ingestion can be fatal for kids under two years old. Pregnant women and people with weakened immune systems are warned against handling cat litter.

The litter itself also takes a toll on the environment. Currently there are several options on the market that use biodegradable materials such as wood chips or recycled newspapers, to help close the recycling loop. These are generally non-toxic and a great choice for litter.

······· YELLOW ● LIGHT ·······

Most scientists and environmentalists warn against composting pet waste. Garden compost heaps do not get hot enough to kill dangerous bacteria like *E. coli*, which may be found in pet waste. Separate pet waste composters are available, but these should be used with caution and the compost should never be used on the garden.

Cleaner Litter

- If you are not composting it, look for litter made from recycled materials like newspaper.

- For a clean litter tray, remove solid waste once a day or every other day as needed.

- Wash the litter tray completely once a month. Use warm soapy water and finish with a disinfecting spray of diluted vinegar.

- Leave to dry and don't fill with litter until the vinegar smell has dissipated, or your cat may trade the tray for your rug in disgust.

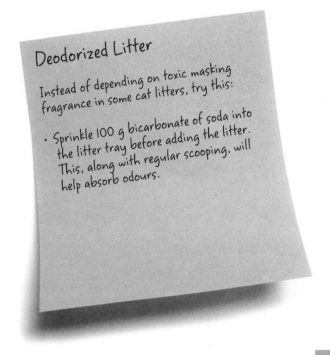

Deodorized Litter

Instead of depending on toxic masking fragrance in some cat litters, try this:

- Sprinkle 100 g bicarbonate of soda into the litter tray before adding the litter. This, along with regular scooping, will help absorb odours.

PETS

163

HOME IMPACT
How to minimize your pet's impact on your home

There's a reason why they call potty training your puppy 'house breaking'. The damage can range from hard-to-remove spots on rugs to ruined sofas. But even fully grown dogs and cats leave their mark on our homes on a daily basis.

Of course, there are products designed for cleaning everything, including pet stains, but they are not likely to make it into our green cleaning kit. Like other carpet cleaning products, these pet stain cleaners can contain the dry cleaning solvent PERC (see page 100) as well as mildewcides, disinfectants and toxic surfactants.

Dander is another pet waste that needs to be controlled. It consists of flakes of your pet's skin, and if it is allowed to accumulate it can trigger allergies and reduce indoor air quality. If your dog or cat moults a lot and you see fur, you can be

Dander and Fur

- To control dander and fur, brush your dog or cat outside once a week.

- For hard floors, dry-mop with a microfibre mop and vacuum or wash as needed.

- For carpeting, vacuum frequently. A HEPA-filtered vacuum with a motorized pet fur attachment is a good investment.

- For clothing, use a reusable lint brush. Brush in the same direction each time so you don't redeposit lint and fur on your clothing.

Furniture

- To protect your furniture, lay down towels, sheets or blankets in your pet's favourite spots.

- For cats that scratch, place a rope scratching post near the chair or sofa the cat likes to scratch.

- Vacuum upholstery each week with a pet-hair-specific vacuum tool or the upholstery attachment.

- Place a pet bed in a sunny spot near the favoured furniture to tempt the animal to lie elsewhere.

reasonably sure that you also have a lot of dander. Dander is harder to spot if an animal does not moult much, but you can assume it's there. Frequent dusting and vacuuming can help reduce dander.

Pets that luxuriate on furniture can dirty and even ruin it with dirty paws, fur oils and nail scratches. Animals can certainly be trained to stay off the furniture, but if you have a hard time enforcing this simple rule, regular cleaning and precautionary measures can minimize the impact.

Another way in which animals can have a negative impact on your home is by chewing or scratching furniture and rugs. While this is pretty normal for puppies and kittens, it can be corrected through training. Keep in mind that exercise and stimulation are the key to well-behaved animals. Take your chewing dog on an extra walk each day or even step it up to a run, and you may find the problem disappears.

Fresh Stains

- Blot stain with a light-coloured rag or towel.

- Mix ¼ teaspoon mild washing-up liquid with 250 ml tepid water.

- Submerge a corner of a towel and blot the stain.

- Rinse with a towel dampened with water.

- Alternate sudsy and plain water blotting.

Old Stains

- If you have pet stains that have been around for a while, try this:

- Apply enzymatic cleaner directly to the stain and use as directed.

- When stain is gone, sprinkle with bicarbonate of soda and leave overnight to further reduce odours.

- Vacuum up the bicarbonate of soda next day.

PETS

165

FLEAS
Flea collars aren't only toxic to the fleas

Of all the ways pets can leave their mark in our homes, fleas are perhaps the worst. They make the dog or cat miserable but can also infest rugs, furniture, clothing and pretty much everything else. If you don't catch the infestation immediately, it's easy to feel as if you've lost the war, which is why we spend so much money each year on flea and tick products to keep these pests off our pets and out of our homes.

However, an American study by the Northwest Coalition for Alternatives to Pesticides found that over two-thirds of the chemicals found in flea control products are neurotoxic and can negatively impact reproductive systems. Half of the chemicals are either known to be carcinogens or are strongly suspected to be carcinogens, and a quarter of them are known mutagens. These products can harm many pets, and

What to Avoid

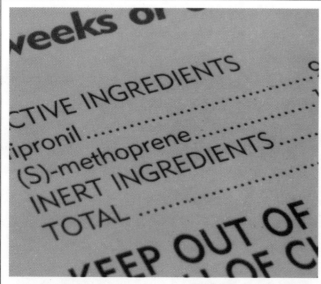

- Preventative flea treatments contain chemicals that are too toxic for us to get on our skin, yet they are meant to be absorbed by our pets.

- Pesticide use in anti-flea products is unregulated.

- Flea collars use pesticides that the pet inhales constantly while wearing the collar.

- Collar manufacturers also warn against human contact with their products, yet most people pet and scratch their dogs regardless of the collar.

Natural Flea Control

- Vacuum floors, curtains and upholstery, and throw out the bag or clean the cylinder after use.

- Wash bedding and rugs often.

- Switch to a cedar-filled bed for your pet.

- Introduce beneficial nematodes to your garden. These insects will kill flea larvae quickly.

- Place lavender, mint, rosemary or cedar essential oil sachets alongside furniture cushions to repel fleas.

humans who apply the products and pet the animals. While we all want our homes and pets to be flea-proof, these toxins do not offer a great green alternative, and it's a good idea to avoid them.

While there are some non-toxic remedies for flea infestation, your best bet is prevention, which can be done by frequent washing of pet bedding, supplementing their diet, and knowing when flea season hits so you can be prepared.

Tools

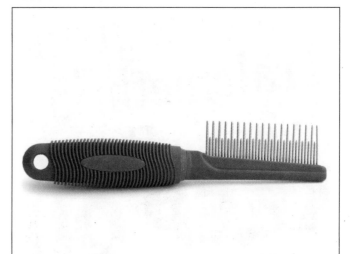

Flea Prevention

• To keep the fleas off your pet, add garlic and brewer's yeast and/or flaxseed oil to your pet's food. This will improve skin health and coat lustre while also repelling fleas.

- To get rid of fleas on pets, you will need a flea comb and a bowl of warm soapy water.

- Comb your flea-infested animal daily with a flea comb.

- After each pass, dip the comb in the bowl of soapy water to ensure the fleas won't jump back on the animal.

- Comb every part of the animal, including the face.

- Regular baths can also help reduce fleas.

PETS

167

TOXIC PESTICIDES
Try integrated pest management for a healthier and pest-free home

If you've gone to the trouble of detoxing your cleaning, the last thing you want to have to do is call in pest control. Pesticides are for killing pests, so there's no getting around the fact that they're toxic.

Mild exposure to pesticides can cause eye, nose, and throat irritation, while more prolonged exposure can lead to central nervous system and kidney damage and increased risk of cancer. Spraying pesticides inside the home without ventilation can compound the already serious dangers they pose.

Integrated pest management (IPM) is a green, chemical-free approach to keeping insect infestations out of your home or getting rid of insect pests that have already taken

Pesticides: What to Avoid

Less Toxic Pesticides

Boric acid

- These products cause severe irritation to eyes, skin and respiratory systems.

- Accidents are common because the propellants are highly flammable.

- Active ingredients include pesticides like permethrin, which is a possible carcinogen and endocrine disruptor. It is also a known neurotoxin that can cause damage to kidney, liver and reproductive systems. Tetramethrin is a carcinogen and known neurotoxin.

- Inert ingredients often include known carcinogens, such as formaldehyde, chloroethane and dichloroacetic acid.

- If you are blowing or sprinkling boric acid in your home, be sure to wear a mask to prevent inhalation.

- Diatomaceous earth (DE) is an irritant when inhaled. Wear a mask when you use it.

- Silica gel is highly absorbent silicon dioxide. It won't irritate skin, but use a mask because it can cause lung damage if inhaled.

- All three are effective for crawling insects that infest homes, especially when combined with other preventative measures.

up residence. IPM takes a lot more strategizing and usually a little more time, but given the risks posed by using pesticides, it's worth it. IPM looks at pest control from every angle to get rid of pests instead of simply pointing and spraying existing insects, which doesn't always stop the colony from coming back.

With IPM, you physically block access using window screens and by filling in cracks and holes. Use insects to your benefit by introducing the appropriate beneficial predator to your garden to control pests, such as using nematodes to control vine weevils. On the inside, IPM practitioners focus on making the home inhospitable to the pest. That can mean everything from clearing clutter and removing food sources to fixing leaks and more frequent washing of all bedding and carpeting. With IPM, use non-toxic baits or traps to catch any insects that have already made it inside.

IPM DIY Ideas

- Install or replace fly screens
- Seal cracks with filler
- Reduce clutter and clean cupboards
- Store pet food and rubbish in sealed containers
- Vacuum and clean often
- Move wood stacks away from house walls

IPM: Questions to Ask Before You Start

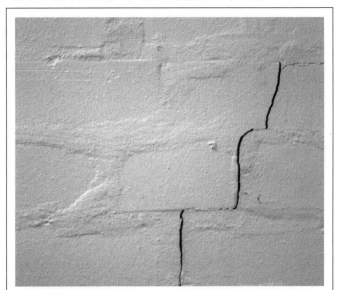

- Specifically, which pest is bothering you?

- What level of damage or danger is there with this insect? A minor nuisance or something worthy of low-grade pesticides?

- What are the habits of this insect? Does it come out at night or during the day? Does it stay hidden or parade across your floor?

- How is it getting in?

- Why is it staying?

ANTS

Locate their entry point and eliminate ants in an eco-friendly way

The worst thing about seeing an ant indoors is knowing that hundreds more are not far behind. While ants are annoying and don't suit the clean green home you've envisioned, they are not the end of the world. Most don't bite or cause structural damage to your home. And since we can see exactly where they are coming from, they're fairly easy to deter.

The labels of most ant-killing products warn against everything from breathing it to getting it on clothing and skin. Among other toxins, many ant control products contain permethrin, which is a strongly suspected human carcinogen. Toxic pesticides tend to backfire because they target only the 5 per cent of a colony that actually ventures out, and

Pharaoh Ants

No Entry

- These tropical ants seek out warm nesting places in centrally heated homes where there are food sources. Eliminate the food source by cleaning up crumbs or spills.

- Keep kitchen worktops and cupboards clean and crumb-free. Wash surfaces with vinegar to break the scent trail the ants leave to track each other.

- Keep all food in tightly sealed containers. Empty rubbish bins daily.

- Store pet food in tightly sealed containers and keep pet eating areas clean.

- Follow the ants to where they are entering your home. Seal the hole or crack to prevent further entrance.

- If you can't seal the area, create a barrier:

- Sprinkle a thick line of coffee grounds or use any combination of cayenne pepper, a citrus-oil-soaked string, lemon juice or cinnamon to create the barrier.

- The ants won't cross, but you may have to replace the barrier every day.

destroying some individuals splits a single colony into multiple colonies, which will then yield more ants.

An integrated pest management approach (see pages 168–69) focuses on deterring more ants from entering your home. For the ants that are already inside, be vigilant about eliminating food sources such as crumbs and pet food. For a green solution, spray the non-toxic ant repellent described here to kill the ants.

Non-Chemical Warfare

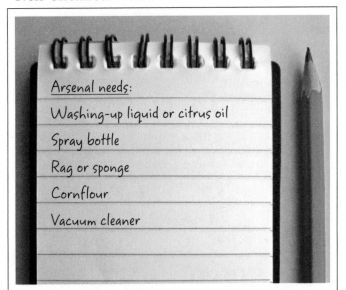

Arsenal needs:
Washing-up liquid or citrus oil
Spray bottle
Rag or sponge
Cornflour
Vacuum cleaner

- For the ants that are already inside, combine a teaspoon of washing-up liquid or citrus oil with water in a spray bottle.

- Spray it on any ants you see and wipe them up with a rag or sponge.

- Alternatively, put cornflour in your vacuum cleaner bag or cylinder and vacuum them up. The cornflour will suffocate them.

- Dispose of the bag immediately.

Carpet Strategy

- If the previous tactics don't take care of the problem, try using diatomaceous earth (DE).

- Wear a mask as you sprinkle DE on your carpet. If you have a rug you can take up, you may want to do this outside.

- Work the powder into the carpet with a broom.

- Leave it for several hours or overnight, then vacuum thoroughly.

FLIES

Keep a clean home to deter flies and prevent infestation

Besides being utterly annoying, a sudden influx of flies needs your prompt attention because they are expert germ carriers. Houseflies feed on waste and sewage as well as rotting food, which makes them prime vehicles for bacteria as serious as salmonella. Fruit flies look for garbage and decaying organic matter in your fruit bowl but also in sink and bathroom drains, under refrigerators, and just about anywhere else. Getting rid of flies and keeping them out is as easy as pest control gets.

The first step is to install fly screens such as mesh panels or chain curtains over windows and doors you want to keep open in summer. Next, and even more important, find where the flies are breeding and clean it up. A good bet is to check

Fruit Fly Deterrent

- As long as there is a supply of rotting matter in your drain, rubbish bin or fruit bowl, fruit fly larvae will thrive.

- To find out if the flies are coming from the drain, place a piece of cling film over the plughole and tape to the sink. Leave overnight and then check to see if fruit flies are stuck to it in the morning.

- Placing a basil plant near where you keep your fruit is a good deterrent for fruit flies.

Fruit Fly Trap

- For a very satisfying science project and fruit fly trap, try this: partially fill a small bowl with cider vinegar.

- Cover with cling film.

- Prick holes that are large enough for the flies to get in but not so large that it's easy for them to get out. The holes should be about 1 cm from the edge of the dish.

- Leave out overnight.

172

your dustbin and the area behind it for any decomposing food. Keep your dustbin and indoor waste bins tightly covered, and empty and wash them frequently. Pick up pet waste in the garden immediately and check your houseplants for decaying material.

With screens as barriers and thorough cleaning, all that's left to do is perfect your swatting technique, and your fly problem will be a thing of the past.

ZOOM

Studies show that when flies are ready for takeoff, they usually jump up and backwards. To swat a fly, aim your swatter about 4 cm behind the fly and you will impress your family and friends with your Zen-like fly-swatting abilities.

Tried and True

- Flies that come in with the breeze and exit as soon as you open the door again are not a serious problem.

- Flies that stay and reproduce mean you have a sanitation problem.

- Empty rubbish frequently and keep it in a covered container. Wash the bin once a week and clean up any other rotting organic matter, such as dog waste in the garden.

- Find a good sturdy fly swatter and perfect your technique (see above).

Make Your Own Flypaper

You will need:

paper bag

50 ml golden syrup

100 g sugar

- Cut the paper bag into four or five strips that are about 5 cm wide.

- Stir together syrup and sugar in a bowl.

- Use a knife to spread the mixture evenly on to the paper strips.

- Hang up the strips but remember to place a bowl or tray under them to catch any drips.

RODENTS

Poison can backfire – try these gentler methods to rid your home of rodents

Rats and mice are not exactly the symbols of a clean green home. If left to their own devices, they can cause damage by chewing through wiring, walls, plastic and furniture. Considering that one pair of mice can produce up to 87 babies in a year and rats can produce more than 35, you need to rid your home of them as soon as possible or you'll have an even more serious problem. It may be tempting to reach for the rat poison, but don't. Rat poison is highly toxic to the rat but also to your family and pets. Poisoning rodents can also make the situation worse, because they tend to retreat into their holes to die where you can't reach them or see them – but you can certainly smell them.

House Mouse

- The common house mouse grows to about 12.5 cm long while rats can be up to 40 cm long.

- A rat or mouse scampering or swaggering across your floor, droppings, and gnawed food packaging, furniture and walls are all signs of infestation.

- You may also see flickering lights because the rodents are chewing the electric wires or hear rustling sounds at night.

- Rat urine is hard to miss because it smells quite strong and it stains.

Integrated Pest Management

Seal the cracks

Eliminate hiding places

Take away the food

Cut off the water supply

- Stuff steel wool into any crack larger than 6 mm wide and seal it into place with filler.

- Clean often and store all human and pet food in covered containers. Don't leave dishes in the sink. Cover rubbish and take it out often.

- Declutter so it's harder for mice to hide, and clean out any cupboard they seem to frequent.

- Don't leave your pet's water dishes out at night, and get rid of any standing water in houseplant trays, etc.

Mice and rats like living with you simply because you provide food and hiding places, so the key to getting rid of them is to stop providing both. A rat needs a hole the size of a 10 pence piece, and a mouse even less to get into your house, so make sure you stop up any holes that you see. Eliminate their food source by tightly covering rubbish and keeping your kitchen worktops and floors extremely clean. Using all-purpose cleaner with peppermint oil (see page 31) deters mice, who find it distasteful.

Trapping is the final stage in the war against rodents and should do the job without chemicals. Start with the most humane traps available and progress from there. Use as many traps as you can and make sure you buy the right size traps for your pest, as rats are significantly bigger than mice. Peanut butter, fruit, bacon and gumdrops are all attractive bait choices.

Live Trap

- Some live traps do not need to be baited.

- For the others, use peanut butter or gumdrops to lure the mice in.

- When you catch a mouse, put on some gloves and take it at least 2 km away from your home so it doesn't find its way back.

- Release the mouse, and reuse the trap to catch the rest of the mice.

Snap Trap

- Snap traps are the next most humane traps after live traps because they usually result in a quick and easy death.

- Choose traps that are the right size for your rodent and place them out of the way of children and pets.

- Bait two or three traps at once. Do not set the traps for the first few nights to accustom the rodent to this new food source.

- Use gloves to avoid getting your own smell on the trap.

REDEFINING RUBBISH
Compost and recycle everything you can to reduce rubbish

The average Briton produces about half a ton of rubbish in a year, of which over 65 per cent goes into landfill. Luckily for the planet, the definition of 'rubbish' gets a lot narrower in a green house. Living according to the order of the three Rs – reduce, reuse, recycle – means that products that are unnecessary or wasteful, such as disposable shower wipes

and temporary, disposable food storage containers, are not purchased in the first place, so the amount of possible waste is reduced. Products such as computers or baby gear are donated for reuse. And anything and everything that can be is recycled, either by setting it out on the kerb for collection or, for food waste, composting it in the garden. When

CLEAN HOME, GREEN HOME

Cleaner Waste Management

- Keeping the waste bin under the sink is common, but the combination of a juicy food source and increased moisture can attract pests.

- It's preferable to create a pull-out system in a separate cupboard that is just for waste. Use covered bins

or keep the cupboard door closed to deter pests.

- Place the rubbish in front and recycling at the back to keep the recycling free of drips and misplaced waste.

- Alternatively, use a lidded rubbish bin that is easy to clean.

Keeping It Clean

- Depending on your household, clean out your bins once every other week.

- Empty the rubbish and recycling as usual and then take the bins outside. Use a sponge, rag or brush to scrub them with soapy water.

- Spray with straight vinegar to disinfect and leave them to dry in the sun.

- If your bag slides down inside the bin and creates a mess, tie knots at the mouth of the bag to create a snugger fit.

176

rubbish collection day comes, you can tell a green house by the small size of the dustbin in comparison with the large size of the recycling bin.

To use the three Rs to redefine and limit rubbish, the first step is to make it easy for everyone in your home to do the right thing with anything they're ready to discard. That means having a functional and easy-to-clean system of separating rubbish from items for recycling, composting and donating.

The 'Great Pacific Garbage Patch' is a startling reminder that rubbish never really goes away. It's an island consisting almost entirely of plastic that weighs about 3.5 million tons and occupies an area twice the size of Texas. It is a huge threat to Pacific marine animals and birds, who mistake bits of plastic for food.

Green Bags

- There are a variety of green bin liners available.

- Look for bags that are made from as much post consumer waste recycled material as you can find, or bags made from non-petroleum sources such as tapioca.

- Biodegradable rubbish bags usually do not biodegrade in landfill conditions.

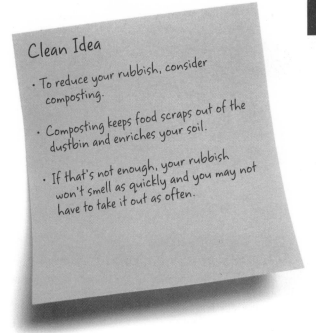

Clean Idea

- To reduce your rubbish, consider composting.

- Composting keeps food scraps out of the dustbin and enriches your soil.

- If that's not enough, your rubbish won't smell as quickly and you may not have to take it out as often.

RECYCLING
Creating the recycling habit in your home means less rubbish going to landfill and less work for you

While it's true that many people recycle, less than 40 per cent of household waste in the UK is either recycled or composted, compared with over 70 per cent in other European countries such as Belgium and Germany. A key part of raising recycling rates is for councils to make it easy to recycle, with coordinated kerbside collections, and making it easy is also the key to stepping up your household recycling programme, to make it so convenient that everyone in the household does it out of habit instead of only with constant prodding.

If your recycling system looks too much like a waste bin, it can often be mistaken for the rubbish, which means you either have to do some unpleasant sorting or throw the

Kerbside Bins

- One sign of a clean green home is that on rubbish day, the recycling bin overshadows the dustbin.

- Put up a list of what is and isn't recyclable, so everyone knows what goes where.

- Reduce the amount of packaging you discard by buying in bulk whenever possible.

- Make buying choices based on whether the packaging is recyclable and choose not to buy products that are overpackaged.

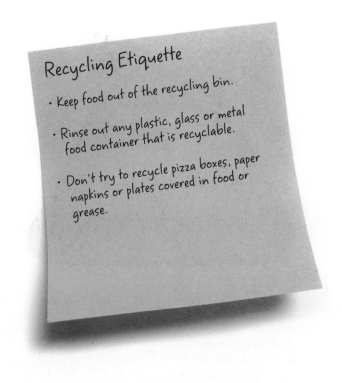

Recycling Etiquette

- Keep food out of the recycling bin.

- Rinse out any plastic, glass or metal food container that is recyclable.

- Don't try to recycle pizza boxes, paper napkins or plates covered in food or grease.

whole mess out. Instead, and to clarify what goes where, offer well-marked bins that are noticeably different from the rubbish. Be sure they are large enough so that they're not overflowing by collection day. Recycling rules require you to rinse recyclables free of food before placing them in bins. However, this doesn't always happen, and spills make this area an attractive feeding ground for pests, so choose bins that are easy to clean. Placing the bins in the kitchen or utility room means no one needs to travel far to do their part.

·····GREEN●LIGHT·····

Make amends for all the energy waste in your home and lifestyle by paying for your greenhouse gas emissions through carbon offsetting, to fund climate-positive programmes like wind turbine construction, solar installation, treatment plants in developing countries and more.

In-House Bins

- Create a clearly marked recycling centre that fits your space.

- If your local authority requires you to sort items, create separate containers for paper, plastic and metal.

- Make sure the containers are large enough not

to overflow, or, if space is limited, create a schedule to empty them midweek before they have a chance to overflow.

- Wash the containers with a hose and soap once a month.

Stackable Bins

- Stackable bins may fit better in a small space, or a situation such as a garage.

- Position the bins so they require the least effort to get to and won't be blocked by cars or other items.

- To make it even easier, leave a tray on the kitchen

worktop where people can put recyclables during the day and then take them out to the bins after dinner each night.

- This cuts down on trips to the bins and drips from the kitchen.

RECYCLING GUIDELINES
What you need to know to recycle effectively

A successful recycling programme is dependent on the proper participation of many people. As soon as you know the rules of how and what to recycle, following them is easy.

These rules vary by region, so get the information directly from your local authority's environmental department. Post a list of what can be recycled clearly next to your bins so there are no grey areas. Some recycling programmes make it easy by not requiring you to sort different materials, making collections every week and accepting a wide range of plastics and other materials in the recycling bin. Other places have strict rules on sorting and are more restrictive on what can actually be recycled.

As a general guideline, be sure to rinse out all containers before putting them in the recycling bins. Don't put in paper

Plastics

- Check with your local authority for the plastics they do and do not recycle, but here are the most commonly accepted:

- Type 1, found in fizzy drinks bottles, is reincarnated as fibrefill for dog beds, winter coats and beanbags, among other uses.

- Type 2 is the sturdier plastic in shampoo, laundry detergent or milk bottles. These will become toys, plastic piping and rope.

- Type 6 is polystyrene or Styrofoam and will become rigid foam insulation, among other things.

Paper

- Newspapers and ordinary paper are accepted in any recycling programme. Brown paper may be accepted with cardboard for composting.

- In some locations you need to tie up the newspaper in string or paper bags.

- Phone books are not always accepted because the thin paper can't be recycled to make more paper – but they can be used to make new phone books as well as paper bags, cereal boxes and paper towels.

products or anything else that is soaked through with food or grease. If you find something that you use regularly that doesn't get recycled via the kerbside collection, try to find somewhere that will recycle it. However, it's important to look at the bigger picture and not drive a long way to recycle a few small items.

Metal

- The most commonly accepted metals are aluminium and steel or 'tin' cans.

- Both are closed-loop recycled because they find immediate use; an aluminium drinks can may go from kerbside to shelf as a new aluminium can in as little as 60 days. Steel may become material for cars and other products.

- Aluminium cans are mainly fizzy drinks cans.

- Steel and tin cans are the thicker metal ones used for tuna, soup and other canned food items.

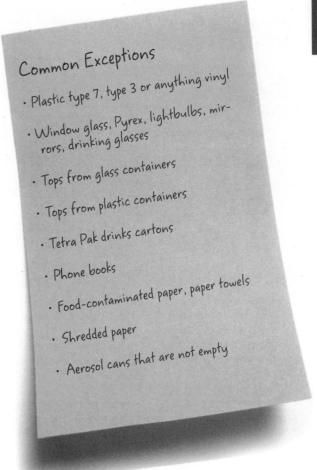

Common Exceptions

- Plastic type 7, type 3 or anything vinyl

- Window glass, Pyrex, lightbulbs, mirrors, drinking glasses

- Tops from glass containers

- Tops from plastic containers

- Tetra Pak drinks cartons

- Phone books

- Food-contaminated paper, paper towels

- Shredded paper

- Aerosol cans that are not empty

SMALL-SPACE COMPOSTING
Composting shrinks to fit even the smallest spaces and busiest schedules

Composting is the ultimate in recycling because it reduces waste going to landfill and even more directly benefits the environment by improving the soil. Compost-enriched soil grows healthier plants but also conserves water by reducing runoff and resisting erosion. But if you live in a flat or a home with no garden, it may seem that composting is not an option. These days, however, there are systems to fit any lifestyle, including bins that fit under your kitchen sink and produce just enough compost to keep your houseplants, and maybe those of your neighbours, luxuriously green and healthy. You just need to find the system that will work best for your lifestyle and take time to learn the ropes.

Worms

- The easiest way to get started with composting is to buy a Can-O-Worms wormery system, which is made from recycled materials.

- This is a set of stacking trays designed so that the worms eat their way up through the layers as you feed them non-meat kitchen scraps and shredded newspaper.

- You can keep them in your kitchen or leave them outside on a patio.

- You'll need the housing, a starter bedding block, and about 1,000 redworms.

Undersink System

- Most indoor systems consist of a bin with a tight-fitting lid and some kind of microbial additive or 'starter' to digest the scraps.

- Start the bin with a layer of additive. Then add scraps and more additive and keep it up until it's full.

- There is a waiting period before you can use the compost or bury it for further decomposition.

- It's a good idea to have two bins and alternate between the two.

If you do choose under-sink composting, keeping the bin tightly covered is key to ensuring that pests don't find this treasure trove of decaying kitchen scraps. Any system will have a tight-fitting lid, but make sure you put it on correctly each time or you could compromise your compost and have a real mess on your hands. Cleaning the whole area regularly will make turning kitchen scraps into 'black gold' a much more enjoyable process.

Compost Tea

Drain compost tea from here

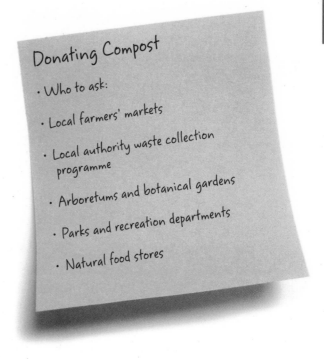

Donating Compost

• Who to ask:

• Local farmers' markets

• Local authority waste collection programme

• Arboretums and botanical gardens

• Parks and recreation departments

• Natural food stores

- Compost tea is basically liquid compost that you can use as indoor or outdoor fertilizer.

- Some composters have spigots that allow you to drain off compost tea easily.

- Making compost tea requires some equipment and science, but you can buy a compost tea brewer that makes it easy for you. The Can-O-Worms also produces liquid compost.

- Apply tea to the soil at the base of your plants to fertilize or spray on the leaves to fight fungus.

GARDEN COMPOSTING
Choose a sunny spot and the tools that suit your lifestyle

For families who do have gardens and produce more organic waste in the form of kitchen scraps, but also more garden waste such as grass clippings and leaves, composting can really pay off. The reduction in waste going into the dustbin is substantial, but enriching your soil with compost helps you reduce or eliminate fertilizers and pesticides because your plants will be healthier and more resistant to disease.

It's important to have a sink-side container to make it easier for everyone to stick to composting. Who wants to traipse out to the compost heap every time they have an apple core or peel potatoes? The container should be large enough to hold a day's worth of scraps and have a lid that seals tightly. There are containers made for this purpose, but a glass bowl with a tightly fitting top can also work.

Sink-Side Composting

- Make it easy for the whole household to compost with a sink-side container.

- It should be big enough to fit a whole day's worth of kitchen scraps.

- Take the crock out to add to the compost heap each night after dinner.

- Look for a crock that seals tightly or use a bowl with a tight lid. Some crocks have charcoal filters to absorb smells, in case you don't get to empty it every day.

Garden Bins

- When looking for compost bins, look for recycled plastic bins with turning mechanisms and tight fitting lids to keep pests out.

- You will also need compost accelerator, which you add to the bin to jump-start the process.

- Effective composting is a balance of 25 per cent green matter from kitchen scraps and 75 per cent brown matter from garden waste.

- If the mix is not right, mould and smells will become a problem.

For your garden compost heap, buy an easy-to-use bin and some compost accelerator, or construct a container for the heap yourself. As in small indoor spaces, it's important to be realistic about your lifestyle so you don't commit to a compost system that's too involved. It's also a good idea to have one person in the family who is responsible for the compost. This role can rotate, but it will ensure that the task doesn't fall through the cracks.

ZOOM

Compost decomposes rapidly in temperatures of 30–60°C, but cold-weather composting one heap may take a year. To allow for this, keep several heaps going at once so you always have access to the rich soil that results from the breakdown. Place compost heaps in a sunny spot in the garden and choose heat-absorbing black-coloured bins with insulation jackets.

25 Per Cent Greens: Nitrogen

- Fruit and vegetable trimmings
- Eggshells
- Rice and pasta
- Teabags or leaves
- Coffee grounds
- Houseplant clippings
- Flowers
- Outdoor plant clippings
- Hedge trimmings

75 Per Cent Browns: Carbon

- Leaves
- Pine needles
- Twigs and branches
- Cardboard egg cartons
- Woodfire ashes
- Straw
- Sawdust
- Tumble dryer lint
- Shredded newspaper

TOXIC SPILLS IN THE HOME
Clean up toxic messes in three easy steps

Even clean green homes may have a few toxins still lurking in garages and cellars that come out every once in a while for the car or the pool. Unfortunately, in the process of moving around these toxins, many inevitably end up on the kitchen worktop. The worktop is a way station for just about everything, but it's also a food preparation surface that should be kept as clean as possible. When antifreeze or pool chemicals leak on to it, there is definite cause for concern.

If this happens, it's important to protect yourself first – even before your granite worktops, I'm afraid. Open a window for ventilation and get protection for your skin and eyes before attempting to clean up the area. It's a good idea to keep a

Protect

- Keep an emergency protection kit under your sink so it's easy to grab in case of emergency.

- If a toxic chemical or pesticide spills, first open as many windows or doors as you can.

- Next, put on eye protection and rubber gloves so you minimize your own exposure to the chemical.

- Any rags you use will most likely be ruined after cleaning up, so don't grab your nicest kitchen towel.

Step 1: Contain

- To protect your floor and worktops, create an absorbent boundary around the chemical.

- You need to act fast here, so flour may be the easiest option. Other options include cat litter and sawdust.

- Generously pour the absorbent material over the top of the spill.

- Use a rag and a piece of cardboard to scoop up the spill. Place the rag and cardboard in a plastic bag.

protective kit under the kitchen sink for emergencies of this type. Next, contain the spill, keeping it from spreading to the floor or other surfaces and absorbing as much as you can with flour, sawdust, cat litter or whatever other absorbent materials you can access quickly.

Use a detergent to clean up the area and to remove traces of the chemical from the worktop. Keep in mind that the chemical and now everything you used to clean it up classify as hazardous waste and need to be disposed of accordingly. Contain the hazardous waste in a plastic bag or covered bucket to be taken to the hazardous waste collection centre. Last, open more windows and arrange fans to increase ventilation and direct any lingering gas or smells out of your house as quickly as possible.

Step 2: Clean Up

- Pour liquid dishwashing detergent or laundry detergent directly on the spill spot.

- Now, reapply absorbent material over the top of the detergent to absorb.

- Scoop up the spill with cardboard and add to the plastic bag.

- Scrub the spot with more detergent and water.

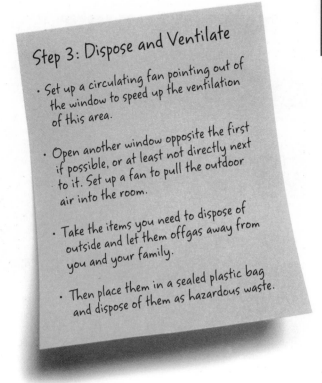

Step 3: Dispose and Ventilate

- Set up a circulating fan pointing out of the window to speed up the ventilation of this area.

- Open another window opposite the first if possible, or at least not directly next to it. Set up a fan to pull the outdoor air into the room.

- Take the items you need to dispose of outside and let them offgas away from you and your family.

- Then place them in a sealed plastic bag and dispose of them as hazardous waste.

DECLUTTER

The first step to keeping any space clean green is to know what to keep and what to throw away

For anyone who has lived in their home for more than a few years, cellars and garages become holding zones for discarded objects that are no longer wanted in the house. Already-read books, old baby clothes, outdated computers and long-forgotten exercise bikes, among other things, tend to get stashed here. The longer we let the clutter build up, the more difficult it is to clean up. What might have been an afternoon project grows into a multi-weekend marathon.

Much of what's stored in these spaces takes little energy to donate or recycle. The books are perfect for a used-book sale. The baby clothes and computer can be donated. And the exercise bike ... well there has to be someone who wants it.

Electronic Waste

- Plastic casings around electronics are usually treated with toxic flame retardants, decabrominated diphenyl ethers (deca-BDEs).

- Monitors, chips, connectors and other materials inside the electronics can contain neurotoxic lead and mercury and carcinogenic chromium and cadmium.

- These items are hazardous materials and should not be thrown in the dustbin.

- But they should also not sit idle in your garage or cupboard.

E-Waste Resources

- The best way to get rid of your e-waste is to donate or sell your item to someone who can use it.

- If the item is too outdated, you'll want to recycle it. First check to see if the manufacturer runs a take-back scheme.

- Some manufacturers do this for free and others charge a small fee for recycling.

- If this isn't a possibility, check with electronics stores for recycling facilities, or look for local authority e-waste collection schemes.

To help you declutter, first move everything out of the storage area to where you can see it and group together items that are similar, such as sports gear or car maintenance tools. Sort the piles according to what you will keep and what you will let go.

Anything that is clearly junk and non-recyclable should be thrown out immediately. Anything that is junk and hazardous should be set aside to take to the hazardous waste centre in your area. Damaged or broken items should be set aside for recycling, repairs or disposal in a green way. Items in good condition but no longer needed or wanted should be set aside for donations.

Once you know what's staying and what's going, decide where the discards will go. With a little research, you can find recycling or donation schemes to fit just about everything. Give yourself a deadline and stick to it.

Sports Equipment Resources

- For old but still functioning sports equipment, check with local schools, after-school clubs, charities and churches to see if they can use it.

- You can also sell sports gear at a garage or car boot sale.

- Or donate it to a local charity shop.

- Or sell or swap it through an online auction site.

Other Ideas

- Cut old T-shirts and flannels into cleaning rags.

- Cut up your old yoga mat to make a knee pad to use while gardening or a mat for your pet dishes.

- Give packing materials to a local mail order company for reuse.

- Donate old books to the local library or school.

DETOX

How to dispose of or store household toxins so they're safely out of breathing range

As you're clearing out the clutter in your cellar and garage, you may come across toxins such as paint, paint thinner, pesticides, transmission fluid or hazardous household cleaners. These are all items that can't just be thrown out with the rubbish or dumped down the drain so their containers can be recycled. If the label tells you it's toxic, corrosive, flammable, reactive or explosive, it's hazardous waste and should not end up in landfill. Read the labels for information on proper disposal, but also research the hazardous waste disposal guidelines in your area.

For the most part, it's a good idea to finish up the product (or find someone who will) and then make your next

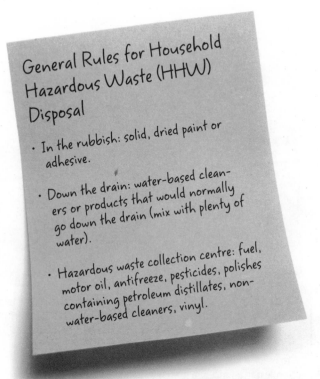

General Rules for Household Hazardous Waste (HHW) Disposal

- In the rubbish: solid, dried paint or adhesive.

- Down the drain: water-based cleaners or products that would normally go down the drain (mix with plenty of water).

- Hazardous waste collection centre: fuel, motor oil, antifreeze, pesticides, polishes containing petroleum distillates, non-water-based cleaners, vinyl.

Antifreeze

- Antifreeze is a staple in many garages and is often stored on a shelf with other car products.

- Yet, this one product is responsible for thousands of child and animal poisonings every year.

- It tastes sweet, so kids and pets will lap up puddles of it, but the sweetness comes from toxic ethylene glycol.

- Store antifreeze in a locked cupboard. Make sure it's not leaking out of your car. For your next purchase, look for a safer antifreeze that uses less toxic propylene glycol instead.

purchase a safer alternative, or find a non-toxic homemade solution. For toxins you aren't ready to let go of, make sure you store them safely where children can't reach them and no one is inhaling them.

A locked cabinet is ideal for most toxins, but it's important to keep flammable products away from corrosives. Products that have warnings about vapours and fumes should be kept in well-ventilated spaces. Keep all toxins in their original containers with the labels intact so they are never mistaken for something non-toxic. Children are poisoned every year from toxins stored in fizzy drinks cans or other old food containers, which make them look like something edible. Make sure the lids are on tightly and the area is dry. If you have rags that are designated to be used with a specific product, store them in sealed containers that are clearly marked with their use.

Storage

- Store hazardous products in a locked cabinet that kids can't access.

- Keep similar products on the same shelves; put pesticides on the top shelf and paint on a lower shelf.

- Make sure the lids are on as tightly as possible. If you smell the chemicals when the doors are shut, check the lids.

- Routinely check for bulging containers and dispose of them properly.

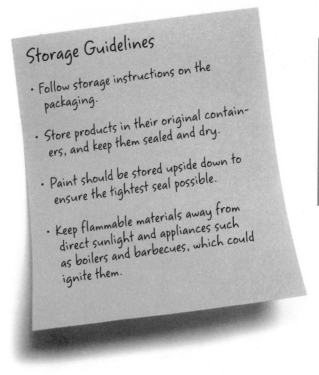

Storage Guidelines

- Follow storage instructions on the packaging.

- Store products in their original containers, and keep them sealed and dry.

- Paint should be stored upside down to ensure the tightest seal possible.

- Keep flammable materials away from direct sunlight and appliances such as boilers and barbecues, which could ignite them.

CLEAN CELLAR

Seasonal cleaning can mean the difference between a healthy home and a colossal mould or pest problem

It's not as visually rewarding as a clean kitchen or bedroom and it's certainly not the kind of cleaning you would do before guests arrive, but cleaning the cellar is crucial to the overall health of your home. Since it is generally one of the least-trafficked areas in the home, it's prime for all kinds of problems, from mould growth to insect or rodent infestation.

Seasonal cleaning will keep you in touch with what's going on (or growing) in your cellar and help you catch it before it's too late.

Depending on how the space is arranged, it may work best to break it down into quadrants when cleaning. That way you can move things over into the next quadrant while you clean.

Ceiling

- Start cleaning at the ceiling to remove cobwebs, dust and dirt.

- Clear the area you are cleaning as best you can so you will sprinkle debris only on the floor.

- Cover anything you can't move with dustsheets.

Wear a hat or scarf on your head and use a face mask to avoid breathing in dust particles.

- Use a straw broom to sweep the ceiling. Try to get into tight spaces and above pipes. Stand on a stepladder if necessary.

Appliances

Dust and dirt build up here

- Move on to the next highest surface – the tops of shelves or appliances.

- Start at the top and wipe them with a damp cloth to remove dust layer.

- Then wash with warm sudsy water. Avoid using too much water on electrical appliances.

- Make sure the areas around appliances are clutter-free. Any boxes or bags of stored items located near an appliance could be a fire hazard.

When you're finished you can slide the stuff back over without too much trouble. As in any room, it's a good idea to start at the top with the ceiling. Cover your head and anything else in the space and use a broom to remove cobwebs and dust. Next, clean any appliances like water heaters or boilers. Wipe these down and inspect them for mould or any loose parts. Dust, vacuum or wipe down shelves, and sweep and wash the floor. A concrete floor can be cleaned with mild castile soap and water. A janitor's broom is excellent for scrubbing.

Floor

- Remove dust sheets, wrapping up debris and taking it outside to shake.

- Use a broom to sweep debris into piles. If you have a wet/dry vacuum cleaner, use it to suck up the piles.

- If not, use a dustpan. Do not use your household vacuum because cellar debris may include larger objects that can cause damage.

- Use a clean broom to scrub the floor with a solution of warm water and castile soap.

Routine Inspections

- While you're cleaning, check the following:

- Stored items for water damage or moisture

- Shelves for evidence of pests like mice or silverfish

- Appliances for fire safety

- The floor and walls for evidence of moisture and cracks

CELLARS/GARAGES

CLEAN GARAGE
Neglected garages may be far from green

While there's no need to slip into the protective suit or dig out the gas mask, cleaning the garage does take some special precautions. Once you've cleared out the clutter and either disposed of or properly stored chemicals, the remaining concern for the environment concerns what's on the floor. Hosing down the floor can seem like a very logical and expedient way to clean, but it means that oil-tainted water flows down your drive and into the storm drain or road, only to be washed into the surrounding environment the next time it rains. Just one drop of oil has the power to pollute 4,000 litres of water. So think twice before you hose off that oil slick under the old Subaru.

Step 1: Cleaning Stains

- Cover the entire stain with a layer of cat litter or sawdust about 1 cm deep.

- Lay down strips of paper or cardboard that are wide enough for your feet.

- Step on to the paper and do the twist! Grind the litter or sawdust into the concrete.

- Repeat whenever you have a minute to do it again. Add more litter or sawdust as needed. It may take up to a fortnight of twisting to absorb the stain.

Step 2: Sweeping the Floor

- Discard the absorbent material and paper or cardboard as hazardous waste.

- Use a broom to sweep the garage.

- Because the garage floor can be a collector of toxic debris from cars and household chemicals, don't just sweep the dirt out on to the drive, where rain can carry it into the drains.

- Instead, sweep debris into piles and use a wet/dry vacuum cleaner to suck up the piles and dispose of it properly.

194

If your car is leaking oil or other chemical fluids, be pro-active by strategically placing trays of cat litter or sawdust to catch and absorb the leaks. When it's time to wash the floor, you'll be able to dispose of the oily litter safely, without risking the water supply. If you've caught it all and the garage floor is oil-free, cleaning it is easy. Wet the surface with the hose, apply a mixture of mild castile soap and water, and use a janitor's broom to scrub and guide the water on to the drive.

For oil slicks directly on the floor, your best bet is to contain and absorb them by pouring on a generous amount of cat litter or sawdust. Place strips of newspaper over the piles and proceed to do the twist – yes, the twist – to grind the sawdust into the floor and increase the absorption. If you do manage to get all the oil up, then washing the floor with water is a possibility. Otherwise, stick to sweeping.

Step 3: Washing the Floor

- Mix a few squirts of phosphate-free detergent and 4 litres of water in a bucket.

- In small amounts, pour the mixture on to the area you are cleaning.

- Use a broom to scrub the floor and repeat in the next area.

- Use the hose and the broom to rinse the floor and push the water out of the garage. Leave the door open for it to dry.

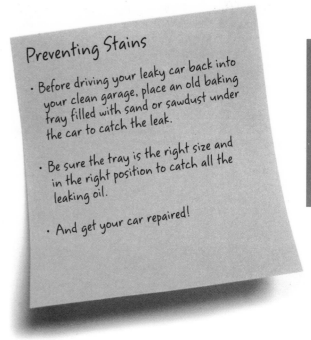

Preventing Stains
- Before driving your leaky car back into your clean garage, place an old baking tray filled with sand or sawdust under the car to catch the leak.

- Be sure the tray is the right size and in the right position to catch all the leaking oil.

- And get your car repaired!

KEEPING IT CLEAN
Organized storage makes cleaning easy and fast

If you have recently cleaned up your cellar or garage, congratulations! Not only have you increased the usefulness and improved the appearance of these areas, but you have also just increased the value of your home. Cleaning out the garage is one of the cheapest things you can do to give a tremendous boost to your home's kerb appeal. If you're not interested in selling your home anytime soon, just take a few more steps to organize these spaces, and they'll remain free of clutter and easy to clean over the long haul.

Setting up well-organized stations for the different types of gear stored there will save you time spent on searching for the correct tool or football, as well as giving you ample

Off-the-Floor Storage

- The best use of space in your garage or cellar is to build shelves to expand vertical storage.

- Install the bottom shelf about 30 cm above the floor to keep your stored items dry and make the whole room easier to clean.

- Designate sections of the walls for different types of items, and structure your shelving accordingly.

- Combine shelves with hooks and bungee cords to accommodate the different items you want to store.

Sports Equipment

- Store sports equipment where it won't be damaged by falling over or getting scratched by car doors.

- Surfboards, snowboards, wakeboards and skis could get damaged or warped by the shelving itself; consider wrapping any hard edges in old towels.

- Hang your most expensive gear where it is least likely to be damaged.

- Use milk crates, clean plant pots, or other recycled bins and containers to hold smaller objects such as balls, gloves, surf wax and bike tyre tubes.

space for household projects like repotting plants or carrying out repairs. In essence, your garage and cellar can actually be spaces you use instead of just storage areas for parking and storing stuff. When all you have to do is back the car out and sweep and vacuum a few cobwebs, you'll be more inclined to tackle those projects more often.

· · · · · · · · · · GREEN ● LIGHT · · · · · · · · · ·

Organizing the garage will probably require more shelving than you have. Since aesthetics don't count for much in these spaces, it's easy to go for the cheapest option. Resist the lure of cheap formaldehyde-emitting chipboard shelves. Try recycled fibreboard shelves that are formaldehyde-free.

Tools

- Organize tools so that you can easily see and grab whatever you need.

- Most pegboard is made of hardboard, a source of formaldehyde and other VOCs.

- Look for companies that offer less toxic choices.

- You can also use shelves, bins and hooks to achieve an organized tool area.

Crafts

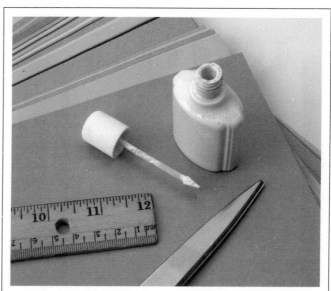

- Use a corner of your basement or other utility room to create a workspace for crafts, sewing or other hobbies.

- Some glues, paints, dyes and other craft supplies are toxic. Choose an area that can be ventilated easily.

- Keep all toxic supplies in a locked cabinet so children and pets can't get at them.

- Be sure to use the vertical wall storage space to give you more workspace.

197

CAR WASHING
Get the dirt off without polluting the oceans

While washing your car every week will most likely help your car last longer, washing the car at home may not be your greenest option. All that water running off the car as you wash contains oil, grease, mud, rubber and petrol, which will now run into surface drains untreated, and eventually enter the waterways and the sea.

On the other hand, professional car washes are required by law to drain their waste water into the sewage system, where it will be treated, reducing the risk of contamination. In addition, car washes can save between 150 and 350 litres of water per wash. These details add up to huge benefits for the environment.

Car Wash Suds to Avoid

Ingredients:

petroleum distillates

kerosene

silicone

mineral spirits

- All of these known carcinogens are found in car wash products.

- As you rinse your car, toxins including brake dust, exhaust fumes and oils join the harsh detergents and carcinogens from the car wash solution.

- They get rinsed down your drive and into the drains or the surrounding soil.

- Washing your car on the lawn acts like a filter, keeping the toxins out of the waterways, but they remain in your own garden.

Car Wash Suds Labels to Look for

- Petroleum-free

- Phosphate-free

- Kerosene-free

- Waterless

- Biodegradable

If you must wash the car at home, try a non-toxic soap such as the recipe given here. Also, resist the urge to run the hose the entire time you're washing. Instead, use a hose attachment that enables you to turn the water on and off without having to run back to the tap each time.

Eco-Friendly Car Wash

If You Must Wash at Home

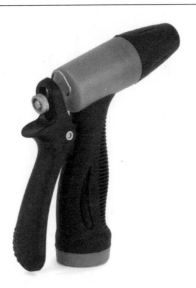

- Any car wash is greener than washing at home because wastewater goes into the sewer where it will be treated.

- Look for car washes that take extra steps to conserve water, such as separating the oil and water and re-using the water.

- A few car washes also use green building practices and alternative energy sources, like solar power.

- Above all, look for a car wash that uses non-toxic cleaners. If they don't tell you what they use, ask.

- Park the car in the shade or wash it in the morning. You'll use less water because the sun won't bake on the soap. Use a hose attachment with a shut-off valve to wet the car.

- Soap up with a large sponge, and use a separate bucket to rinse the sponge so you minimize detergent use from changing dirty buckets.

- Rinse the car thoroughly but without going overboard and wasting water.

- If your car is fairly clean to begin with, try a waterless product.

CAR

CHROME

Keep your chrome looking showroom-new with a few items from your kitchen

If you're lucky enough to have a car that hasn't traded in all its classic shiny chrome parts for plastic, then you'll need something to bring out the shine. If you neglect chrome, oil or grease can bake into the surface, making cleaning difficult. A better option is to clean chrome regularly so it maintains its shine. Before cleaning, look closely at the metal to be sure it's actually chrome. Some carmakers use polished aluminium, which resembles chrome but does not clean up the same way. If the surface has tarnish or pits in it, it's most likely aluminium.

Specialized chrome cleaners can contain ethylene glycol, a neurotoxin that can also damage the reproductive system, kidney and liver. Of more immediate concern, it can irritate

Chrome Polish Ingredients to Avoid

Ingredients:

ethylene glycol

ammonia

1,1,1-trichloroethane

triethanolamines (TEA)

fragrance

- Ethylene glycol is toxic to the nervous and reproductive systems; it's also a respiratory irritant that can cause kidney, blood and liver damage.

- Ammonia is a respiratory irritant and 1,1,1-trichloroethane is a neurotoxin.

- TEA can combine with preservatives to form nitrosamines, which are carcinogenic.

- 'Fragrance' represents a whole host of chemicals, including phthalates, suspected endocrine disruptors.

Polish Technique

- For best results, use a soft flannel cloth to avoid scratching the chrome.

- Dip the cloth in cider vinegar.

- Move in the direction of the metal grain. Do not move in circles or you could scratch the chrome.

- Use a second clean, dry, flannel cloth and buff the chrome to a shine.

your throat and lungs. These cleaners can also contain other irritants and neurotoxins along with carcinogens and synthetic fragrances. What's more, they're not even necessary when you have vinegar or lemons on hand. These non-toxic techniques will help minimize the impact of washing your car yourself by reducing the amount of toxic products you need to have on hand for the task.

Alternative Technique

- Cut a lemon in half, and cup it in your hand.

- Wipe the chrome with the lemon in the direction of the metal grain.

- Buff with a clean, dry, flannel cloth.

Old Corroded Chrome

CAR

- If your chrome looks impossibly corroded, try this shine-saving technique:

- Use fine steel wool, as coarse steel wool can damage the chrome further.

- Rub the steel wool across the chrome in the direction of the grain, and flip the wool often.

- Use some elbow grease for this task, and work it until it shines.

201

CAR WINDOWS
Step-by-step tips to non-toxic, crystal-clear windows

Although the spatters on your car windows can be as different as bugs and milkshakes or tree sap and road salt, cleaning them off effectively is easy. Soda water makes a perfect cleaner because its bubbles help to break up the stuck-on goo, but it doesn't leave a residue when you've finished, like other glass cleaners. Other cleaners can also leave streaks,

especially when they come into contact with the special water-repellent coatings on your windscreen.

Frequent cleaning will keep this job manageable without requiring too much elbow grease. It will also help you to avoid the always-dirty squeegee and toxic blue solution at the service station.

Step 1: Start at the Top

- Lower each side window just enough to enable you to clean the top edge of it.

- Spray soda water on scrunched-up newspaper or a T-shirt rag.

- Do not use paper towels for this job – they leave fibres on the window and it's a waste of paper.

- Wipe in straight lines from side to side.

Step 2: Work Your Way to the Bottom

- Raise the window so you can clean the very bottom of the window.

- Spray more soda water on to the newspaper and continue wiping in straight lines down the window.

- Take one more pass with a dry side of the newspaper to get rid of any streaks.

- Be sure to clean the frame around the window as well.

202

If you live in a colder climate and are constantly battling foggy windows and ice build-up on the windscreen, here's another easy green solution. Mix 120 ml of white vinegar with 350 ml water in a spray bottle. Spray generously on the windscreen and leave it to air-dry. Do this twice a week, and you'll notice that both the fog and the ice become much less of a problem. While other de-icing products can harm your car's paintwork, this basic solution will not.

Step 3: Exterior Windscreen

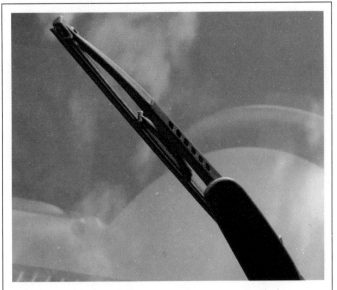

- Pull wiper blades off the window so they are sticking straight out.

- Start with the driver's side of the windscreen. Spray soda water on your newspaper and wipe in long overlapping lines halfway across the windscreen.

- Be sure to wipe below where you can see out of the windscreen and around the wiper blades, which can catch a lot of dirt.

- Take another pass with dry newspaper to eliminate streaks, then repeat on the other half.

Step 4: Interior Windscreen

- Kneeling at an angle on the front seat can help make cleaning the interior of the windscreen a less awkward job.

- Spray the soda water on newspaper instead of the window and wipe in straight lines.

- Be careful around the rearview mirror. If it is attached by glue it can be dislodged fairly easily.

- Split the window and do one side at a time. Take a final pass with dry newspaper to eliminate streaks.

CAR

SHINE AND PROTECT
Revive and preserve your car's finish with non-toxic polish

Regular cleaning and occasional polishing can protect your car so it looks newer longer. Unfortunately, many polishes contain chemicals that are irritants and can damage your central nervous system, cause dizziness, headaches and nausea. But road debris, weather, and pollution do take their toll and protecting your car is still important. A growing awareness about toxins in the automotive industry is leading to the appearance of new products that are less toxic to our bodies and the environment.

In the past, car polish and wax were completely different products. Polish was used to remove impurities, remedy surface scratches and make your paint look brighter, while waxing protected the paint from chips and scratches caused by normal everyday use. As car paint technology advances,

CLEAN HOME, GREEN HOME

Car Polish to Avoid

- Like other polishes, car polish contains petroleum-based chemicals, such as petroleum distillates, known neurotoxins.

- It carries the second most serious hazard warning, 'Danger', meaning it could cause permanent tissue damage to the skin, mouth, throat and stomach.

- This product is also 'combustible' or able to catch fire and burn easily.

- Because paint technology has progressed so far, polish is less and less necessary. Using no polish is a better option than using this type of toxic product.

What to Look For

Ingredients:
water
coconut oil
beeswax
carnauba wax
banana essence oils
no petroleum distillates
no kerosene

- If you have a lot of plastic on your car, be sure to read the label. Some polishes are not appropriate for this.

- Look for no-rinse cleaner-polish combinations. You save packaging, water, toxic runoff and time.

- These products are most effective for routine cleaning. If the car has not been washed for months, take it to the car wash and then wash every other week with the rinseless cleaner.

polish is less important and its abrasiveness can now actually harm a clear-coated finish. The result is that polish and waxes have been combined into a single product designed for the new paint. The combination helps to reduce the number of products you need to buy and the plastic packaging they require. Yet the problem chemicals remain.

This homemade car polish and wax is a little more involved than other recipes in this book, but it works very well. Otherwise, look for non-toxic, biodegradable products.

Beads mean the car is well protected.

Water Test

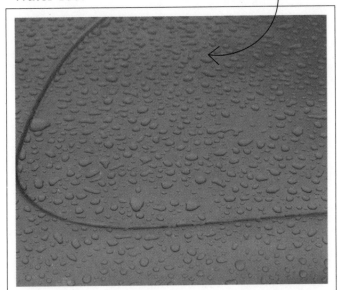

- If you see the water bead on the surface, your paint is protected and you don't need to wax it.

- No beads means it might be time to take it to the car wash to have it professionally waxed.

- The more you wash your car, the less need you'll have of protective waxing.

- It is possible to overwax. If you do it too often, you can dull the finish on your car.

Homemade Polish/Wax Technique

- Before you begin polishing, the car should be out of direct sunlight and freshly washed.

- Working on one section at a time, apply a coin-sized circle of polish to a clean flannel or microfibre cloth.

- Rub the polish on to the car in a circular motion and leave to dry until it looks cloudy.

- Use a dry flannel or microfibre cloth to buff the polish to a shine. Repeat on the next section of the car.

CAR

205

INTERIOR

Re-invent the 'new car smell' by minimizing toxins

People either love or hate that 'new car smell', but what is it exactly? Unfortunately, it's a toxic mix of chemicals that are offgassing from different parts of the car's interior. Even more unfortunately, a large part of this smell comes from PVC.

You might expect to get that smell if you bought a car with vinyl seats, but even cars with leather or fabric seats usually contain PVC on the backs of seats, armrests, steering wheel and door trim. As we've seen, PVC contains phthalates (see page 36) and is strongly linked to cancer as well as problems with reproductive development and fertility. Given that the average car owner spends 100 minutes or more a day in their car breathing this stuff, it is definitely cause for concern.

If you're planning to buy a new car, avoid vinyl seats and look for cars with the least PVC content you can find. If you

Gearshift

- Attach the crevice tool to your household or wet/dry vacuum cleaner.

- Vacuum either from the top of the stick shift down or, for automatic cars, the length of the gearbox.

- If you have a soft leather or vinyl base to the gearshift, use your other hand to stretch it taut as you vacuum.

- Finish by wiping down the area with a cloth dampened with castile soap and water. Wipe dry.

Dashboard

- Your best tool is a micro-fibre cloth or a just damp T-shirt rag to make sure you are not just scattering the dust.

- Use a clean paintbrush to dust the vent slats, joins and any other hard-to-reach places.

- After dusting, use a damp, clean sponge to wipe down the dashboard.

- Use soda water sprayed on a clean rag to wash glass surfaces.

already have a car that contains vinyl, try using this recipe to minimize the smell, and leave your car windows open when the car is in the drive or garage, so that offgassing can happen without you being there to breathe it.

Washing the interior of your car should not add toxins to the mix. Use your vacuum attachments to minimize dirt and dust and non-toxic cleaners like this vinyl deodorizer (right) for deeper cleaning.

'Baking Out' Vinyl

- To get rid of the vinyl car smell, try this. Leave the car in the hot sun for at least 3 hours with the windows open a few centimetres. The heat will speed up the chemical emissions from the car.

- Next, open the windows all the way and let the car air thoroughly without you in it.

- Vacuum thoroughly.

- Finally, use the vinyl deodorizer (above) with a microfibre cloth, and finish by wiping with a clean damp cloth.

Leather Seats

- Vacuum the seats and wipe with a microfibre cloth to ensure you've picked up all the dust and debris.

- Avoid toxic leather cleaners and stick to the basics. Use leather furniture cleaner (see page 119) as you would on your sofa and buff to a shine.

- Alternatively, lather a bar of moisturizing soap on a clean wet cloth.

- Apply to the leather. Do not rinse. Buff with a clean cloth.

CAR

207

UPHOLSTERY AND CARPETS
Vacuuming can reduce the need for cleaning products

Most carpet in cars, as well as the glues and sealants used to install and protect it, is petroleum-based and contains off-gassing VOCs that pollute interior air. Carpets and upholstery also trap dust and make an inviting home for dust mites. Don't make matters worse by using more toxins to clean them.

Regular vacuuming with a quality filter can help reduce the toxins lingering in your car's dust. Vacuuming also helps to reduce the need for cleaning products, because dirt doesn't have time to get ground into the fibres. But for most people, ice cream cone drips and coffee spills are inevitable. Have a stain-cleaning kit handy (see right) so you can treat spills quickly when you'll have a better chance of removing them.

When it is time to clean your car upholstery more deeply, look for products that are fragrance-free to minimize your

Maintenance: Clean Floor

- Remove the floor mats from the car and shake them out.

- For rubber mats, hose them down and scrub with a brush and warm soapy water. Castile soap or washing-up liquid is fine for this.

- For carpet mats, vacuum thoroughly. Sprinkle with bicarbonate of soda and leave them out as you wash the rest of the car. Vacuum again before replacing them in the car.

- Using a flat tool and crevice tool, vacuum the entire floor of the car.

Maintenance: Clean Seats

Don't forget in here

- Vacuum your car frequently to keep the dirt from getting ground in or staining.

- Use the upholstery tool for flat surfaces. Pull the tool from top to bottom in long slow, overlapping strokes.

- Use the crevice tool for uneven surfaces and to get into tight spaces, including the space between the headrest and the seat back.

- Also use the crevice tool to get the areas on the floor alongside the seats where crumbs and other debris can fall.

exposure to phthalates and other toxins. For an easy non-toxic deodorizer, sprinkle bicarbonate of soda on your car's carpet and upholstery and leave it overnight. Next day, use your vacuum cleaner's upholstery attachment, preferably one that includes a rotating brush, to vacuum up the bicarbonate of soda.

A vapour cleaner, or a steam cleaner with a non-toxic solution, are great options for deep-cleaning your car's carpet and upholstery (see page 119).

(see page 119).

Food Stains

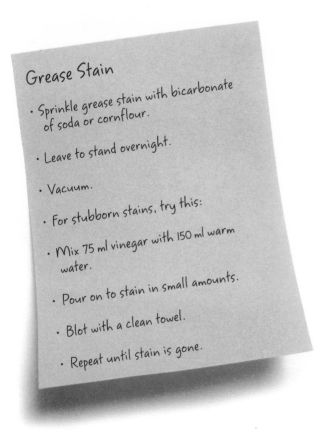

Grease Stain

• Sprinkle grease stain with bicarbonate of soda or cornflour.

• Leave to stand overnight.

• Vacuum.

• For stubborn stains, try this:

• Mix 75 ml vinegar with 150 ml warm water.

• Pour on to stain in small amounts.

• Blot with a clean towel.

• Repeat until stain is gone.

• Scrape off any unabsorbed spillage with a knife. Pour soda water on the stain and blot with a clean towel. Repeat until the stain disappears.

• If the stain is still there, repeat process with white vinegar and water and another clean towel.

• For stubborn stains, mix ½ tsp washing-up liquid in 250 ml water. Blot and repeat.

• As a last resort, repeat using this mixture with hydrogen peroxide. Test for colour-fastness first in a hidden area.

CAR

OUTDOOR WOOD FURNITURE
Choose green and easy to clean

Wood is the obvious choice for natural and environmentally friendly garden furniture. It's a renewable resource and can be cared for with the ultimate in non-toxic cleaning products: mild soap and water.

For hardwoods such as teak and oak, an occasional cleaning is all that is necessary, and the wood will age to a nice shade of silver grey. Woods like cedar are naturally resistant to pests and rot, but look best with an occasional sealing. Softwoods, such as pine, require annual sealing to keep the moisture out and prevent rotting.

There are many different types of wood sealants and protective finishes available. Oil-based formulas are best for outdoor furniture, especially because the alternatives typically contain ammonia and should not be exposed to direct

Choosing

- Look for wood furniture that is FSC-certified to be confident you're buying a green product.

- Otherwise, look for non-exotic woods; instead of teak go for western red cedar, which is naturally bacteria-, fungus- and insect-resistant.

- Reclaimed or recycled wood furniture keeps wood out of landfill and the trees in the forest.

- Look for 'secondary species' that are less popular and therefore less harvested.

Cleaning

- To clean, first sweep off the furniture with a straw broom.

- Work the broom into tight spaces where cobwebs and other debris may have collected.

- Mix castile soap or mild washing-up liquid and warm water and wash. A sponge will work well. Avoid using harsh brushes or scourers, which may damage the finish.

- Rinse and dry thoroughly.

sunlight. Many of the available products emit VOCs, which can combine with other substances in the air to produce hazardous gas like ground-level ozone, a major contributor to smog. These products also can contain 1,4-dioxane, a suspected carcinogen, and toxic solvents like xylene and toluene. Some also contain insecticides. Instead, look for a product that has low VOCs and is plant-based.

Preserving

- To preserve your furniture, look for products that do not contain petroleum-based chemicals and are low-VOC.

- Less toxic products contain linseed oil, beeswax or tung oil, but check that they don't include toxic solvents and heavy metal dryers.

- Copper and zinc compounds are other less toxic preservative ingredients.

- Follow the label for application, but most products suggest you clean furniture thoroughly and apply a thin coat of the oil. Wipe the furniture dry with a clean T-shirt rag.

Natural Ageing

- If you already have teak furniture, you can oil it regularly and maintain its original colouring.

- But you can also let it age naturally and avoid using any product on it at all.

- When left alone with the weather, teak will age to a silver-grey colour. Cracks can develop, but they will not weaken the structure of the wood.

- Oak and cedar also do not need regular preserving.

OUTDOORS

OTHER OUTDOOR FURNITURE
Look for durable, recycled or fast-growing materials

For covered areas or furniture that you're willing to store away during the months of harsher weather, fast-growing grasses like bamboo or vines like rattan transformed into wicker serve as alternative green options that deliver the natural look of wood. If you prefer furniture you can leave outside year-round without too much worry, recycled plastics and metal are probably your best options.

Look closely at your wicker furniture before cleaning it. Much that is sold as outdoor furniture is actually not made of natural materials but is woven plastic, like vinyl or resin. The most common wicker vine is rattan, but it can also be made from cane, bamboo or willow. These are fast-growing, renewable resources so wicker qualifies as a green choice. However, it's not quite as durable as other options.

Wood- or Vine-Based Wickerwork

- Wicker will last longer if it is not soaked, either by rain or hose.

- To clean, use a brush vacuum attachment or a broom to remove dust deep inside the weave.

- Clean with a small amount of castile soap and water. Scrub with a brush to get into the fibres.

- Wipe with a clean damp cloth and leave in the sun to dry.

Resin- or Vinyl-Based Wickerwork

- If your furniture is very dusty or dirty, start with your vacuum or a broom to get dirt, dust and cobwebs out from the fibres.

- Otherwise, use the water pressure from the hose to penetrate the fibres.

- Turn the hose off and scrub with castile soap and water.

- Rinse with another blast of the hose and leave out in the sun to dry.

Both bamboo and rattan wickerwork should be cleaned regularly, because dust can build up in between the fibres and cause wear, and mould can develop in these spaces as well, particularly if furniture is stored in a damp shed in winter. Vacuuming with a brush attachment is your best option for routine cleaning. You can also wash the furniture with a damp sponge or rag and mild soap. Avoid soaking with a hose unless absolutely necessary.

Metal Furniture

- Aluminium, steel and wrought iron are your primary choices for metal outdoor furniture.

- Aluminium is durable and can tolerate being wet.

- Iron and steel are more inclined to rust, especially if you live near the sea.

- If rust begins to develop, sand the area with 600-grit sandpaper until you see the metal again.

- Wash with castile soap and water, but be sure to dry thoroughly.

Plastic

- Recycled plastic outdoor furniture is extremely durable and closes the recycling loop for recycled milk cartons and other HDPE plastic.

- To clean, hose down and then scrub with castile soap and water and a brush.

- Rinse with the hose and leave to dry in the sun.

- Plastic furniture can stay out in harsh weather, but if you know you won't use it for an entire season, it's best to store it out of the elements.

OUTDOORS

BARBECUES AND FIRE PITS

Whether you use gas or charcoal, regular cleaning reduces pollution and increases efficiency

Another seemingly eternal debate amongst the environmentally conscious is whether to go with gas or charcoal for barbecuing. Although the debate is far from over, it's clear that neither option is perfect. Charcoal releases greenhouse gases, produces ground-level ozone and contributes to deforestation. Typical charcoal grill accessories such as lighter

fluid and self-lighting briquettes can give off petrochemical VOCs as well. On the other hand, gas barbecues, which run on bottled propane, require a non-renewable resource. Gas contributes pollution on its own, but far less than charcoal.

If you prefer charcoal, look for briquettes that don't have chemical additives, and use a chimney starter instead of

Proactive Step

- To reduce the need to clean the barbecue often, take this simple step each time before you use it.

- Fill a pump spray with an oil with a high smoking point, such as safflower or grapeseed oil.

- Before you light the barbecue, spray the cooking racks with oil so food will not stick to them.

- Or brush the racks with oil, but be careful not to pour it into the barbecue itself.

Easy Clean

- When you've finished cooking your meal, turn off the gas and close the lid of the barbecue to keep it hot while you serve the food.

- After your meal, come back to the barbecue and use the grill brush. You could also use aluminium foil for

this – it's a great way to recycle used foil.

- Brush or scrub the hot racks to get rid of any pieces of burnt food.

- Tap the brush a few extra times to ensure that it's clean when you finish.

lighter fluid to get it going. It's also important to keep the barbecue as clean as possible to prevent extra smoke, which means extra pollution.

Whether you use gas or charcoal, regular cleaning and maintenance of your barbecue will keep it functioning efficiently and safely.

Deeper Clean

- Remove racks and soak in warm soapy water.

- Remove coal grate for charcoal and everything but the burner for gas barbecues. Brush out the inside of the barbecue.

- Dip a stiff wire brush in soapy water and gently

scrub the inside of the barbecue, removing any debris. For gas barbecues, brush the briquettes and metal flame shield in warm soapy water.

- Scrub and rinse cooking racks, reassemble and leave the cover open to dry.

Fire Pits

- Clean fire pits regularly to reduce the particulate matter they release as pollution into the air. Cleaning also helps keep them safe.

- Remove any leftover wood and add the ash to your flower borders.

- Spray the pit with water and scrub gently with a soft brush and warm soapy water.

- Rinse the pit and leave it in the sun to dry.

OUTDOORS

215

DECKING CARE
Practise eco-friendly seasonal cleaning and take protective steps

An outdoor patio or wooden deck can offer the promise of carefree, peaceful days spent reading or barbecuing with family and friends. But some decks require a few extra steps before they can be entirely worry-free. Until recently, many wooden decks were constructed from arsenic-laden pressure-treated wood – treated with chromated copper arsenate (CCA) – and many of us still have that decking in our gardens. The problem is that this treated wood leaches arsenic and other toxins into the earth, groundwater and your body. If you do still have CCA wood in your garden, it's important to seal it regularly with a low- or no-VOC sealant to reduce the leaching.

Winter Proactive Step

- Winter neglect can make a lot more spring work for you.

- Weight from snow and debris can harm your decking, as can months of exposure to moisture. To prevent damage, clear decking after a snowstorm.

- If snow is deep, shovel it in shallow layers rather than digging all the way to the bottom.

- As you get down to the wood, shovel more gently so you don't nick and cut into the decking.

Summer Scrub

- Sweep your decking weekly to get rid of any debris that may trap moisture and cause mould or rot.

- Use a knife or screwdriver to remove any debris caught between boards.

- Wet the deck with a hose. Power washers are effective but can strip and damage the wood.

- Scrub with castile soap or washing-up liquid and water using a broom or a deck brush. Follow the direction of the grain. Do this early in the morning so it can dry in the sun.

If you decide to replace your decking, look for reclaimed timber. It's easy to clean, but does require additional care, such as finish and sealants. Composite decking is another green option. It's made with recycled wood and plastic and doesn't require extra maintenance. It also resists moisture, has a long life, and is fully recyclable.

For regular wooden decking, it's important to remove any accumulated debris to prevent the growth of mould and rot. Cleaning your decking is a great opportunity to inspect the area for loose boards or soft or rotting wood and replace any that you find. Pay attention to any signs of infestation by insect pests.

For regular cleaning use mild castile soap and water, scrub with a janitor's broom, and rinse off with the hose.

Decking Sealer to Look For

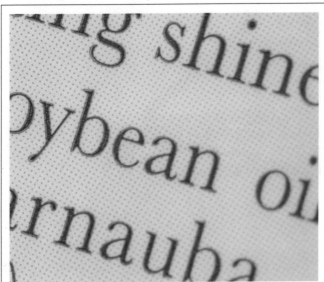

- You know it's time to reseal your decking when water no longer forms beads on the surface.

- It's important to choose a safe sealant.

- Decking sealers contain pesticides and petroleum-derived ingredients to penetrate and weather-proof the wood.

- Less-toxic products rely on plant-derived oils, safer solvents like isoaliphate, and contain no preservatives.

Sealing Decking

- Check the weather forecast to ensure it won't rain for at least two days.

- Follow the label instructions. Most products suggest you strip the old sealant off the wood by sanding it. Wash the sanded decking, and give it time to dry completely.

- Use a paint roller with a long handle to apply an even coat to the boards.

- Remember to start furthest away from your exit and work your way off the decking.

GARDEN WORK

Clever planning makes green garden maintenance a breeze

Routine garden chores can take a toll on the environment. It's estimated that petrol-driven mowers, strimmers and other landscaping tools are responsible for 5 per cent of urban air pollution. Amateur gardeners tend to use pesticides more frequently and more strongly than farmers, resulting in disrupted ecosystems and contaminated land and water. And a perfectly manicured, weed-free lawn of velvety green grass requires the application of tons of water and additional fertilizers and weedkillers.

'Beneficial landscaping' is key to changing this situation. It means choosing native plants and grasses that typically need less supplemental watering. Native plants are also more resistant to pests on their own, without the need for pesticides. Keeping your lawn area to a minimum makes it possible to switch from

Grass Alternatives

- Look for drought-tolerant grass varieties, which will require less water and less pest control.

- Consider whether you need a lawn, or reduce its size and use the space to plant a vegetable garden to help feed your household.

- Plant native, drought-tolerant shrubs and trees instead of a lawn. Position them strategically to form wind breaks or cool your home by providing shade where you need it.

- Use rain barrels to catch water and use it to irrigate your garden.

Eco Grass Cutter

- Push mowers with spinning blades are perfect for small lawns and require only you to power them.

- Mower blades need sharpening periodically. Check your area for sharpening services before buying this type of grass cutter.

- Electric mowers pollute less than petrol-driven ones and in the long run cost less to operate.

- Take off the grass box and leave grass cuttings as mulch for your lawn to help it retain moisture so that it needs less water.

a powered mower to a person-powered push mower. Letting the grass grow longer between mowings also helps, because deeper root systems mean less watering and healthier grass.

While feeding is important, look for non-synthetic and non-fossil-fuel-based options that won't add nitrates and phosphates to waterways. Contamination can kill fish and birds that inhabit those areas. Your own compost is the best and most effective fertilizer you can use, and it doesn't cost you more than the bin and the compost starter.

Fertilizers to Avoid

- Studies show that fertilizers contain many of the most toxic heavy metals, along with dioxins.

- Synthetic fertilizers dump all of the nutrients at once and in large doses.

- Fertilizer chemicals contribute heavily to algal blooms in waterways, which kill fish and vegetation because the algae reduce the oxygen in the water.

- Avoid fertilizers that also contain weedkillers. These are not good for your health or the environment.

Organic Fertilizer

- Overfertilized lawns are not healthy lawns.

- Instead of synthetic fertilizers, let the grass grow to at least 7.5 cm so it absorbs more sun and will develop a deeper root system. Deeper roots mean less watering over time.

- If you're composting, you have all you need for a healthy lawn.

- Leave the grass clippings on the lawn as mulch and try seeding the lawn with a mix that includes Dutch clover, which naturally fixes nitrogen in the soil.

OUTDOORS

PEST MANAGEMENT

Choose ladybirds over carcinogens for effective pest control

With an integrated pest management approach (IPM), garden pest control does not have to be toxic. Instead of neurotoxins and carcinogens, your pest management arsenal can consist of non-toxic products such as liquid soap, cooking oil, horticultural-grade (as opposed to pool-grade) diatomaceous earth (DE), neem oil and ladybirds.

To prevent infestation, beneficial landscaping can be key. Any new plants you add to your garden should be native to your area and, therefore, naturally resistant to local pests. Providing appropriate care without overwatering or overfertilizing also helps, because the plants are healthier and better equipped to resist pests.

Aphids

- Aphid infestation is not pretty, but the damage is largely superficial. From an integrated pest management viewpoint, toxic intervention is not worth the risk.

- Check plants before you buy them to make sure you're not bringing home aphids.

- Reduce the use of fertilizer, because new growth attracts aphids. Sustained, slow growth is healthier and makes plants less vulnerable to this pest.

- Introduce ladybirds and lacewings, who feed voraciously on aphids. Encouraging birds into the garden is also helpful.

Mites

- Plants that are hot and dry are particularly vulnerable to spider mites.

- To test for mites, look for yellow or white specks on leaves. Or hold a piece of paper under the leaves and shake the plant. If tiny bugs appear on the paper, you have mites.

- Remove infested leaves immediately.

- Wipe both sides of each remaining leaf with a damp cloth once a week to eliminate the dust and webs the mites use to protect their eggs.

Strategic planting is another IPM approach, if you do find pests accumulating on specific plants. For example, plant nasturtiums, which black aphids love, right next to a plant you want to be aphid-free. When the nasturtiums fill up with aphids you can pull them out and take the aphids with you.

Introducing beneficial insects that eat destructive pests is also an easy and effective solution. For example, ladybirds love to dine on aphids, weevils, whiteflies and mites among others. Green lacewings prefer aphids, mealy bugs, spider mites and whiteflies. Do some research before introducing your beneficial insect of choice to make sure your garden and climate is well-suited to their needs.

Snails and Slugs

- These pests can cause major damage to your garden by eating leaves and sometimes the entire plant.

- Pick off snails and slugs whenever you see them.

- Look for them in the dark spaces of your garden – the undersides of leaves as well as walls shielded by plants, inside or underneath containers, your compost heap, etc.

- Some research has shown caffeine to be toxic to slugs. Use your coffee grounds as a mulch and see if the slugs retreat.

Deer

Deer-Resistant Plants
Boxwood
Coneflower/Echinacea
Holly
Iris   Spruce
Marigold   Strawflower
Nasturtium   Yucca
Snapdragon   Zinnia

- There are a million techniques for trying to defend your garden from munching deer, including fencing, scents, dogs and rotten eggs.

- Even when they do work, it's usually a temporary fix. Then the deer are back.

- The best defence is to choose plants that deer don't like.

- You may still have the pleasure of seeing them pass by, without the frustration of knowing what they just did to your garden.

OUTDOORS

PHOTO CREDITS

Chapter 1
xii (left) Stasys Eidiejus/shutterstock
xii (right) Carsten Reisinger/shutterstock
1 (left) (left) Bomshtein/shutterstock
1 (right) oblong1/shutterstock
2 (left) © Scott Van Blarcom | Dreamstime.com
2 (right) © Krzysztof Wiktor | Dreamstime.com
3 (left) © Feng Yu | Dreamstime.com
3 (right) Johanna Goodyear/shutterstock
4 (left) Graca Victoria/shutterstock
4 (right) stocksnapp/shutterstock
5 (left) © Karin Lau | Dreamstime.com
5 (right) © Randy Mckown | Dreamstime.com
6 (left) Courtesy Soil Association
6 (right) Courtesy Fairtrade Foundation
7 (left) Courtesy Leaping Bunny
7 (right) Courtesy Forest Stewardship Council
8 (left) photos.com
8 (right) © Kirill Roslyakov | Dreamstime.com
9 (left) Courtesy of The American Soybean
Association
9 (right) Yusaku Takeda/shutterstock
10 Liz Van Steenburgh/shuttterstock
11 Elena Elisseeva/shutterstock

Chapter 2
12 (left) Carole Drong
12 (right) Jonathan Vasata/shutterstock
13 (left) Domenico Gelermo/shutterstock
13 (right) Carole Drong
14 (left) Courtesy of Gaiam
14 (right) © Shaday365 | Dreamstime.com
15 (left) Wikipedia
15 (right) matka_Wariatka/shutterstock
16 (left) Liette Parent/shutterstock
16 (right) HomeStudio/shutterstock
17 (left) K Chelette/shutterstock
17 (right) Courtesy of Gaiam
18 (left) serthom/shutterstock
18 (right) rj lerich/shutterstock
19 (left) R McKown/shutterstock
19 (right) © beth ponticello | Dreamstime.com
20 (left) © Flashon Studio | Dreamstime.com
20 (right) Bashkirova Marina /shutterstock
21 Ruben Enger/shutterstock
22 (left) photos.com

22 (right) Deborah Reny/shutterstock
23 (left) rebvt/ shutterstock
23 (right) Liv friis-larsen/shutterstock

Chapter 3
24 (left) photos.com
24 (right) IoanaDrutu/shutterstock
25 (left) K Chelette/shutterstock
25 (right) photos.com 24 (left): Anna Adesanya
26 (left) oblong1/shutterstock
26 (right) Carole Drong
27 (left) Aleksei Potov/shutterstock
27 (right) Hugo de Wolf/shutterstock
28 (left) Courtesy of Kohler Co
28 (right) Courtesy of Kohler Co
29 Courtesy of Kohler Co
30 (left) UrosK/shutterstock
30 (right) © Varyaphoto1000 | Dreamstime.com
31 (left) Courtesy of Kohler Co
31 (right) Courtesy of Marble.com
32 (left) Courtesy of Maytag
32 (right) Sandra Rugina/shutterstock
33 (left) © Pat Choinski | Dreamstime.com
33 (right) © Thesupe87 | Dreamstime.com
34 (left) Stephen Coburn/shutterstock
35 (left) TheSupe87/shutterstock
35 (right) Carole Drong
36 (left) photos.com
36 (right) © Design56 | Dreamstime.com
37 (left) © Rafa Irusta | Dreamstime.com
37 (right) R. Gino Santa Maria/shutterstock

Chapter 4
38 (left) Mark Stout Photography
38 (right) © Igor Terekhov | Dreamstime.com
39 (left) Courtesy of Ikea
39 (right) photos.com
40 (left) FSC Trademark ® FSC Forest
Stewardship Council
40 (right) Stasys Eidiejus/shutterstock
41 photos.com
42 Patricia Hofmeester/shutterstock
43 © Kotiki | Dreamstime.com
44 (left) Courtesy of Ikea
44 (right) Courtesy of Build Direct
45 Courtesy of Ikea

46 felix casio/shutterstock
47 (left) Carole Drong
47 (right) Graca Victoria/shutterstock
48 Kiselev Andrey Valerevich/shutterstock
49 (left) Matka Wariatka/shutterstock
49 (right) ahkim/shutterstock

Chapter 5
50 (left) Courtesy of Kohler Co
50 (right) Courtesy of Kohler Co
51 Courtesy of Kohler Co
52 © Milanlj | Dreamstime.com
53 © Edward Sporbert | Dreamstime.com
54 (left) photos.com
54 (right) Marie C. Fields/shutterstock
55 Anthony Berenyi/shutterstock
56 (left) Courtesy of American Standard
56 (right) © Marc Pinter | Dreamstime.com
57 (left) photos.com
57 (right) Carole Drong
58 (left) photos.com
58 (right) Konstantin Sutyagin/shutterstock
59 (left) Courtesy of Gaiam
59 (right) photos.com
60 (left) Carsten Reisinger/shutterstock
60 (right) photos.com
61 photos.com

Chapter 6
62 (left) Courtesy of White Lotus Home
62 (right) Factoria singular fotografia/
shutterstock
63 (left) Courtesy of Coyuchi
63 (right) Courtesy of VivaTerra
64 (left) shutterstock
64 (right) Piotr Skubisz/shutterstock
65 (left) shutterstock
65 (right) Courtesy of Gaiam
66 Courtesy of Gaiam
67 (left) Courtesy of VivaTerra
67 (right) Courtesy of Gaiam
68 Svetlana Larina/shutterstock
69 Courtesy of VivaTerra
70 (right) Deborah Reny/shutterstock
71 (left) Andrew Kroehn/shutterstock
71 (right) Pattie Steib/shutterstock

72 (left) © Heide Hibbard Reed |
Dreamstime.com
72 (right) Gravicapa/shutterstock
73 shutterstock

Chapter 7
74 Ali Ender Birer/shutterstock
75 (left) Steve Cukrov/shutterstock
75 (right) Milan Vasicek/shutterstock
76 Carole Drong
77 (left) matka_Wariatka/shutterstock
77 (right) Courtesy Soil Association
78 (left) Carole Drong
78 (right) Carole Drong
79 (left) Carole Drong
79 (right) Elke Dennis/shutterstock
80 (left) Michal Kram/shutterstock
80 (right) Carole Drong
81 (left) Serghei Starus/shutterstock
81 (right) wheatley/shutterstock
82 holligan78/shutterstock

Chapter 8
84 (left) Elena Schweitzer/shutterstock
84 (right) Marcel Mooij/shutterstock
85 elaine hudson/shutterstock
86 (left) Kim Ruoff/shutterstock
86 (right) Annmarie Young/shutterstock
87 (left) sagas an/shutterstock
87 (right) Anita Patterson Peppers/shutterstock
88 Ramona Heim/shutterstock
89 Losevsky Pavel/shutterstock
90 (left) Oleg V. Ivanov/shutterstock
90 (right) Galushko Sergey/shutterstock
91 Artem Efimov/shutterstock
92 (left) Alexan66/shutterstock
92 (right) The Mary Cordaro Collection™
93 (left) Courtesy of Coyuchi
93 (right) MalibuBooks/shutterstock
94 (left) ostromec/shutterstock
94 (right) evan66/shutterstock
95 (left) shutterstock
95 (right) Barbara Delgado/shutterstock

Chapter 9
96 Courtesy of Maytag

98 (left) Glenda M. Powers/shutterstock
98 (right)Péter Gudella/shutterstock
99 (right) Stephen VanHorn/shutterstock
100 (left) Carole Drong
100 (right) Johanna Goodyear/shutterstock
101 (left) Sarah Bossert/shutterstock
101 (right) STILLFX/shutterstock
102 Courtesy of Maytag
103 (left) shutterstock
103 (right) Abel Leão/istockphoto
104 Chris Howey/shutterstock
105 (left) Dan Bellyk/istockphoto
105 (right) Bocos Benedict/shutterstock
106 Courtesy of Maytag
107 (left) AGA./shutterstock
107 (right) GoodMood Photo/shutterstock

Chapter 10
108 (right) David Andrew Gilder/shutterstock
109 (left) Courtesy of Stacks and Stacks
109 (right) Andrew McDonough/shutterstock
110 (left) Mike Flippo/shutterstock
110 (right) Jyothi Joshi/shutterstock
111 Courtesy of Stacks and Stacks
112 Gareth Roelofse/shutterstock
113 Courtesy of Stacks and Stacks
114 WizData, inc.
115 (left) Chris Rodenberg Photography
115 (right)Ferenc Szelepcxenyi/shutterstock

Chapter 11
116 (left) Stephen Coburn/shutterstock
116 (right) PeJo/shutterstock
117 Losevsky Pavel/shutterstock
118 (left) Greg Henry/shutterstock
118 (right) Courtesy of Greener Lifestyles
119 William Milner/shutterstock
120 (left) Kuznetsov Alexey Andreevich/
shutterstock
120 (right) Kenneth C. Zirkel/istockphoto
121 (left) Lara Barrett/shutterstock
121 (right) James Pauls/istockphoto
122 (left) Matej Krajcovic/shutterstock
122 (right) Elena Elisseeva/shutterstock
123 (left) Thomas Sztanek/shutterstock
123 (right) Margie Hurwich/shutterstock

124 (left) Courtesy of Gaiam
124 (right) dainis/shutterstock
125 (left) Joseph Gareri/shutterstock
125 (right) christine balderas/istockphoto

Chapter 12
126 (left) shutterstock
126 (right) Carole Drong
127 (left) Robert Elias/shutterstock
127 (right)Kruchankova Maya/shutterstock
128 silver-john/shutterstock
129 (left) Caitlin D/shutterstock
129 (right) Adiasz/shutterstock
130 (left) Denis Miraniuk/shutterstock
130 (right) Auter/shutterstock
131 Feng Yu/shutterstock
132 (left) Don Tran/shutterstock
132 (right) Konstantin Remizov/shutterstock
133 photos.com
134 (left) DUSAN ZIDAR/shutterstock
134 (right) Pattie Calfy/istockphoto
135 Courtesy of Ikea

Chapter 13
136 Amanda Penton/istockphoto
137 (left) Emrah Turudu/istockphoto
137 (right) Emrah Turudu/istockphoto
138 Carsten Reisinger/shutterstock
139 (left) Dietmar Klement/istockphoto
139 (right) ian francis/istockphoto
140 (left) Courtesy of Gaiam
140 (right)istockphoto
141 Daniel Krylov/shutterstock
142 (left) Graça Victoria/istockphoto
142 (right) Carole Drong
143 (left) Carol Gering/istockphoto
143 (right) shutterstock
144 (left) photos.com
144 (right) © Andrea Church | Dreamstime.com
145 (left) photos.com
145 (right) Kimberly Hall/shutterstock

Chapter 14
146 (left) Stveltlana Larina/shutterstock
146 (right) Marie-france Bélanger/istockphoto
147 (left) terekhov igor/shutterstock

INDEX